"A philosophical tour de force, touching the heart and challenging the mind."

—JON MEACHAM, AUTHOR OF *THE SOUL OF AMERICA: THE BATTLE FOR OUR BETTER ANGELS*

"With a deeply moving vulnerability, Baird challenges us to be present and patient in our lives, lest we miss the wonder that grace bestows."

—MONICA C. PARKER, BESTSELLING AUTHOR OF *THE POWER OF WONDER*

Praise for *Phosphorescence*

"A book such as this one—one that aims to provoke delight and wonder and comfort, that is at its heart trying to find answers or modes of connection, or light—is of the moment in the best possible way." —*The Guardian*

"Intelligent and emotionally astute . . . Many will find sustenance in reading it." —*Sydney Morning Herald*

"This book is beautiful. A book of tough hope. A light in the dark. A thing of beauty. Phosphorescence itself. Life, nature, hope. You should treat yourself." —Matt Haig

"Friendships and family, climate change and world affairs—Baird tackles them all with warmth and grace." —*Big Issue*

"That is the beauty of this profound book. It transports you into all the deep, inner yearnings you've had for a long time, and then articulates them for you. . . . I could rave about this gem of a book forever. We need this book. You need this book. It is the perfect gift for us all right now. It is perfect." —*Better Reading*

Praise for *Victoria*

"Julia Baird's exquisitely wrought and meticulously researched biography brushes the dusty myth off this extraordinary monarch. . . . The book thrums with authority."
—*New York Times Review of Books*

"Baird nails Victoria, with sympathy but not uncritically. There can be no higher praise." —*Sydney Morning Herald*

"Monumental . . . [An] important and at times enthralling study."
—*Australian Book Review*

"It . . . will forever change the way you see the world, and in particular the role of women who live in it."
—Caroline Overington, *The Australian*

"A triumph. Genuinely fresh insights into one of history's most intriguing figures, impeccably researched and beautifully written."
—Leigh Sales, ABC TV anchor

"It's Baird's gift as a storyteller, her knack for human detail and the idiosyncrasies of the era, that make this book so superb. . . . An extraordinary story, told with brilliance and tenderness by one of Australia's most perceptive writers." —Annabel Crabb

"A thoroughly contemporary biography . . . Baird brings the figure of Victoria richly to life, with all her contradictions . . . Lively, intelligent." —*Books+Publishing*

"A stunning achievement . . . A remarkably lucid, endlessly engaging account of Queen Victoria's life and rule." —Amanda Foreman, author of the bestselling *Georgiana: Duchess of Devonshire* and the chair of the judging panel for the 2016 Man Booker Prize

"Frisky, adventurous . . . exhilarating."
—Janet Maslin, *New York Times*

bright shining

how grace changes everything

JULIA BAIRD

HarperOne
An Imprint of HarperCollinsPublishers

HarperCollins books may be purchased for educational, business, or sales promotional use. For information, please email the Special Markets Department at SPsales@harpercollins.com.

Originally published as *Bright Shining* in Australia in 2023 by HarperCollins*Publishers,* Australia Pty Limited.

FIRST HARPERONE EDITION PUBLISHED IN 2024

Design adapted from the Australian edition designed by Kirby Jones.

Library of Congress Cataloging-in-Publication Data has been applied for.

ISBN 978-0-06-341435-8

24 25 26 27 28 LBC 5 4 3 2 1

For my brothers
and my father
oak trees, all three

When we've been there ten thousand years,
Bright shining as the sun

—from the hymn "Amazing Grace"

Grace has a grand laughter in it.

—Marilynne Robinson, *Gilead*

This book was written on land first inhabited by Aboriginal people, most likely the Gayamaygal, Guringai or Cameragal. I would like to pay my respects to the custodians of this saltwater-encircled country, who lived in harmony with the sea and the land, fishing, painting, carving and clearing bush with fire, and to all elders of this ancient country's past, present and future. I'd also like to acknowledge the importance of telling the truth about our history, which has been warped, denied and dismissed for too long, so that enduring harms can be reckoned with and so our future may shine bright.

Contents

Part IV: Our Sins

Part V: Our Senses

Introduction

When the Shadows Fall Behind You

GRACE IS LIKE THE SUN: it warms us, fuels us and unerringly brings light. At first and, perhaps, second glance, though, the world seems to have been drained of it. Try to recall the last time you saw a public act of grace or an unexpected, extraordinary decency. Presidents trash talk, commentators brawl and spit, vitriol is a currency of clicks, outrage is a profitable algorithm, and hate fills online pews. Rage flows thick, daily, through well-worn tributaries on social media.

But something has happened in the past few years, both subtle and seismic. During the pandemic, millions of us squinted, shifted our lenses, started looking further and asking for more, for better. We began to imagine a different way of life, of being, and of relating to each other. I wrote a book about the importance of hunting awe and wonder, of living deliberately and with purpose, of stout-hearted friendship, of finding an inner light when the world goes dark, and was astonished by the number of people who wrote to me to say, "Me too. I feel the same." Others, too, wrote columns, books, blogs, tweets and posts about the need for rest, for silence, for stillness, and for each other. We paused.

At the same time, I was struck by something else that was not easy to articulate. It was something a little more mysterious and hard to define. People were talking about a need to reckon with our own smallness, a need to find meaning and dignity in connection, and to better understand each other. I had been stunned, too, to read the results of a recent study on the science of awe (defined as "being in the presence of something vast and mysterious that transcends your current understanding of the world"). In it, Dacher Keltner from the University of California, Berkeley conducted research into what the most common sources of awe are, surveying 2,600 people across 26 countries. Would it be nature, art, music, sports games, the ocean? He found it was seeing moral beauty—"the exceptional virtue, character and ability"—in other people. Many of the stories they told were stories of grace. I saw also a desire to more readily acknowledge—and build on—our shared humanity, to be kinder, bigger, better, more forgiving. Which isn't always easy when we're tired, overwhelmed and worried about this melting planet.

To me, this read also as a desire to see, experience and express *grace*. Something that might look and sound good but is not easy. How—or why—should we willingly do something that costs us when the world is full of enough pain? Why should we be decent to idiots, kind to narcissists or tolerate, or even forgive, those who hurt us?

The answer is that grace isn't a form of capitulation or complacency, isn't about weakness or politeness. It requires grit and strength, and, somehow, can change everything.

This is what I became determined to understand. My quest has become even more urgent given that we live in an era when grace is an increasingly rare currency. The silos in which we consume information dot the media landscape like skyscrapers, and the growing distrust of the press, politicians and public figures has in some ways choked our ability to cut each other slack, to allow each other to stumble, to forgive one another. The rows of guillotines on Twitter attest to the fact that apologies or remorse are very rarely viewed with anything but cynicism.

Think, too, of these trends: We are getting lonelier, angrier and less tolerant. Trust in institutions and in each other has corroded. We report having fewer close friends. We are also becoming less empathetic. One study, analysing data from 1979 to 2009, found that the empathy of American students had dropped by almost 50 percent, with the decline accelerating over time. (Over the same period, narcissism has apparently increased.) The statements the students responded to included "I often have tender, concerned feelings for people less fortunate than me" and "I try to look at everybody's side of a disagreement before I make a decision." Asked to find reasons for this dramatic decline in empathy, the leader of the research, Sara H. Konrath of the University of Michigan at Ann Arbor, points to growing social isolation—in many Western countries, the number of people living alone has doubled in recent years, and we are less inclined to join communities such as churches, scouts, unions and political parties. Social fabric is fraying, like patches decaying on quilts. (We are also, incidentally, reading far less—something that has been shown to impact empathy.) It seems obvious to say, but research tells us that those who report being more empathetic do actually respond more to the needs and concerns of others.

Lonely people are more likely to cheat, think worse of others, and suffer from a range of physical and mental health issues—even moderate loneliness can make us sick. And, curiously, the lonelier we are, the less wise we are. Researchers compared loneliness in two starkly different populations, one in Cilento, in rural southern Italy, and one in San Diego, in the United States. In both groups, they found that the more wisdom an individual had, the less lonely they felt. The study defined wisdom as having several components—all of which stoke grace—including empathy, compassion, self-reflection and emotional regulation or discipline, with the first two having the strongest inverse correlation with loneliness. Be kind to people, listen to people, try to understand their point of view, and you will be wiser and less lonely. Wisdom also meant people slept better and were healthier. The designer of the study, Dr. Dilip Jeste, Distinguished Professor of Psychiatry at the University of California, San Diego, says wisdom and loneliness do not seem to coexist: "In other words, wiser people don't feel lonely and vice versa. Obviously, this doesn't prove that increasing wisdom will *reduce* loneliness, but it certainly points in that direction. . . . It is logical to expect that wisdom will counter loneliness."

This all makes sense, and researchers are now working on ways to increase people's compassion and in turn improve health. A 2021 study even showed how loneliness and wisdom—including compassion—relate to gut microbial diversity and composition.

Some find empathy too hard, too taxing. But empathy is integral to grace, and something I believe to be integral to a life well lived. "Turn your face to the sun," goes the old saying, "and the shadows fall behind you."

❋

SO, WHAT IS GRACE? When I ask people that question, I find that they generally mourn its absence. Of course, religious circles are where people speak most often of the concept of grace, especially Christians who read in the Bible that their sins are forgiven by grace alone. This forgiveness, the wiping of the slate clean, is not deserved and can never be merited; it is a kind of unfathomable gift. This is why Christians are called to forgive unconditionally, because they have been forgiven themselves. By this teaching, humans are fundamentally unworthy but are nonetheless lifted up: this is the core of the faith, and why the word "grace"—the grace of God—is used so liberally in churches.

But I want to draw the circle far wider, because we all know, instinctively understand and experience grace—the grace shown by people. What many people think of are acts of compassion: the kindness of strangers, of good Samaritans who pay for people's groceries, of ordinary people in extraordinary pain who somehow learned to forgive, who show what Franciscan author Richard Rohr calls "an unexplainable goodness."

But grace is more than simple kindness. Grace is both ineffable and utterable, which is why so many thinkers have grappled with it for decades. It's not esoteric, it's wrapped in the everyday, but it is still extraordinary. It spawns generosity, compassion and empathy. It involves understanding, recognizing another person's humanity and walking in another's shoes, which can pave the way for forgiveness. Poet Mary Oliver wrote that where other people might use words like "chance," "luck," "coincidence" or "serendipity," she would choose "grace," even though she didn't know exactly what it was. Anne Lamott said: "I do not understand the mystery of grace—only that it meets us where we are but does not leave us where it found us." There are no "delicate silver bells" announcing grace's arrival, she says, "it's clog and slog and scootch, on the floor, in the silence, in the dark." American author Jonathan Rauch says, "Regardless of the context, [grace is] always at least a little unexpected and out of the ordinary."

In public jargon, there are many competing definitions of, or facets to, grace. When Lutheran pastor Nadia Bolz-Weber asked her followers how to define grace in plain language, the answers were astute:

When someone sees your dark side and says, "I got you. Here's some light."

Grace is honoring another person's humanity even when they don't honor yours.

Grace is extending a hand even when a fist might be more deserved.

A deep self-giving love that causes the most true and best parts of a person [to come] out of themselves, even if, and especially if, they have wronged you or someone else.

The chance to be wrong and mess up and that not to be the end of our story. (Or: Grace is the space where your fuck-ups are a beginning instead of an end.)

Seeing people as more than the sum of their mistakes.

Grace gives space for flaws and forgives unconditionally.

According to Helen Garner, grace is much like happiness. She wrote in *The Guardian* that it had taken her eighty years to figure out that happiness "is not a tranquil, sunlit realm at the top of the ladder you've spent your whole life hauling yourself up. . . . It's more like the thing that Christians call grace. You can't earn it, you can't strive for it, it's not a reward for virtue. . . . It's something you glimpse in the corner of your eye until one day you're up to your neck in it."

Many see grace twinned with gloom, as origin or destination. Cormac McCarthy wrote in his novel *The Road*: "All things of grace and beauty such that one holds them to one's heart have a common provenance in pain. Their birth in grief and ashes." Bolz-Weber sees grace evident when "God makes beautiful things out of even my own shit." Some see it as a state of being. Aviator Anne Morrow Lindbergh called it a word "borrow[ed] from the language of the saints," meaning "an inner harmony, essentially spiritual, which can be translated into outward harmony." Others, like Catholic religious sister and anti–death penalty campaigner Helen Prejean, see it as selfless social activism: "When we're called to leave this little ego-centered thing of our lives, to pour ourselves out in something bigger than ourselves, to help justice come into the world, you know that's grace in you." Friedrich Schiller described a person living in a state of grace as "a beautiful soul," the highest form of human.

Author Marilynne Robinson grasps it perfectly. "Love is holy because it is like grace," she wrote in her novel *Gilead*, "the worthiness of its object is never really what matters." She defines grace as "an understanding of the wholeness of a situation," and says it includes the fact that we live in an unfathomably interesting universe, and we "amazingly" add things to that "great plenum."

This conclusion thrills me—the idea that we add things to the universe. When I was about sixteen, and arguing with my Ancient History teacher about something, she walked slowly over to me, put her hands on the edge of my desk and stared into my eyes. "There is nothing new under the sun," she boomed in her deep voice as rebellious thoughts began to knot in my brain. I appreciate this statement of hers was not original, but I was so angry that she would say to a teenager, a young woman trying to make sense of the world, that there was nothing she could do that might be fresh, unique or in any way new.

I'm with Robinson.

My own definition of grace is: First of all, to be fully, thrillingly alive. None of us has done anything to earn the awe and wonder we witness on this planet, the ability to wander through the natural world and be both diminished and expanded by its glory. To dive into the depths of the sea on a single breath, swim alongside whale sharks, plant seeds into soil and watch green push through brown, or climb through clouds on mountain peaks to observe gorillas in their natural habitat is, in many ways, to exist in a state of grace.

Second, and most fundamentally, grace is something undeserved. In its crudest interpretation, karma is getting what you deserve. Grace is the opposite: forgiving the unforgivable, favoring the undeserving, loving the unlovable. With grace you get something you have done nothing to earn. It is mercy, not merit. And grace, in giving people another chance, the benefit of the doubt, an opportunity to learn and change, can unravel people, redirect futures, melt hearts, heal family rifts, transform lives. We can see some of this in restorative justice.

Third, it is the ability to see good in the other, to recognize humanity, to tolerate difference and to continually plough lives, conversations and public debates with a belief that people can change, and that what we fight for is joy and beauty, as well as equality.

Grace is, in most of its forms, fleeting and often overlooked; it reveals itself in flashes and glimmers. But these are moments that illuminate and transcend. So the fundamental question must be: How different would our lives be if they were defined, or lit, by grace? What would happen to our hearts, our health?

I must stress that I am not writing a definitive guide to grace, to what it is and how to find it; I am merely writing about ways in which I and others have seen and known it. Nor am I writing from a point of possession, of a person who doles out grace like porridge to all who ask for it or need it. I don't claim to be full of grace, but full of wonder at what it does, at what it is. How it makes people whole. How it means the terrible can exist alongside the beautiful, in every person, every life and country. How it means we can live a life less burdened by vengeance, envy and greed. I want to write about the different forms it takes, and what it might mean if we reached for it more often, and aspired to show it, without expectation of applause or thanks.

There is often a cost in showing grace to someone who is undeserving, unworthy or hurtful, who warrants savage punishment, even if it just means turning away from them. It takes sweat. It's not pious or glib or easy. It can be a chore to attain a state of grace, and even harder to stay there. Gravity often pulls us back to the gratifying cushion of meanness, judgment, superiority, dislike, hate. We might act graciously but do so reluctantly, through gritted teeth. It cannot be expected, earned, demanded or coerced. It especially cannot be demanded of women, who for centuries have been praised for "grace"— which most often means compliance, quiet, and not complaining about their lot. There is also a mystery to grace because on one level—that of ledgers and weighted balances, of an eye for an eye, of law books, quid pro quo and retribution—it makes no sense.

Grace is, arguably, the antithesis of cancel culture. That's not to say that you should just give racists a cuddle, or forgive dickheads for blind acts of narcissism, thereby creating a culture of impunity and stasis. But every great reform movement, every great movement of justice in history, has been fueled by a simple gracious belief—that people can change, or be persuaded. That we can appeal to what Abraham Lincoln called "the better angels of our nature." To believe that of everyone you meet is an incredible gift—for you and for them.

IN MY RESEARCH, I have been struck by the fact that the greatest examples of grace come from people who have been oppressed and continue to fight, to ask for change and for understanding. In Australia, this is seen most clearly in our First Nations people's request in the *Uluru Statement from the Heart* that non-Indigenous people walk with them and join with them in a *makarrata*—a coming together after a struggle. To continue to ask for this after a history of murder, slavery, exploitation and humiliation—and not seek to retaliate, rage and burn in return—is a stunning act of grace.

In this context—one of systemic racism and historical and current oppression—asking about forgiveness is frequently the wrong question, and one that continues to burden the victims, or the oppressed. Survivors of the Stolen Generation, having spent decades trying to heal from the trauma of being torn from their families, their culture and their country, being dipped in chemicals used on sheep to "clean them," having their mouths washed with sandy soap or worse, and being the subjects of a grotesque national experiment to erase their color—a trauma that has had devastating impacts and flowed down through generations—told me repeatedly that the word "forgiveness" was almost incomprehensible to them. "I am already dealing with my own burdens; why do I have to deal with theirs?" asked Aunty Lorraine Peeters, who has spent her life healing herself and other survivors.

Sitting in on one of her workshops on intergenerational trauma, I was struck by how she has spun horror into healing, how she survived suffering to help others do the same. Forgiveness, says Aunty Lorraine, is "a word I hate." But she works tirelessly to educate people, Black and white, and holds hope that, with the next generations, those better angels will emerge.

※

IMANI PERRY, AUTHOR AND a professor of Women, Gender and Sexuality, and African and African American Studies at Harvard University, told Krista Tippett, host of the podcast *On Being*, that it is hard to advocate for an insistence on joy and delight when fighting against ugliness, hate and injustice. But, she said, "It's really the thing we're fighting for. It's the human experience that we're fighting for the proliferation of, so that life is not defined primarily, for so many people, by suffering in violence and hardship, but actually that thing that all of us possess, which is this incredible capacity for joy and beauty."

At its core, grace is about recognizing each other's humanity. Former civil rights leader and statesman John Lewis said he trained himself in the way of nonviolence by trying to think of the good in every person. In his own interview with Tippett, he said, "In the bosom of every human being, there is a spark of the divine. . . . We, from time to time, would discuss if you see someone attacking you, beating you, spitting on you, you have to think of that person, you know, years ago that person was an innocent child, innocent little baby." Then you need to ask, he says, what happened? "Something go wrong? Did the environment [cause it]? Did someone teach that person to hate, to abuse others? So you try to appeal to the goodness of every human being and you don't give up. You never give up on anyone." Doing this is incredibly hard. Aren't some people beyond repair?

As French philosopher Simone Weil noted, the world is defined by grace *and* gravity—and it is the latter that defies the former. She wrote: "All the natural movements of the soul are controlled by laws analogous to those of physical gravity. Grace is the only exception." Grace is flight, beauty and dance, and gravity is the granite, the hardness of everything that pushes against it, the cold truth of what we have to work against to achieve—even fleetingly—a state of grace. To get there, we often have to fight parts of ourselves, as well as other people.

✳

WHILE WRITING THIS BOOK, I have been wrestling with the opposite of grace: my bodily gravity, the weight of a chronic, recurrent illness that keeps bringing me back to earth, that has filled me with despair, uncertainty, fear and grief. This has been my gravity. And it has made my search for grace even more pressing—my search for the moments when we transcend the worst of ourselves, and witness or experience a moment of clarity or beauty, like a *glisk*, which, as nature writer Robert Macfarlane tells us, is a Scots word meaning "glimpse" or, more specifically, "sunlight glimpsed through a break in the clouds" or, figuratively, "a glimpse of the good, a brief burst of warmth or hope."

I have written these paragraphs, meditating on moral beauty, in between appointments with grim-faced surgeons, GPs and hospital nurses, with my arms punctured and bruised by the constant taking of blood and inserting of cannulas, and my veins pumped full of contrast dye as I slide in and out of scanning machines that search my insides for lumps of cancer and keep lighting up: *Bingo, bingo, bingo, your card is full.*

And outside these sterile medical rooms, I have gone to remote reefs for solace, floated rapidly along currents, mimicking flight with my arms outstretched, seeking peace, seeking grace in motion, in nature, in beauty, in silence, in loving, in fighting, in the chance to live another year, or day.

Grace is elusive and hard, and it's everywhere, shining bright like the sun.

PART I

Our Souls,
Our Selves

"Really into waterfalls": On a state of daily grace

All her life she would believe that moments of beauty,
pleasure and human connection, no matter how fleeting,
had a life-transforming power.

–Ann-Marie Priest on poet Gwen Harwood

In a little Salvation Army hall near my home one Sunday, I found myself sitting around a table with a small group of people, a motley crew of drifters and seekers. I'd come to this place because I'd grown bored of conventional church and wanted to roll my sleeves up.

The Salvos run a soup kitchen and a range of outreach programs, so most of those who turn up on Sundays have needs they bring to the community: mental health, homelessness, disabilities, dementia. It means that when we sit around and talk about life, and what it means, no one pretends to be anything other than who they are—just people trying to get by. This strips our conversations of clichés or pat rhetoric, and I love it.

On this day, the minister—or officer—asked everyone to pull a card from a back table, and each card had a question

17

on it that we all had to answer. Next to me was J——, who read his card with a loud voice: "Describe a beautiful place you have been to."

He went first. "Well, anyone who knows me knows I have psychiatric problems, and sometimes I go to the hospital for treatment. Outside the corner of the main room there, it looks onto a concrete slab, and when it rains, the sound of the water hitting the concrete is just . . . incredible." His entire face lifted, lit. "It sounds like a waterfall. I am really into nature, and waterfalls, so that place is pretty special."

I looked at him. "I bet that is really calming to listen to."

"Yeah, exactly, calming, I love it."

The way rain splashes onto cement and stone: a beautiful place.

❄

BEING OPEN TO WATERFALLS IS, surely, being open to grace. So is being open to other human beings. There is no prescription for being open in this way; it means tuning our ears to the possibility of wonder, and awe, and to the importance of acts and attitudes that go beyond the punitive, exacting and self-righteous. It also means recognizing beauty is part of what we strive for and need—beauty and art and leisure and music.

Rebecca Solnit, author of the delightful book *Orwell's Roses*, highlights this perfectly. Orwell, "our great prophet of totalitarianism, the man famous for facing unpleasant truths," planted roses. He fought intellectually for equality and also cared about and nurtured beauty. This reflects beautifully the slogan of the suffragette movement, "Bread for All, and Roses too," which meant that women were fighting for not just physical needs but also music, education, nature, art, leisure and books, for "pleasures as well as necessities, and the time to pursue them, the time to have an inner life and freedom to roam the outer world." Solnit told *The Nation*: "We all know what 'bread' is: food, clothing, shelter, the bodily necessities, which can be more or less homogenized and administered from above. But 'roses' was this radical cry, in a way, for individualism, for private life, for freedom of choice—because my roses and your roses won't be the same roses, you know? It's saying that people are subtle, complex, subjective creatures who need culture, need nature, need beauty, need leisure."

I'd add moral beauty too—witnessing it, and experiencing it.

Often, it's the beauty that we miss. We in the media can become so intent on capturing horror, on exposing problems and untold inequalities, that we forget the beauty and the joy, the ways we look after each other, the reasons we have to stay alive. Actor and writer Brett Goldstein, who plays the curmudgeonly Roy Kent in the TV series *Ted Lasso*, said he had a "profound moment as a creative" when he went to see a critically acclaimed movie—"five stars everywhere"—and found it profoundly bleak and depressing. After he and a friend had sat watching horrible things happen, including a lingering moment of sexual violence, he turned to his friend and joked, "That's entertainment."

"And I thought, What are we doing?" he said on NPR. "Why have we paid to see this thing?" He decided the film was bad art, he said, because there was "no glimmer of light in it," and no humor. "This isn't how life is," he went on, even though it was a true story. If you have survived horrific events, or read the accounts of those who have, he said, "there are always, always jokes in them, there's a moment where they laugh, there's a moment where they held each other, there's a moment of connection, of love, of light, in everything, and if you make something that doesn't have any of that I think it's bad art, I think you've not watched life."

The chapters in this section are about watching life, and watching each other. Watching for those moments of connection, of love and of light, and moments when we hold and care for each other in the midst of everything. And noticing, too, that Orwell's roses still bloom today.

Chapter 1

21.3 Grams

We must remove the word "empathy" from the
[news]papers and put it into practice.
Our humanity is thirsty for affection, care and attention. . . .
We must do it without expecting anything in return.

—Brazilian nurse technician Semei Araújo Cunha

THE TIME OF DEATH is not, apparently, when the last breath is taken, when the lungs or legs give way, when the internal organs collapse, when a bullet punctures the skin. It is when the heart stops. Some studies have shown that brain activity can continue for some time after the heart stops, though, which is wild to contemplate. (The functions that linger longest, by the way, are the sense of touch and hearing, which is important to know when holding the hand of—and whispering to—a person who is dying.)

Activity is, of course, not the same as awareness, but some researchers have found people can be aware they are dead after their heartbeat stills. In a 2017 study of the near-death experiences of 2,060 patients who had suffered cardiac arrest and been brought back to life, some patients said they had even heard their doctors declare them dead. Of the survivors, almost half had memories of that time, with seven major cognitive themes:

Fear
Animals/plants
Bright light
Violence/persecution
Déjà vu
Family
Recalling events post-cardiac arrest

Nine percent had had "near-death experiences" they could recount. Two percent recalled "seeing" and "hearing" events that were part of their resuscitation. Some felt peaceful, others felt they were being dragged under water.

The study concluded: "[Cardiac arrest] survivors commonly experience a broad range of cognitive themes, with 2 percent exhibiting full awareness. This supports other recent studies that have indicated consciousness may be present despite clinically undetectable consciousness." This is genuinely mindboggling, and might prompt some to ask if it suggests we possess souls, separate from our bodies.

This idea preoccupied one particular American doctor a century ago, because he was intent on trying to measure the weight of a soul as it left the body at death. In 1907, Dr. Duncan Macdougall of Massachusetts wrote a report of his controversial experiment, entitled "Hypothesis concerning soul substance together with experimental evidence of the existence of such substance," for the April issue of *American Medicine*. He had incorporated a particularly sensitive beam scale in a bed in a tuberculosis hospital in Boston. One by one, he placed six terminally ill patients on the bed just before and after the time of death (awkwardly, one actually died there). With the very first patient, he told a reporter, "the instant life ceased, the opposite scale pan fell with a suddenness that was astonishing—as if something had been lifted from the body."

The difference in weight was three-quarters of an ounce, or 21.3 grams, and, while the drop in mass varied in his subjects, Macdougall pronounced that this was the weight of a soul. When he repeated the experiment on fifteen dying dogs, he found no difference in weight, thereby sadly concluding that dogs did not have a soul.

These findings caused a sensation. When the study was reported in the *New York Times* under the headline "Soul Has Weight, Physician Thinks," another doctor sank his teeth into its credibility, at first by claiming a body no longer cooled by lungs would sweat, thereby shedding some weight from the body. This sparked a dispute that roiled for a year. Macdougall, described in the *Times* as a "reputable physician of Haverfill," claimed to have ruled out the possibility of it being the weight of air from the lungs or any expulsion of bodily fluids, but this was received with skepticism.

Four years later, Macdougall expanded his experiment. While attempting to photograph what he believed to be the soul leaving the body at the time of death, he claimed to have captured the glow of an "interstellar ether" around the head. But the scientific community remained doubtful. The sample size of Macdougall's first study was very small, and his inconsistent results have been considered scientifically implausible ever since. The term "21 grams" has endured, though, with most references dropping the 0.3 from the finding, as in the title of the film *21 Grams*. It seems an odd thing to do, to round down a soul.

THE ATTEMPTS OF SCIENTISTS to somehow measure the spirit seem to have impressed the prize-winning American poet Laura Gilpin, who finished her second book of poetry, *The Weight of a Soul*, in Fairhope, Alabama, a century later, just before she died in 2007. Coming from a gifted poet who had spent decades working as a registered nurse, Gilpin's words are striking for their empathy, their concern for the human soul, and for the care of people at their most vulnerable, desperate and, often, shy.

The fact that she devoted her life to advocating for better patient care will surprise no one familiar with her work. Her poems radiate tenderness. Take this one, called "Two-headed Calf":

Tomorrow when the farm boys find this
freak of nature, they will wrap his body
in newspaper and carry him to the museum.
But tonight he is alive and in the north
field with his mother. It is a perfect
summer evening: the moon rising over

the orchard, the wind in the grass. And
as he stares into the sky, there are
twice as many stars as usual.

The perfect night, in a field, facing death. But, in truth, instead
of facing death, the calf is facing life. It's a superb summation of
the grace of life, of relishing the simple miracle of a moment on
this earth. A lingering one.

As a twenty-six-year-old poet, in 1976, Gilpin won the
Walt Whitman Award for her book *The Hocus-Pocus of the
Universe*. Shortly afterward, she abandoned writing for nursing
and later she would become a founding member of Planetree,
an organization dedicated to ensuring hospital patients are
treated humanely. In 2003 she published an article with Roger
Ulrich called "Healing Arts: Nutrition for the Soul," in which
they described the important role art has played in healing,
historically, and how necessary it is for restoring the will to live.
Patients needed to be treated, they argued, not just as broken
bodies, but souls thirsting for beauty. "In the centuries before
Hippocrates, the healing temples of ancient Greece surrounded
patients with music, poetry, storytelling, painting, sculpture,
gardens, and fountains," they wrote. "An environment rich
with art was seen as therapeutic, providing a means to alleviate
physical discomfort, emotional distress and spiritual crisis. In the
absence of science, the arts were vital in restoring the will to live
and enhancing the healing process." Gilpin and Ulrich argued
for the capacity of nature to soothe and comfort, especially calm
scenes of trees, flowers and water, as well as, curiously, the sight

of a kind face: "Evolutionary theory proposes that . . . humans are genetically predisposed to pay attention to, and be positively affected by, images of smiling or sympathetic human faces."

❋

AUTHOR AND PHYSICIAN MICHELLE Johnston tells me that the busy Perth hospital emergency department she works in is, on the whole, "riot and mess and stab vests and meth and rage and the debris from the crumbling fabric of society." Yet, she says, she witnesses "a thousand tiny acts of grace every day, every beat of the heart. Most unnoticed by the bigger, glossier world, but they add up." When I asked her for an example, she described a patient from her latest shift, "a newly paralyzed man, [after a] silly accident, just starting out as a schoolteacher, comprehending his future in a single moment [and] only caring about the words we would choose to tell his wife, not for himself."

One room in the emergency section of hospitals is usually set aside for distressed relatives, where people are placed before staff deliver awful news. Johnston tells me: "As we are a trauma center, not infrequently the news is utterly unexpected. Not long ago, I walked the long corridor to tell a mother her son was irretrievably brain-injured. He was the same age as my son. I felt fragile breaking the news. She could tell, and she held and supported me as much as I [did] her, as I outlined all the terrible details and prognosis."

Often, Johnston says, moments of grace are "virtually imperceptible, mighty in intent but easily missed if you aren't paying attention." In this environment, you see "people at their lowest, their most frightened, ripped open and vulnerable, caring for the welfare of others: their children, their spouses, the cat at home." She continues:

Acts of grace also come in microscopic encounters. The forgiveness of a patient in pain if you miss getting a drip in, the stoic understanding when you explain it will take twelve hours to find the patient with newly diagnosed breast cancer a bed, the gratitude people express for the time you take to sit on their bed with them and talk. These are the acts of grace that slay me. When people should be ranting about the parlous state of public medicine in the richest country imaginable, they are gracious themselves, giving and understanding.

I find some of the staff perform acts of grace on a constant, endless basis. The nurses, moving from holding the hand of someone dying, to checking the boxes on a useless bureaucratic piece of paper, to getting yelled at by a supervisor, to cleaning up bodily secretions, to going into the next patient to whisper calming words to them, reassuring them, making them feel safe. If that's not grace, I don't know what is. The physiotherapists patiently walking elderly patients, the pharmacists gently correcting a drug chart, a chaplain sitting in the rubble of grief with howling relatives. Sure, these people are all paid, but these are acts of grace, every single time.

❄

THE TITLE POEM OF Laura Gilpin's collection *The Weight of a Soul* was inspired by a story the poet heard of a doctor who is said to have experimented and determined the soul to weigh a fraction of an ounce. The poem follows the passage of a soul, "weighing slightly less than an airmail letter," as it rises out of a hospital patient's body with his last breath, hovers then slips into the hallway, past hobbling patients, nurses, doctors, and a janitor sloshing his wet mop, and then out an open window. The soul rises up into the evening air over the hospital car park, over the rush-hour traffic on the highway, and back to the patient's home, lightly touching the heads of his children as they play tag, and his wife as she packs pajamas to take to him in the hospital: "He touches her so lightly she feels only the evening breeze." How many medics think about the soul of their patients returning to touch the people they love?

In the same volume, Gilpin writes about bathing a woman "while she sleeps in a far place beyond my reaching." But she continues to talk "in case she hears me (believing that hearing is the last to go)"—about the weather and the seasons—as she washes the woman's arms and legs and works her way around her body:

She offers no resistance
except that of gravity,
the earth pulling her down
while I lift, as though something between us
is being weighed.

Then I turn to wash her back
talking to her about what seems to matter
in this life—though I make no promises.

Only this morning
the promise of spring was in the air
and I tell her that.

In that lift, surely, is grace. The kind that so many of us who
have tended to sick children, friends, family, or aging parents can
understand. The kind that seeks to comfort and dignify. Little
wonder Gilpin campaigned forcefully against what she saw as the
sterility of many hospital environments. She died aged fifty-six,
of multiple glioblastomas, her death notice in the *New York Times*
recording that she was honored for her "indomitable spirit, her
kindness, her droll humor, her brilliant intellect and her love of
celebrations."

❄

NURSES HAVE BROUGHT ME immense comfort in the past
few years. Most of us who frequent hospitals can quickly tell
the difference between a competent, caring nurse and an
indifferent one (and the vast majority, in my experience, are the
former). Little things give it away. Like one nurse bringing me
a single ice-chip when I was not allowed to let anything pass
my lips. Or another letting me sleep in the middle of a hubbub.
One who looked at me without judgment when my body was

malfunctioning. Another who spoke soothingly when I quietly despaired about my ability to heal and work again. A nurse who, when I started crying one day after my children visited because I was missing them so much, grabbed my arm, yelling, "You are okay! You are a strong and intelligent woman! Just like David Marr!"—and I burst out laughing at this reference to my fellow writer and then colleague. When in pain, I am inordinately grateful for both expertise and small kindnesses: an extra heated blanket tucked in over exposed toes, laughter at one of my bad jokes, an eye trained to see pain when I'm too spent to complain.

This is part of the reason I am always astonished when doctors treat nurses with disregard, or people patronize them. A couple of years ago, a friend of mine, Caitlin Brassington, was at her local shops in her scrubs after a long day at work and bumped into an acquaintance, who said she had not realized Caitlin was "*just* a nurse." That morning Caitlin had left three kids asleep in the hands of a babysitter who would get them to school and daycare so that she could go and do her nursing work. She came home that night and posted the following message on Facebook:

I have helped babies into the world, many of whom needed assistance to take their first breath, and yet I am just a nurse.

I have held patients' hands and ensured their dignity while they take their last breath, and yet I am just a nurse.

I have counselled grieving parents after the loss of a child, and yet I am just a nurse.

I have performed CPR on patients and brought them back to life, and yet I am just a nurse.

I can auscultate every lung field on a newborn and assess which field may have a decreased air entry, and yet I am just a nurse.

I can educate patients, caregivers, junior nurses and junior doctors on disease states, prognoses and treatment plans, and yet I am just a nurse.

I have been a lecturer in a school of medicine, teaching medical students how to perform a systematic physical examination of a patient, and yet I am just a nurse.

I am my patients' advocate in a health system that does not always put my patients' best interests first, and yet I am just a nurse.

I can take blood, cannulate, and suture a wound, and yet I am just a nurse.

I can manage a cardiac arrest in a newborn, a child or an adult, and yet I am just a nurse.

I can tell you the dosage of adrenaline or amiodarone based on weight that your child may need to bring them back to life, and yet I am just a nurse.

I provide comfort, compassion, emotional and social support to patients and their families in their darkest times, and yet I am just a nurse.

I have worked twelve-hour shifts without a toilet break or a cup of coffee, to ensure that the best possible care is given to my patient, and yet I am just a nurse.

I have been screamed at, vomited on and urinated on, but I will still come to work and do my job, and yet I am just a nurse.

I have the experience, knowledge and competence that has saved and will continue to save people's lives, and yet I am just a nurse.

So yes, lovely acquaintance in the corner store, if I am "just a nurse," then I am ridiculously proud to be one!

Damn straight. Who else will care in such a way for strangers? For our sisters, fathers, brothers, mothers, lovers, children? Who will treat patients as human beings, possessed of sensitivity, of hurt and love and longing? We don't talk much about souls these days. It's a word loaded with woo-woo vibes, with connotations of sound-baths and self-appointed healers robed in floaty garments. But the oldest word for soul, I understand, is the Greek term *pneuma*, which means "breath" but also "spirit" or "soul"—in other words, our deepest selves. To recognize all people have souls is to treat them with dignity and respect, as they, too, breathe and yearn, strive, love and lose. They, too, are someone's child, someone's love, someone's friend.

❋

THE MOST WRENCHING PART of the pandemic that squeezed the air out of a locked-down globe during 2020 and 2021 was the lack of human touch: we could not hug each other, could not visit our older relatives, could not sit by the bedsides of people we loved as they were dying, or rest our cheeks on their brows. It was crushing. The stories of heartbreak were relentless: elderly husbands being placed in ambulances as their wives of fifty years waved them off, their faces hidden behind masks, prevented from throwing their arms around them to say goodbye, perhaps never to clap eyes on them again; patients lying on narrow hospital beds, intubated, hooked up to beeping machines and unable to speak to family or have contact with loved ones in their final moments. One nurse posted on Twitter: "My biggest trauma from this whole pandemic is one of my dying patients only feeling my gloved hand holding theirs as they passed. It wrecked me for months."

In Brazil, in an emergency care unit in Vila Prado in the city of São Carlos, two nurse technicians, Semei Araújo Cunha and Vanessa Formenton, decided to try to do something about this. Sitting together at lunchtime one day, overwhelmed by the suffering they were witnessing, they were looking at their phones when an old nursing technique that had been forgotten popped up on a social network. They walked back into their wards, determined to put it into practice.

Despite the nonchalance of the country's COVID-denying president, Jair Bolsonaro, who said the virus was a "little flu," there was, at that time, intense and growing anxiety about the number of people dying from COVID in Brazil, which was pushing hospitals to the brink of collapse and exhausting the already stretched frontline medical staff, who lacked basic diagnostic testing kits and beds to put patients in. In 2020 there had been a total of 22.3 million positive cases. By March 2021, almost four thousand Brazilians were dying from COVID every day, and at the end of that year Brazil became the second country in the world to exceed six hundred thousand deaths; a Brazilian congressional panel had recommended the president be charged with "crimes against humanity" for his botched response to the pandemic.

Back in São Carlos, Vanessa and Semei filled two latex medical gloves with hot water, closed them at the wrist and then tied their fingertips together. Then they slid them over the hands of patients so they would feel as though someone was there, next to them, holding their hand. It was the most stunning, heart-wrenching act of grace. The gloves came to be known as "the little hands of love," or, individually, as "the hand of God." Semei said: "What we could observe was the improvement in the perfusion and the vital signs of our patient, and what caught our attention the most was to see that in the midst of a pandemic isolation we could give a cosiness, that is, a caress with a warm hand. . . . It was as if the hand were welcomed or held by two other hands; it brings like a human warmth, a form of affection."

The two women then took the technique to other hospitals, and repeated these results. After Semei posted descriptions and images of her "gloves of love" on her social media accounts, their gesture—both professional and intensely, intuitively personal—was reported across the globe, to the nurses' astonishment.

With the help of my Brazilian friend Suzana, I recently managed to find these two women, who continue to work as nurses in São Carlos. Still reeling from the fervid global response to their gesture, Semei told me she had found the attention quite scary, but that they had also had the honor and pleasure of being recognized by Dr. Tedros Adhanom Ghebreyesus, Director-General of the World Health Organization. "It is a reason for enormous satisfaction," she said, "a feeling of accomplishment." She also hoped their innovation had helped "alleviate the suffering that this pandemic has brought us, whether physical or psychological."

What was most striking about the "hands of love" was that it was an entirely voluntary and unprompted gesture of love and affection from strangers. I am constantly grateful for nurses whose empathy allows them to walk among people in pain, and whose competence enables them to lessen that pain. (I also love their black humor, like the nurse who called out to another as I lay in the ER one day, "Well, I just gave a glass of orange juice to a naked man in a shower, if you want to know how my day is going.") I'm not the only one. Author Helen Garner wrote recently that rather than hanging about waiting for an evasive happiness, she has decided to settle for "small, random stabs of extreme interestingness—moments of intense awareness of the things I'm about to lose, and of gladness that they exist." One of the things she listed was "the theatre nurse gripping my hand at the moment the anesthetic knocks me out."

Vanessa and Semei embody a vocation of care beautifully. Semei told me:

Sharing knowledge and what is good and what works is very important; it gives us joy and peace in the soul, because that day it was for someone we didn't know, and that was someone's lover, mother, wife, daughter, niece, friend, neighbor. With this, we saw positive results, it was splendid. It is very good to treat people as we would like to be treated, or as [we would like them to] treat our loved ones. We must remove the word "empathy" from the [news]papers and put it into practice. Our humanity is thirsty for affection, care and attention. . . . We must do it without expecting anything in return. And everything we do, wherever we put our hands, we must [also] put love, affection, attention. We don't know when it will be our turn; life is too short, let's enjoy it and do it with joy, affection, care, dedication and love.

Two kind women, tending to strangers, loving them as though they were their own, without expecting anything in return. Looking after them as though they do not have just physical needs, but a soul: 21.3 grams of life. Such are the multitudinous acts of quiet love that happen every day in the hospitals, aged-care homes, daycare centers, often unrecognized, unseen, but reminding us of why we live, why we need to stand guard, and why we matter so much to each other.

Chapter 2

Anonymous Samaritans

PROFESSOR BARBARA MASSER THROWS her hands up and laughs: "I am baffled!" After many years of in-depth academic study into the reasons why people give blood, she says, "One of the things that has always mystified me about this behavior is that I can't understand logically why people do it, but they do." Donors need to voluntarily go to a place where they will have a needle stuck into their arm and are asked all kinds of questions about their behavior when there is nothing wrong with them. Nevertheless, says Masser, "People do it time and time again, and it is kind of baffling as to why—we've been searching for that answer for some time."

"They are the most amazing individuals," notes Masser, who is Joint Chair of Donor Research at Australian Red Cross Lifeblood. "It's absolutely joyful to be in a donor center—watch people give their blood and their time, have a biscuit and a drink." The shortest explanation for why they do it, Masser says, is "because it makes people feel good and they know they are doing good."

Can there be a simpler example of grace? These are anonymous donations: you don't know who your blood will go to and what exactly it will be used for, whether the person into whose veins your vital fluid is infused will be a teacher, a sex worker, a typist, a snake handler or a real estate agent. You don't know if or how they vote; if they are good sons, daughters, parents, wives or husbands; if potted plants wilt or bloom under their touch; if they believe in horoscopes or conspiracy theories, raw-meat diets or the power of human kindness. You don't know if they send mean tweets, refuse to give way to other cars in traffic, bully their siblings or cheat at Monopoly. All you know is that there is a need, and you can meet it. It is just as Thomas Merton wrote, that our job "is to love others without stopping to inquire whether or not they are worthy."

In a series of interviews with "super donors," I was struck by several things. First, most started donating in their teenage years, usually because another family member was doing the same; second, many relish the anonymity; and third, all seem to just want an opportunity to help people. Nick Woo, an arborist in Darwin, first gave blood aged eighteen, with his mother, who had also begun donating at that age. As a "pretty shy, introverted type," he says, he loves being able to help people in a quiet way. "The anonymous nature of blood donation I think is a sort of comfort: you're making a lifesaving difference but it's indirectly, and you don't expect some direct reward or congratulations. Good for someone like me who avoids award ceremonies and stays out of the spotlight at all costs!"

Recently, Woo took a workout supplement, unaware that it had not been approved by the Therapeutic Goods Administration. The local blood authorities needed to investigate whether he could still donate or whether he may have to be barred for as long as five years. He was surprised to find himself devastated by the prospect. "It really had me tearing up, thinking, 'I can't do the thing I do every fortnight, and it's a really big part of my life.' It really affected me." Happily, he was cleared.

Now thirty-nine, Woo has given well over four hundred blood donations (425 at the time of writing), and has convinced many mates to sign up, even organizing busloads of fellow university students when he lived in Canberra. Super donors tend to be very proud of their numbers, and some compete with themselves to reach ever-higher goals.

❄

I WILL NEVER FORGET the first blood transfusion I received, in 2015. I had just endured a fifteen-hour surgery, and was fading afterward, in ICU. For days, I was depleted, exhausted, hallucinating and in pain. I remember a nurse gripping my hand, leaning over my shoulder, and whispering into my ear as they hooked the blood into my arm and began the infusion. She was talking to me about my writing, and about purpose and about people who cared for me, like we were in the most intimate bubble—until I lost consciousness. When I came to, I felt stronger, and I wondered whose blood it was that was now racing through my veins, injecting me with life. I have absolutely no knowledge of them, of their views, their lives, their hopes. It's a strange and magical experience.

Australian Red Cross Lifeblood estimates that three in every hundred people give blood in Australia, and one in three people will need that blood. A recent prevalence survey estimated that approximately 10.5 million people (57.3 percent of eighteen to seventy-four-year-olds) were eligible to donate blood in Australia, but only 14.2 percent of those eligible reported donating blood in the past two years. "Demand for plasma is high and growing," says Masser, "and we need more donors."

Eighty-two-year-old Jack Champion has given almost eight hundred donations, and his wife, Mary, whom he encouraged to start donating after they were married, another five hundred. He also began at eighteen, when he was living in a hostel in South Africa and was asked if he'd like to donate blood. He remembers the date of his first donation: Friday, September 25, 1959, in Port Elizabeth. At that time, "there was no sharing of blood between white and other races—white blood went to white people—apartheid times, so it was just stupid."

Now the elderly couple donate in Chatswood in Sydney every second Thursday. "Somebody's got to do it," says Jack. "We're just in the habit now; it's something we do, I can't say why. We might need it someday. At the moment I am donating because I want to get to eight hundred!" After doing an apprenticeship as an electrician, Champion worked around Sydney Harbour with the navy for thirty-six years, setting up systems to protect ships against magnetic mines. Today, he and his wife plan their holidays around a donation date, and volunteer to give blood wherever they are: Cairns, Hervey Bay, Hobart, Western Australia.

At 850 donations, Paul Jenkins, from Melton, Melbourne, is Australia's second highest active donor. He turns seventy-one this year, and has been donating—blood then plasma—since he was nineteen, when a mobile blood unit came to the ammunition factory he was working in. He never skips a week, and still donates when he goes on holidays, so he can describe how they take blood at a host of places: Tucson, Albuquerque, Wyoming, New Orleans, New York, Washington State, San Francisco, Miami, Naples, Hawaii.

When Jenkins reached his eight hundredth donation, his local center celebrated by bringing in a woman suffering from Guillain-Barré syndrome who relied on frequent plasma donations (including many from Jenkins) to keep her alive and enable her to walk. The hug she gave him made him happy. "Although I had no intention of stopping, that was an inspiration after fifty years," he recalls. "I take no medications at all. I'm lucky to have the health I have. I don't like that some people don't have that luck. I believe everybody should give back to the community in some way and this is my way." With plasma, he notes, children and cancer patients are significant users, while those with faulty immune systems are the greatest beneficiaries: "I don't want to see anyone else needlessly [suffer]." Now he is hoping to reach a thousand donations. "If I could, I would go seven days a week. . . . I'm a bit of a blood-bank junkie."

Australia's most legendary donor, James Harrison, donated 1,173 times, earning him a place in the *Guinness Book of World*

Records for the most donations made by an individual. "The man with the golden arm" is credited with helping save the lives of more than two million Australian babies. His blood contains a rare antibody that can be used to make Anti-D medication, which is given to mothers whose blood (from a negative group) may develop antibodies in pregnancy that could damage their baby's red blood cells and cause a miscarriage, as well as severe anemia and brain damage. According to the Australian Red Cross, about 2.4 million doses of Anti-D containing Harrison's blood were given to mothers who have this particular negative blood type, protecting the same number of babies.

When he was fourteen, Harrison had major surgery involving the removal of one lung. Blood transfusions kept him alive. He strongly disliked needles but vowed he would start donating as soon as he was old enough to do so. At eighteen, he began, turning his head away from every injection he has ever had, staring at the ceilings, the nurses, anything to distract him, for sixty-two years. Saving the lives of millions of infants—including his own grandkids—is an astonishing legacy.

Academics talk about different kinds of altruism, and the purest form is the kind that involves no return at all—it is simply giving. With another kind, called "impure altruism," the recipients experience satisfaction or joy from their giving, known, and felt, as a "warm glow" or, in Harrison's case, a "shiver." Woo says he still gets "that warm feeling" every time he gives blood, as most donors seem to. It's odd that this is defined as somehow impure, or a selfish pleasure, because that warm glow should be sought and encouraged, stoked into fire at every opportunity.

I understand that altruism can be impure when people seek accolades or acknowledgment, some kind of reputational glossing from giving, but if it is just a good feeling from helping someone, then burn, burn, burn. After all, studies have found that trying to make others happy is more cheering than pursuing your own happiness, even in scenarios such as feeding money into a parking meter without meeting the beneficiary.

❅

WHEN TIANA BREMNER-KOSTRZEWA GAVE birth to two premature baby boys—who arrived three months early and suffered brain bleeds—she lost so much blood that she was unable to donate blood to them, even though she was a match. She would have preferred their lives to be saved rather than her own, but she was not given a choice, despite her wishes, as their mother. It still hurts her that their entire lives, lasting just one week, were "needles, injections, hospitals, nothing but pain and discomfort."

Bremner-Kostrzewa had long been a donor, after starting as a teenager alongside her father, and has now been giving blood for twenty-six years. She is a biosecurity dog handler, and when she lived in Darwin she had her plasma donation every second Friday written into her work contract. She's now resident in Tasmania, and weeks before she got married she bet the staff at the Devonport Australian Red Cross Lifeblood center that she would wear her special donor socks on her wedding day, in February 2023 in chilly Wisconsin. She even asked the photographer to take a shot of her blue socks under her wedding dress—her "something blue"—to prove it. "[Giving blood] is a nice thing I can do for random strangers," she says. "I will never know these people and the difference it makes, but for somebody it could be the difference between their child growing up and not. It's a great feeling, because I wasn't able to do it for my kids."

Of course, there are people who come to the aid of others every day: paramedics and emergency workers pumping chests, blowing breath into airways, checking pulses, calming, reassuring, caring. Author and curator Gill Hicks was the last living victim rescued from a train carriage after a teenage terrorist triggered a suicide bomb in the London Underground in 2005. The blast ripped off the bottom halves of her legs, her skin was charred and she lost about 80 percent of her blood. She sat in what she remembers as "a blackened, smoke-filled, indescribable 'room' of destruction and devastation" for an hour waiting for help, talking to others, drifting in and out of consciousness. What she was aware of, though, was that, as the emergency services arrived, every person who came to her aid did so without knowing anything about her.

"To them it didn't matter if I was rich or poor, Black or white, female or male, Muslim or Jew, religious or not," writes Hicks. "What mattered to the police, the ambulance [crew], the paramedics, the surgeons, the nurses and all [those] who never gave up the effort to save my life was that I was a precious human being. I arrived at the hospital as 'One Unknown'—an estimated female" (meaning the burns were so bad the medics couldn't be sure). In the midst of the chaos, her hand was "held tightly," her face "stroked gently." She felt loved. That love, and a knowledge of "the brilliance of humanity," Hicks says, is why she has not felt hatred or sought retribution.

In *Middlemarch*, George Eliot described the impact of the heroine Dorothea Brooke on the people who knew her as "incalculably diffusive: for the growing good of the world is partly dependent on unhistoric acts." Likewise, most blood donors give blood in unhistoric fashion, completely unheralded; they are simply good people who are prepared to walk, drive or catch a bus to their local center, month after month, and allow strangers to drain their blood in the hope that someone, somewhere, might have a chance to live a little better, or longer, and that they might just add some good to the world.

PART II
Our Circles

Our beating hearts

On the edge of a pretty, deserted beach on the Japanese island of Teshima sits a small building housing the heartbeats of thousands of people. Precisely 81,192 of them when I visited with my friend Cath and our two teenage boys, and 81,196 when we left. Since 2008, French artist Christian Boltanski has been gathering heartbeats for *Les Archives du Coeur (The Heart Archives)*, an installation that has traveled to many countries, including South Korea, Sweden, Britain, and Finland; but this remote island houses the permanent collection.

Boltanski, whose Jewish physician father hid for eighteen months under the floorboards of his Paris home during the German occupation in World War II, has a body of work that focuses on the lost, the forgotten and the suffering, and what *The Guardian* called "a tireless engagement with death." In 2010, at the Grand Palais in Paris, I had seen his installation *Personnes*, which consists of an enormous room with a large pile of clothing in the middle of it. As we watched, a tall crane dropped garments, one after another, onto the heap as the sound of heartbeats thrummed around us. In French, *personne* means both "person" and "nobody," and it was impossible to avoid the sense that the garments belonged to people who lost their lives either in concentration camps or elsewhere. People once here, then gone.

There are three rooms at the archives on Teshima. In the first, you can listen to the heartbeats of other people by typing in names or searching randomly by country or year. They sounded like a metronome, and, to my surprise, differed markedly. Our workhorses pumping blood in our chests do so sometimes quietly, sometimes robustly, occasionally jumping a little. Soft beats, loud beats, some erratic, some muffled like distant drums.

The second room, called Heart Room, contains a solitary lightbulb hanging down in a long, dark space and flashing with every pulse of a stranger's heart. Walking into this room, expecting to be moved by a gentle rhythm, we were thrown. The pulse sounded unnerving, like a dark techno beat. The room made me think of the place Boltanski's father would have inhabited, his heart banging loudly in his chest as he feared being found in the dark, dusty, confined space that seems to have captured the imagination of his son, born ten days after Paris was liberated. My own heart started to beat harder, my chest tightened, I began to feel anxious and trapped. It was a reminder that hearts pulse with love, and life, but also fear and horror. That we are rarely conscious of our own heartbeat unless we are scared, or exercised, or afraid. The boys danced jerkily to the beat, and we stared at our reflections in the black glass squares on the wall, which acted like mirrors, then left. My chest clenches again, thinking about it.

Asked by the Dazed Digital website why he had created the archives, Boltanski said: "You always try to capture people you love with photos: You know, you take a photograph of them to keep as a memoir? The recordings of the heartbeats are like photographs: they capture a part of someone. Two or three years ago, I was asked by Mr. Fukutake of Benesse Art to visit this island in Japan. I was inspired to make a library of heartbeats because it was so beautiful. It was very quiet and isolated, and you could hear the heartbeats of the person you love in a very quiet way." He continued, more grimly: "After a few years . . . you will find that the heartbeats all belong to dead people. [Teshima] will become the island of death, in fact. The idea of the piece is that it's impossible to preserve something: you can record the heartbeat of somebody, but you can't stop them dying." In Stockholm, a man contacted Boltanski and said, "I love my dog so much. Please can you put his heart in the library?" He did.

In the third room, you can record your own heart, with a microphone close to your chest. Mine sounded steady but muted, with the odd skip. We were able to leave a message with our heartbeats, once they were placed on the register. Sitting at a desk with a pristine view of the beach, I flicked around the archives to listen to different people and read the words they had written:

Chauwei Yak: "To feel alive again."

Roman Alonso: "I left my heart here."

Samara Eguchi: "Take it easy."

Ann Hayashi: "This is how my heart sounds on a happy day."

Jordi Armengol: "Just some beats but the most important for me."

Hon Erik: "Can you dance to my beats?"

Eddie Lin (who had a strong, steady thump): "I am healthy. I am a good heart man."

Spencer Zubtow: "Heartbeats are the music of life, each a different song, melody, never played the same twice."

My fourteen-year-old left his message blank. His mate wrote, "Bum."

❄

THERE IS A GRIM POIGNANCY to the idea that we cannot love forever, that our hearts might beat strongly but will stop one day, but there is also a beauty to it. If we think of those beats as steps, as steady metronomic clicks, blasts of fire, a sounding of horns, how astonishing is it that we exist at all? That our four-chambered hearts pump away despite all we endure and suffer and see, and that we can walk alongside the other precious, fragile, finite pounding hearts and occasionally hear them.

What of heartbreak? When she conducts an echocardiogram, a cardiologist friend of mine is often asked by her patients if she can see the breaks, the fissures, the hurts. She usually smiles and says, "Just a few little cracks." Perhaps a more important measurement, and one that might enhance our understanding of others, would be that of the love felt beforehand. From the outside of relationships, people often see couples locked in odd patterns, in dysfunctional behaviors or in overt displays of affection, but from inside you might see meteors punctuating dull skies, or a tender morning kiss that makes you forgive the boredom of the night before. It's like walking past a nightclub or pub and seeing dancers gyrate and bounce without hearing the music: you might think they were insane. It is only with the music, heard by a few, that we begin to understand the rhythm of the bodies and the movement of the limbs.

The best way to be alive—vividly, loudly alive—is to be conscious that every day we cross off the calendar is an enormous gift. To know we have a finite number of beats—none of us know how many—is to honor the beats we have, the time we have with each other, with our parents, our children, our siblings, our best friends, our lovers, our tribe, all of whom have pulsing hearts, all of whom are stepping alongside us, quietly pumping blood, in and out, in and out, in and out.

To listen, truly listen, to another's heart is the most intimate act of grace.

Chapter 3

Grace Inherited

THE MOMENT MY MOTHER died, in the thick black of night, my two brothers and I were leaning over her, barely moving, trying to listen for a breath, or sigh, eyes focused on the rise and fall of her chest. My older brother, Mike, had woken with a start, just before she took her final breath, and tugged on our feet to wake us. We'd all jerked upright, and stood by her body, still, straining to hear.

We stayed there, a frozen tableau, for what felt like an hour, with only lamplight falling on her face. Nothing. I leaned forward to stroke her cheek; under my hand, her skin was growing cool. The thought of this still lands a cannonball in my stomach. My mother's skin, cold under my fingers. I think it's because I would ordinarily have rushed to warm her, pile on blankets, fill up a hot-water bottle, throw my arms around her. It's also because she had always represented warmth—we are created in the living heat of our mothers' wombs, then nurtured by their bodies and their touch.

But she was gone, she was cooling. And we had walked as far as we could go with her.

❄

ON WHAT WOULD BE her last night, the three of us had sat by her bedside drinking red wine, alternating between gravely watching her and teasing each other, and arguing about whether our childhood home had in fact been haunted. This theory was new to me, and my best friend from school now firmly believes the suspicious bangs in the night my siblings heard were actually the sounds the two of us made sneaking out to parties, or tiptoeing back up the driveway, carrying shoes, muffling laughter.

As we'd prepared to sleep, my brothers were lying on inflatable mattresses on the floor of the aged care home our mother had been living in for the past four years. I was curled up in a big chair next to Mom, resting my head alongside hers. Eventually, my younger brother, Steve, and I rolled into balls and began to nod off, only to be interrupted by Mike—who had, typically, been checking the sports results (all sports, any sports) on his iPad—saying we had failed to say a proper goodnight. So we did that formally, like the Waltons, and went to sleep smiling, if on edge, ears tuned to Mom's long, dry breaths.

It was 4:19 a.m. when Mike woke and roused us. After we knew she'd gone, we cried, prayed, cried again and sat quietly, stunned and overwhelmed. Then we texted our father, who arrived an hour later.

It comforted me to know that in her last hours she would have heard the voices of her three children, laughing and weeping and bent on showing our love for her during her final walk off the very boundaries of this earth. Our mother, now supine and silent.

That dawn stayed with me for days as a kind of calm before the mad flurry of funeral organizing, the millions of decisions, the numbness of grief.

The next night, as we were walking along the beach from the church to my father's apartment, a large pink moon slid above the horizon, dusting the sand with rosy colors. It felt like the presence of my mother, gentle and strong. Like the woman who, to me, embodied and exemplified grace in a way that indelibly marked all of us, branding our cores. She had a wicked sense of humor and adored a prank, but she loved friends and strangers alike with generous openness and quiet steel. It made me wonder if we can inherit that kind of virtue, in our marrow, if one person can season generations with an awestriking kind of goodness, sustain offspring through trauma and sorrow, model strength and compassion. Can humans reflect the light of others, in their own lives?

Harvard professor Imani Perry says we carry grace down through the generations, "same as the epigenetic trauma of a violent slave-master society. But," she notes, "the grace is the bigger part. It is what made the ancestors hold on so that we could become."

There is now a significant amount of evidence showing that children can inherit trauma from their parents and grandparents, through changes to DNA (not necessarily its sequence, but its form and structure), so-called epigenetic modifications. Researchers from the University of California conducted a study of thousands of the children of US Civil War prisoners of war and found these soldiers' sons—but not daughters—had higher rates of mortality than their peers. The consequences of starvation and severe stress echoed for decades, but the authors noted that, in the next generation, "adequate maternal nutrition could counter" the impact of the trauma, and concluded that "while we cannot rule out fully psychological or cultural effects, our findings are most consistent with an epigenetic explanation."

Studies in epigenetics have revealed how particular genes in DNA can be turned on and off by environmental influences. Globally, a host of researchers are examining and trying to understand adults who house in their genes the shadows of the wars, famines, genocides, rapes and other traumas that their parents endured. It is known that childhood trauma can lead to greater risk of behavioral or psychiatric disorders in those who experienced it—kids who grow up in poverty can be at greater risk of depression as adults, for example—although it can also enable some to develop greater resilience too.

But what of these questions: If trauma can pass through genes, can its opposite do the same? Can positive experiences—more than just the absence of trauma or adversity—be transmitted generationally? Can parents serve as circuit breakers in any way, or at least as buffers against the negative impacts of trauma?

Isabelle Mansuy, professor in Neuroepigenetics at the University of Zurich, is studying this question. In 2016, she published a groundbreaking study showing that the progeny of traumatized mice brought up in an "enriched environment" did not inherit the trauma of their parents—or at least did not exhibit any of the symptoms of it. "Long after the traumatic experiences themselves, living in enriched conditions reverses the behavioral symptoms in adult animals and also prevents the transmission of these symptoms to the progeny," Mansuy says. In other words, if a mouse that had a traumatic early life later lived in a low-stress, good, safe environment, then their behavior and that of their offspring returned to "normal." The changes in behavior are linked to a change in the level of the glucocorticoid receptor in the hippocampus—the part of the brain that we use for cognition and responses to stress—which binds together stress hormones (like cortisone, for example). Epigenetic alterations to the gene encoding this receptor can occur in harmful scenarios, and, it appears, at least in mice, be reversed in positive ones. Since then, Mansuy has been working on an expanded form of this research, telling *Science*, "Environmental enrichment at the right time could eventually help correct some of the alterations which are induced by trauma." The possibilities are incredible. Imagine that kind of healing occurring *in our genes*, and that the effects of harmful environments could be thereby altered, or even reversed.

Associate Professor Catherine Suter, former head of the Epigenetics Laboratory at the Victor Chang Cardiac Research Institute in Sydney, has conducted a study with mice showing that epigenetically inherited traits respond to selection. "In this way," she has noted, "you can have a trait that can rapidly pervade a population, but also not be so 'hardwired' (in the form of a genetic mutation, for example) that it cannot be reversed should conditions change." While speculating on my question of whether goodness could be genetically inherited, Suter said: "I do wonder if there has been some evolutionary pressure applied to goodness over the last millennium or longer. I mean we don't generally eat each other anymore, right? And things like gladiator sports and brutal public executions are (in most cultures) no longer in favor. It's nice to think that goodness might propagate itself, and all the selective pressure you need is the good vibes that flow . . ."

One of the most explosive studies in genetics was undertaken back in the early 2000s, when Canadian behavioral scientist Michael Meaney gathered two groups of rats together. The first were affectionate mother rats—those who were attentive to their newborns, licking and grooming them often. The second were undemonstrative mothers who displayed little interest in their offspring. He found that those raised by the nurturers were less likely to get stressed when they were older. They were calmer, more curious and relaxed. The ignored pups were more likely to grow up anxious, frightened and neurotic. The landmark conclusion was that the affection of the mother actually turned on genes that make molecules in the brain that suppress stress. Without this affection, the gene remains silent. Which is extraordinary, as is the entire field of epigenetics.

Meaney's work was controversial when published in *Nature Neuroscience* in 2004, but has since become one of that journal's most cited papers. It is still hotly contested, with some arguing the data is correlative and does not factor in the role of families, fathers or social context. Professor Naomi Priest, a social epidemiologist from the Australian National University, says, "While recognizing the vital importance of early caregiving to future well-being, we need to exercise caution before holding mothers solely responsible for their children's stress and early environments, instead of looking at what can be done to better support mothers." A host of behavioral scientists have pursued the science further, and many of the studies have yielded fascinating results.

❋

IT WAS ONCE THOUGHT—IN Europe from roughly the seventeenth to the nineteenth century, and in various other cultures—that bad thoughts, dreams or experiences of pregnant women would deform, or delay the growth of, their children. What was called the "maternal imagination" could cause "monstrous births," doctors argued, as well as stains, warts, birthmarks or anything else considered anomalous. The best-selling medical book *Aristotle's Master-Piece*, or *The Secrets of Generation*, published in 1684, stated:

> Many Women there are, that seeing a Hare cross them when great with Child, will through the strength of Imagination bring forth a Child with a hairy lip. Some Children again are born with flat Noses, wry Mouths, great blubber Lips, and ill-shap'd Bodies, and inoft ascribe the reason to the strange conceit of the Mother, who has busied her Eyes and Mind upon some ill shaped or distorted Creature; therefore it greatly behoves all Women with Child to avoid any monstrous sight, or at least, to have a steadfast mind, not easily fixed upon any one thing more than another.

The mother of John Merrick, known in Victorian times as the Elephant Man, was almost stomped on by an elephant at a fair when she was pregnant, and it was believed that this caused his disfigurement. The source of his condition is still unknown, though the most common explanation is that it was Proteus syndrome, which results from a genetic mutation and causes excessive, disproportionate growth of bones, skin, organs, and tissues. (In an apt reflection of a life of public exploitation, his bones were bleached so heavily before being displayed at the Royal London Hospital that DNA tests resolved nothing.)

Of course, the thesis of maternal impression—now widely disfavored—is, on one level, an older version of today's tendency to blame mothers for the problems of their children. Discussion of it was also a way to police and control female behavior and exculpate men from the responsibility of caring for offspring deemed to have been so affected by their mothers. Professor Marilyn Francus, author of *Monstrous Motherhood: Eighteenth-Century Culture and the Ideology of Domesticity*, told me that the fact that "pregnancy was a female activity out of male control was a cause for considerable anxiety." The British doctor John Maubray, who championed the idea of maternal impression, advised women not to spend too much time with their pets when pregnant, so that their children did not emerge from the womb resembling cats or dogs. He was significantly embarrassed, though, when the highly publicized and scandalous case of Mary Toft, who claimed to have given birth to a series of rabbits in 1726 after being startled by one, was revealed to be a hoax. (She had, with help, inserted animal parts into her uterus, later expelling them in the presence of doctors and in the grips of "labor pains," in the hope of financial gain. Understandably, this caused a national commotion.)

More superstition than science, the theory of maternal impression was gradually abandoned once genetic theory emerged and more was understood about the way embryos are shaped, nurtured and grown in the womb. Pregnant women could finally feel at ease petting rabbits or dodging wild boars without fear of imprinting their experiences on their children's faces.

Victorian doctors, with their leeches and laudanum, have been rightly lambasted for their ignorance about the female form. And in truth, while they were pondering rats and rabbits, something much more profound was happening, not in the imaginations of mothers, but in their marrow.

❄

MOTHERS DON'T JUST HOUSE our children in our bodies, we meld with them. The volume of blood in our bodies almost doubles; we pool and brim with plasma, cells and platelets. Our hearts work harder and more efficiently as the blood carries nutrients to the fetus, even growing bigger and beating faster. Our pelvic bones separate. A dark line trails down our stomach, dividing us in two. Our pulse rises. Our sense of smell sharpens. Our feet grow longer and wider as our arches flatten out, often permanently. For some reason I also shrank, by two centimeters.

As women create children, children bring about changes in us. Fetal cells migrate into our pregnant bodies, into our blood and tissues, and can stay for decades. We knew that cells traveled from the fetus to the mother as far back as the late nineteenth century, but not that they could remain there for so long. This was first discovered in 1994, when male DNA was found in the body of a woman a year after she had given birth to her son. In 2012, researchers found, when examining the brains of deceased women aged between thirty-two and one hundred and one, that the majority contained male DNA, presumably as a result of having birthed sons.

The process is called fetal microchimerism—after the chimera in Greek mythology, a female monster that breathes fire and has the head of a lion, the body of a goat, and the tail of a serpent. Fetal cells have been found in maternal blood, skin, liver, bone marrow and even the heart and brain. Which means children change women not just in a physiological, or mental, way, but at a molecular level.

This is something mothers know instinctively.

Work is now being done to ascertain what this means for the health of the mother, given evidence that these cells can both expose the mother to and protect her from risks—greater risk of autoimmune disorders and pre-eclampsia, for example, but also protection from rheumatoid arthritis, and help in healing wounds and boosting milk production. Fetal cells may also improve longevity and fertility. In 2017, researchers from Cincinnati and Hamburg published a paper that found that "the bidirectional transfer of genetically foreign cells between mothers and their offspring during pregnancy is probably not accidental. Instead, microchimeric cells that express familially relevant traits are purposefully retained to promote genetic fitness by improving the outcome of future pregnancies." Astonishing.

Not only do we carry our children. We also carry our mothers. We also, I think, carry their mothers too. According to an article in *Scientific American*, "Women may have microchimeric cells both from their mother as well as from their own pregnancies, and there is even evidence for competition between cells from grandmother and infant within the mother." How far back does this go? Women are their mothers, their children, themselves. And Walt Whitman was the one who thought he "contained multitudes." *Oh Walt*, I snort.

❄

MY MOTHER WAS THE epitome of grace, possibly even to a fault. To be clear: while I would love to have inherited my mother's grace, and hope I have at least inherited an understanding of it by observing her, I am a far more judgmental and demanding character. Mom got nervous whenever I told her I was asking my boss (any boss) for a pay rise ("They are so good to you there!"), she frequently failed to invoice people for work she did because she felt sorry for them, and she insisted everyone was capable of great goodness. I thought this last claim might be tested when she spent time working in prisons with a Christian group called Kairos, but instead it was somehow affirmed. She would return with stories of tears and vulnerability after days spent with women who had master-minded multi-million-dollar drug trades or decapitated men. She would speak of the abuse and violence they had suffered, of how they mostly struggled to forgive themselves, of how they lit up when someone baked a cake for them, or broke down when someone expressed genuine care.

One person I never imagined she would cast a gentle eye on was Katherine Knight, who was jailed for life in the high-security, notoriously violent Mulawa prison (now Silverwater Women's Correctional Center) after she killed her boyfriend, skinned him and boiled his body parts. The grotesque nature of the crime made Knight notorious; the trial ran prominently in the media in 2001 and several books were written about her, but none of the authors or journalists were able to secure an interview with her. Meanwhile, my mother got to know her well, and would come home and confide in me that Knight was a very cheerful, affectionate person who would sing hymns loudly—like "When the Saints Go Marching In"—and hug the women from Kairos with abandon. She had, apparently, converted to Christianity.

I was agog. Then, one day, my mother called me to tell me she had had a profound experience with Knight when talking to her about the things that bothered her most. My mother told Knight she was busy and exhausted, and worried about falling asleep when she was trying to pray. Knight put a hand on her arm and told her not to worry about something like that, that she was obviously tired, that God would understand. My mother was startled by what she saw as Knight's gentleness, or wisdom, and her ability to comfort.

It was hard to reconcile. After Mom told me this story, I went online and looked up the court judgment to find out why

Knight had been the first Australian woman to be convicted for life without parole, "never to be released." The facts were horrifying. After a lifetime of cruel and violent acts, and angry that her boyfriend, John Price, wanted to break up with her and would not give her a share of his house, she had stabbed him thirty-seven times, piercing organs and spilling deep, wide pools of blood. Knight, who had spent years working as a meat slicer in a slaughterhouse, then skinned Price and hung his skin on a meat hook. After that, Knight decapitated Price, put his head in a pot on the stove with some vegetables to make a "sickening stew," and carved off and cooked sections of his buttocks, planning to serve them to his children, accompanied by malicious notes.

I mean . . . does this woman merit *hugs*? The scene was so horrendous that, Justice Barry O'Keefe said, several highly experienced police officers—veterans in examining crime scenes—needed to take stress leave "because of the situation with which they were confronted when examining the crime scene at Mr. Price's house." O'Keefe was unsparing in his summation, concluding: "The fact that the murder was premeditated, the prisoner's long history of serious violence, malice, vindictiveness, possessiveness, cruelty and dangerousness to the community if released, and her ongoing incurable borderline personality disorder [mean] the case is marked out as one for which the maximum penalty of life imprisonment would, subject to any subjective matters in mitigation, be appropriate." He considered her likely to commit further acts of violence, even murder, against "those who cross her, particularly males."

The premeditated murder was made worse by the glee with which Knight sliced up his cadaver. "Not only did she plan the murder," said O'Keefe, "but she also enjoyed the horrific acts which followed in its wake as part of a ritual of death and defilement." Nor did she show any mercy or regret.

❉

IN PRISON KNIGHT SEEMED transformed. She was not allowed knives or even cellmates, whom it was thought she might kill. But reports emerged of her painting artworks and knitting. When Catholic Archbishop George Pell—who was facing his own allegations of abuse—visited the prison in 2009, photos showed a beaming, elderly woman with gray hair and glasses standing with her hand on the churchman's shoulder.

Who wouldn't be cynical about such a conversion? Though surely tyrants and murderers are capable of being nice occasionally, of doing handiwork, and smiling for cameras. After Victoria Schembri served time at Mulawa for tax fraud, she emerged with stories of a "very close" friendship with Knight. Schembri, a former stripper and Penthouse Pet, said she and Knight "had an extremely special relationship, one of the closest I've had in my life."

According to James Phelps, who wrote *Green Is the New Black: Inside Australia's Hardest Women's Jails* in 2018, Knight was then the most popular inmate in the prison. Schembri told him: "She is a gentle soul and not a criminal to me. She is a mediator at Mulawa. She would stop girls stealing from each other, and stop girls from fighting. But she never did it by standing over anyone.

She never raised her hands to anyone. She was just someone who everyone loved."

An unnamed prison officer told Phelps that Knight was the "top boss" among the inmates, who were the most violent in the state. "No, she has never raised her hands in prison," the officer said. "Not once. I think she has that level of respect because of her crime. Because she was so brutal. She has a lot of respect in the inmate population, that's for sure. They simply do not f*** around with her, and that's a fact. . . . Even the guards respect her a bit. She's the boss, put it that way."

Schembri told the *Daily Telegraph* that she believed Knight was nothing like the evil woman she was depicted as in books. "She is really nurturing, really caring, and it's so hard in all honesty to put the person I met with that monster. We called her Nanna, like grandma, she was so amazingly caring and considerate. On a Friday we'd have our buy-up come in . . . we'd all be there rolling up bread and making dim sims and spring rolls—everyone buys their bit for the buy-up, some people would do cheesecakes—and she would be there, sharing everything with everybody and making sure no one missed out or was left out."

I tried repeatedly to make an appointment to talk to Knight about my mother, but she was not interested. She sent a message through the governor of the jail, saying that she could not remember Mom. Which makes my mother's openness even more remarkable.

❊

I CAN UNDERSTAND A murderer, even one who premeditated a diabolical crime, having a decent side. I can understand Knight, like others have done, grew up with abuse and magnified it. I can also understand that one key to humanity is understanding, or reckoning with, the environment, or society, that fosters abuse, or creates "monsters." I don't understand, though, how true psychopaths can be forgiven, without reparations and an attempt at redemption.

This is why Sister Helen Prejean's work is important. Known for her role as a spiritual adviser for prisoners on death row, and for her book *Dead Man Walking*, Prejean says grace compelled her to show love to the most wretched, reviled and ugly characters on earth: murderers, rapists and Nazi sympathizers. She told *The Table* podcast: "Where the moral failure is, is to identify a human person completely with an action. Everybody is worth more than the worst thing we've ever done. That's human transcendence."

Sister Prejean has tried to find a morsel of humanity in the remorseless, tried to allow for the possibility that love can transform. She sat with the murderer and rapist Robert Lee Willie—later played by the actor Sean Penn in the movie *Dead Man Walking*—for hours, trying to get him to see what he had done, and reckon with his acts. All the while, she sought dignity for him. As she tells it:

I said to Robert Lee Willie, what if somebody killed your mama, what would you want to do to them? To just get him to cross out of himself into the pain that he had inflicted on these families. And he said "I'd sure as hell want to kill 'em." . . . And then, when he was working on his last words as to what he would say, he was going to come out with all kinds of tough stuff . . . and I was just saying, "Robert, you know it's your chance," and then he said, "Well, look, I really hope my death gives them some peace, the victims." And, boy, I latched on to that. I knew that was a little part of this soul that could be built in terms of . . . because he was thinking of others. And it was really a wish—it was a love wish for other people that perhaps his death could give them peace.

Imagine if we flipped our standard of judgment from magnifying shortcomings to searching for "a little part of this soul that could be built." Scrabbling through dirt when you see a tiny glimmer of light.

The responsibility of a justice system is different from the responsibility of a nun. But both mete mercy. (And mercy cannot be understood without context. A University of Michigan review of the 7,482 death sentences handed down between 1973 and 2004 estimated that more than 4 percent of people sentenced to death in the United States are innocent.) What Sister Prejean challenges us to think about is what shapes a person.

Take James Coddington, a prisoner she recently championed on death row. In 1997, he killed a man called Al Hale, who was both a friend and a colleague, at a car parts store during a crack-cocaine binge. In pleading for clemency, supporters pointed to three things: his remorse, his model behavior as a prisoner, and his background. His parents had been in and out of jail, and his mother had been imprisoned when he was six weeks old. He'd passed between the dilapidated and cockroach-infested homes of his father and grandparents. At his grandmother's, the bathtub was used as a toilet. When he was a few months old, his violent, alcoholic father poured beer into a baby bottle and gave it to him to stop him crying. He also gave him whisky. His brother told a court the "buzz" the baby got was amusing.

James was cared for by his half-sister, who ran away with him when she was fourteen and he was fifteen months old, but she did not change his diaper or properly feed him. His skin became raw, and he was covered in insect bites by the time the children came to the attention of the social services. After a few days of foster care, James was sent back to his father, who spent all his money on booze and later left all his kids when James was seven, by which time James had already developed issues with substance abuse. Soon he was addicted to crack. In 1997 he visited Hale to ask for money to buy cocaine. When Hale refused, Coddington, who was in a drug psychosis, hit him on the head with a hammer.

New York Times columnist Nicholas Kristof commented: "The story of James Coddington is like many of those on death row. These are people who suffered greatly and who in turn inflicted great suffering on others. Without diminishing in any way the brutality of their crimes, in many cases we failed them before they failed us." Prison can be a terrible place for people who have experienced trauma, and can exacerbate instead of fixing behavioral problems.

When the Oklahoma Pardon and Parole Board reviewed his case, Coddington apologized, expressed remorse, and said: "I'm clean, I know God, I'm not a vicious murderer." Former director of the Oklahoma Department of Corrections Justin Jones said

Coddington's time on death row was "a story . . . of remarkable transformation." He added that he was "firmly convinced that Coddington is a person who makes his prison community a better-functioning place for both correctional staff and other prisoners," and that "it would not be in the best interests of the state of Oklahoma to execute someone who manifests such redemption."

The board recommended clemency—and that the death sentence be reduced to a life sentence without parole. Sister Prejean was thrilled, saying this decision was one that "recognizes our human capacity for change and growth, and our ability to forge a new life out of wreckage if given a chance."

Governor Kevin Stitt disagreed. Coddington was executed on August 25, 2022. In the moments before his execution, lying on a gurney, he thanked his supporters then said: "Governor Stitt, I don't blame you, and I forgive you."

Funny, the cracks where grace leaks through.

Twenty-five executions were scheduled for the next twenty-eight months, although in 2023 this slowed to one every sixty days instead of one every thirty days, to prevent over-taxing prison staff.

❊

IT'S GOOD TO CARRY a healthy skepticism about famous last words. Most last utterances are actually whispers, grunts, single words and repetitive, delirious phrases, not perfectly crafted, poetic witticisms. The exceptions tend to come from people who have had time to deliberate on what they want their last words to be, including people who know they are fatally sick or injured, or about to be executed. Some opt for bad jokes. Upon being strapped to an electric chair in 1928, convicted killer George Appel is widely—and probably erroneously—believed to have said, "Well, gentlemen, you are about to see a baked Appel." In 1958, James French, having been convicted of strangling a fellow jail inmate, apparently offered up a headline for the next day's paper before he was electrocuted: "French fries." In 1995, murderer Tom Grasso offered a complaint: "I did not get my Spaghetti-O's, I got spaghetti. I want the press to know this."

Others apologize, or express love for their families and God. An analysis of death row statements archived by the Texas Department of Criminal Justice (going back to 1976, and covering 534 prisoners, 117 of whom chose not to speak) found that 63 percent of all speakers used the word "love"—an average of 1.7 times per prisoner. The second most used word was "family," uttered by almost half. Eighteen percent mentioned their mothers. "Heart" was used by 14 percent of prisoners, and "care" 11 percent.

But few people have sufficient warning, or clarity, to make last statements, despite the romantic myths. And why are we so intent on believing in a uniquely profound deathbed lucidity anyway? As one doctor told *The Atlantic*, many people often just say, "Oh fuck, oh fuck."

❄

WE DO KNOW THAT many people call for their mothers in their closing hours. German author Hajo Schumacher said a hospice nurse told him the last words of dying men are often similar: "With their last breath, almost everyone calls for 'Mutti' or 'Mama.'" In other research, published in the *Journal of Aging Humanities and the Arts* in 2010, hospice workers reported that between 10 and 25 percent of elderly people call for their mothers when they are dying. Soldiers on the battlefield during the American Civil War were reported to have done the same. This still happens in battle today. One Ukrainian surgeon reported: "When soldiers are dying, they all say the same thing: they call for their mother or their fellow soldiers." All of which must cause every mother's heart to clench.

Likewise the mother of forty-six-year-old George Floyd, who called for her while he lay dying, as the knee of a police officer crushed his neck for an agonizing eight minutes and forty-six seconds. "Momma!" he cried. "Momma! I'm through." And the mother of Tyre Nichols, aged twenty-nine, who called for her three times during a night of police brutality in 2023, before dying three days later. Nichols, the father of a four-year-old, had the name of his mother, RowVaughn Wells, tattooed on his arm. At a press conference, she told the policemen who'd killed her son: "You . . . disgraced your own families when you did this." Her heart broke, RowVaughn said, to hear her son had spoken her name: "For a mother to know that their child was calling them in their need, and I wasn't there for him. . . . My son was a beautiful soul."

When I speak here of mothers, I don't mean to downplay the importance of fathers at all. It seems to me that relationships with the people who birthed us run so deep that, in ways we barely understand and scientists can barely begin to measure, we exist with them in a state of grace. It's a state in which anything can happen—when parents find unknown strength to lift rolling cars off toddlers, when the faintest infant cry can flood bodies with adrenaline, when a mother's impending last breath can jerk us awake in the middle of the night, when the sound of a family member's voice can right the world again, where love endures pain, when the unforgivable can be forgiven, when the greatest lessons are learned, and where, when relations are broken, we yearn for them to be mended again. Where our very bodies exchange cells, our hearts pump the same blood. The connection can be so formidable and potent, and the love so profound, that often we don't even know we are in it, until we lose it.

❄

AS I SAT DOWN to write today, a package landed on my front porch. It was a photograph of the sails of the Sydney Opera House silhouetted against a pink moon, printed onto glass, a late Christmas present from my friend Martha. It was, she wrote in an email, in remembrance of my mother. A few minutes later, I realized it was *the* pink moon, the very one that had appeared that evening after my mother died, the super pink moon that rose over the ocean on Tuesday, April 27, 2021. (These moons are called "super" because they appear enormous, as the moon is at its closest position to Earth.) In the image, three silhouetted birds are flying across the sky.

Martha had hunted for months to find a photo of this particular moon, and was especially pleased with the image because the three birds could be seen to represent my brothers and me, carrying our mother to the edge of the earth. Or my two kids and me, walking in the light of her legacy. I thanked her for her thoughtfulness, and she wrote in response:

Perhaps it's just—as you are, so acutely—being alive to the way the world offers so much consolation and companionship. I spent those nights when you were with your mom, and when she ascended, looking at the moon growing fuller and fuller, talking to and, in a way, *being* with you and her, as quietly and steadily as I could, through its light, as she grew closer and closer to the threshold. So now when I walk at night, I do the same thing. This image seemed to express that cycle of reflection and return and her continuing presence and I wanted to find a way to share that with you.

Grace in a friend, in a mother, in a moon, grace everywhere. Before she became a nurse, a young Laura Gilpin wrote a poem called "Night Song," in which she describes a woman waking suddenly in an empty room "crying mother, mother," just as:

the moon, watching
at a distance, rose
over her bed
and stayed there
until she was
asleep.

Chapter 4

Icarus Flew

I believe Icarus was not failing as he fell,
but just coming to the end of his triumph.

—Jack Gilbert

TWO WEEKS AFTER I had started my job at a news magazine in New York, with a breast pump for a six-month-old baby girl slung over my arm, I woke to a flurry of voicemails and messages from Australia. My ex-boyfriend Morgan was missing. He had been on a plane in Indonesia that had overshot the runway, skidded across a road and onto a field, and burst into flames, and he was not accounted for. My phone trembled and vibrated with messages for hours as I sat and stared into space. I nursed my baby in silence, got dressed and made my way through the snow to the subway. In between meetings, I sat in my office overlooking a snow-white fairy-tale Central Park, feeling sick, and tried to concentrate on editing my pages. On the television at the end of my desk, footage of a burning, skidding plane played on a loop as the world tried to fathom what had happened and who was lost.

Morgan could not be found. Morgan, from whom I had separated less than two years before. Morgan, who had asked me to marry him in the mountains of Morocco. Handsome Morgan, the tall surfer with salt in his veins and a ready grin, who had worked on the other side of the newsroom from me, in the business section. Morgan, who had stayed with me at the office Christmas party one year until we were, finally, alone; I folded into him when he told me he had a crush on me. He was direct, strong and certain: he was content to let me write and stay out late dancing when he wanted to get up early to train for triathlons, and he took time off work to help me finish my PhD, sourcing photographs. He called himself "Captain Sensible," although sometimes he would burst out and be the wildest and happiest person in the room.

Morgan was less interested in what people thought of him than anyone I have ever met. "You can't have everyone like you," he'd say when I fretted about something uselessly, "that's just not possible." He often rubbed people the wrong way, appearing remote, and shrugged it off as their problem. We were not, ultimately, meant to be together, but I adored him and curled up in his calm and contentment as we lived together happily for years. He was detached, sometimes, from people: he had a wide circle of acquaintances, but he believed he only had a handful of true friends. The creature he doted on most was Otis, our Burmese cat. He fussed over that chocolate lunatic, allowing him to sleep on his stomach under the covers and racing home after work to play with him. He wrote me simple cards of love: *All I need to be happy is to be near you*, and *I love you more every day, and will forever.*

But Morgan, the man who had once been *my* Morgan, could not be found. The Beatles lyrics about hearing the news today kept recycling through my brain, over and over, as I waited. Oh, boy. We had broken up such a short time ago, after a year of counseling and wrenching frustration, knowing we loved each other but couldn't fix things in the way we needed to in order to last. As I cried before leaving, he said to me, "Well, I think that is very sad," and I cried some more.

Since then, he had traveled the world, won a Walkley Award for his journalism and dated a cluster of pretty women; I had quickly fallen in love, got married and gone to America and had a baby, at almost unseemly breakneck speed. Which meant that, when Morgan could not be found, the memories of him, of him and me curled up together in our home, were still warm, that the imprint of his hand in mine was still fresh. Five years we had spent together, four of them living in a sweet, old run-down apartment overlooking Bronte Beach in Sydney's east. Now, in New York, I stayed up through the night as my then-husband slept, checking my email and news reports for scraps of information about the reporters who had been following the Australian foreign minister on his tour of Indonesia and had been on that plane, Garuda Flight 200.

But he was gone. Burned alive in the fire. One of twenty-one people to die in that horrible crash near Yogyakarta Airport, just after dawn. A man in his prime, fit and upright, just days before his thirty-seventh birthday. His poor assistant had had to identify his remains, after panicked hours spent searching for his body near the wreckage and in the hospital. *Oh, boy.*

I had to stay late at work that Thursday night to edit my first cover story. I locked myself in my office and wept, thinking of Morgan's daring, his decency, his fun, his kindness, his courage, his laughter, of how much he had still to do and be, of the stupid bloody waste of it all. Of the times we scuba-dived on the Great Barrier Reef, danced in tiny bars in Spain, trekked the mountains of Morocco, drank wine in Paris. I called his mother, his sister, his mates. I emailed my friends, puzzling over the senselessness of the accident. "He was obsessed with safety." I wrote to one, "He drove a Subaru."

So where is the place in grief for a former girlfriend, one who lived with a man who has just died, who had almost married him? In the days to come, I would see him being recast as a rogue and a ladies' man, not the self-reliant introvert who was true and kind. All kinds of people would claim him, people he barely knew, and the women he had spent time with jostled for a place in online tributes. I quickly realized how competing incomplete narratives of grief can add further layers of pain for the grieving. I became fascinated by his Indonesian girlfriend, Nila Tanzil, largely because so many in Australia seemed to dismiss or overlook her in their clamoring recollections, while she insisted she be known. She wrote sweet, sad blog entries talking about how he'd wanted her to dance for him—now a newspaper correspondent and a TV host, she had once been a traditional Javanese dancer—and how she only did once because she was too shy.

When Nila went to her office on Wednesday March 7, her colleagues had all crowded around a television, watching footage of the crash. She'd cried: "Oh my god, Morgan's on the plane!" His maid said his ticket was for another flight, so that day was one of confusion until one of Morgan's friends called and said his ID card had been found.

Nila flew to Sydney for the funeral, which was quite an event, attended by politicians and editors at a big cathedral. In quiet moments, I read reports of this dainty woman standing to speak at Morgan's wake. Boldly, she took the microphone at the morning tea after the service and told the gathered crowd: "He was my best friend, my partner, my personal editor. It was my privilege to be with him on his last days." I cheered her on from New York. Morgan loved relationships and respected women, and so many of the public recollections had made him seem like a player. At the same morning tea, Morgan's editor at the *Financial Review*, Glenn Burge, said: "He had a great sense of humor, a great ability to stir the people around him—particularly the women."

As Australian women he had dated laid claim to Morgan in online forums with varying timelines and acknowledgments, Nila insisted on reminding them he'd had a girlfriend in the months leading up to his death, one he saw every day and stayed with every night. This seemed important, somehow. In a speech to his colleagues, Laura Tingle, his bureau chief in Canberra, spoke about how he'd made his relationship with me his first priority, leaving the parliamentary gallery every Thursday afternoon like clockwork to drive back to our home in Bronte, and not returning until Monday.

As I sat there in New York, tuning magazine copy, reworking headlines and captions, and conferring with the lead writer, I received an email from Burge, saying the police were trying to find out who his dentist was, and could I help? His teeth. They needed to identify his remains by his teeth.

I cracked.

❄

PEOPLE OFTEN TALK ABOUT a hierarchy of grief, whereby those who loved and knew a person best grieve the loudest and clearest, but it often does not happen this way. As with biographies, side players and supporting actors frequently race to share fragments of their recollections, to insert their stories in the broader narrative of a life beautifully, imperfectly lived. It's especially striking when it happens to someone you love.

At any rate, an ex-girlfriend is just that: an ex, gone, the stuff of rumor, conjecture and history. I had nothing to say; I was mute with grief and struggling to recognize the character newspaper reports were describing. No one mentioned how much Morgan loved spending time in silence, how much he loved the wild—the seas, mountains, rivers. How, the further he drew away from cities, the happier he became. How much he wanted to be "honorable" in life, how important the word "honor" was to him. How interested he was in time—his oft-expounded theory of aging was that as we grow older, time speeds up—and how he always tried to do what Kenneth Slessor said: lean against the "golden undertow" of time. How preternaturally calm he was, the calmest person I have ever met. How focused and disciplined he was, at least when it came to his training for triathlons and adventure races, but how every now and then what a friend called a "party tiger hiding in the long grasses of sobriety" would emerge, and cut loose. How much space he required on a dance floor: he once almost punched a waiter at a Soho bar with a flailing limb. How he danced at home, all the time, in his bathing trunks, to make me laugh. And how he encapsulated his dreams for the future in a single word: "relaxing."

I kept thinking of the poem the self-described American "serious romantic" Jack Gilbert wrote about Icarus, "Failing and Flying." In it, he asks why we are so glum about relationships that don't last, why we don't recognize that some relationships soar before fading, and tells us that that is what we need to remember, and hold. Otherwise, why would we ever dare to love? And why do we assume an ended relationship must be defined by its end, not its beginning, or its heights?

> Everyone forgets that Icarus also flew.
> It's the same when love comes to an end,
> or the marriage fails and people say
> they knew it was a mistake, that everybody
> said it would never work. That she was
> old enough to know better. But anything
> worth doing is worth doing badly.
> Like being there by that summer ocean
> on the other side of the island while
> love was fading out of her, the stars
> burning so extravagantly those nights that

anyone could tell you they would never last.
Every morning she was asleep in my bed
like a visitation, the gentleness in her
like antelope standing in the dawn mist.
Each afternoon I watched her coming back
through the hot stony field after swimming,
the sea light behind her and the huge sky
on the other side of that. Listened to her
while we ate lunch. How can they say
the marriage failed? Like the people who
came back from Provence (when it was Provence)
and said it was pretty but the food was greasy.
I believe Icarus was not failing as he fell,
but just coming to the end of his triumph.

I wanted to fly back for the funeral, but, given the distance, and circumstances, I decided to stay in the shadows. I was a mother, living in another country. I was worried that, like Nila, I would want to grab the microphone and say, "No, that's not right, he was more than that," though I felt petty and shitty and small to even be raising eyebrows at other people's stories, wondering if they were distorting their own role in his life. See? It sounds awful. I knew also that Morgan was many things to many people.

He died sixteen years ago, but I cried again writing this. Imagine the life he could have lived.

❄

FIFTEEN YEARS AFTER THAT Garuda plane overshot the runway, I walked into the Boatshed Café in South Perth one Tuesday morning to meet Nila for a coffee. While writing this, I had looked her up, discovered she had gone on to do some astonishing things, and emailed her out of the blue while sitting on my bed watching the sun set over Exmouth. I'm not even entirely sure why. I'd asked her how she was, if she was okay now, and how she had coped with the grief. She wrote back almost immediately, with a warm gust of words, spoke of crying three times a day for two months after Morgan died, and asked if I would ever be in Perth and could we meet? Coincidentally, I was due to arrive there a couple of days later.

Nila told me she'd had to leave her job at a public relations firm after Morgan died, because so many media contacts were friends of his and were daily reminders of her loss. Three months after he died, she took a job trading bonds at a securities company, before being poached to work in Singapore. After two years there, she said, "I felt my heart was healed." Not 100 percent, but better. "Now, if I think of him," she said, "I smile."

Today a mother and a force, Nila left her job in finance to establish a not-for-profit group that has set up a long chain of libraries for children in regional Indonesia. She has been an Eisenhower Fellow and an Atlantic Fellow, and is now partway through a PhD in education at Curtin University.

Nila was sweet, candid and funny, often breaking into laughter. She was glad to talk, she said, because she had buried a lot of the sadness, as she had not known how to process it at the time, and had not yet discovered meditation. She recalled that after she had flown to Sydney for the funeral she had sat in her hotel room, enraged—how could this happen? Why? The week before Morgan died, he'd glowed with rude health and joy, she said, remembering how she looked at him one morning as he was dressing and thought it was like he was lit up: "Wow, my boyfriend is really handsome."

❄

HE WAS. AND FATE was, is, cruel. People often describe early, sudden deaths as senseless, as though the opposite, life, makes sense. When people who fall ill ask, "Why me?", it always perplexes me—why someone else and not you? Why should the foul vagaries of sickness, accident and misfortune only fall on others? But it is particularly difficult to stomach an early death—of an infant, a child, or a strapping thirty-six-year-old Australian man making a decent fist of creating a life he loved. The sheer randomness of it was exacerbated by the fact that he wasn't meant to be on that flight, that a shift in the foreign minister's schedule had meant he'd changed airlines at the last minute, to Garuda, which he thought would be safer than the other local carrier, Adam Air.

The Jewish Italian chemist and writer Primo Levi wrote of the shock of having a primal, if irrational, belief in the kindness of destiny before he was captured and taken to Auschwitz in 1944:

This time last year I was a free man: an outlaw but free, I had a name and a family, I had an eager and restless mind, an agile and healthy body. I used to think of many, far-away things; of my work, of the end of the war, of good and evil, of the nature of things and of the laws which govern human actions; and also of the mountains, of singing and loving, of music, of poetry. I had an enormous, deep-rooted faith in the benevolence of fate; to kill and to die seemed extraneous literary things to me.

Cynthia Banham referenced these words of Levi's in her book *A Certain Light*. Cynthia, then a foreign affairs and defense correspondent for the *Sydney Morning Herald*, was sitting across the aisle from Morgan as the plane slammed into the fields, but she somehow managed to drop out of the bottom of the plane and haul herself to safety through the muddy rice fields. She lost both of her legs, broke her back and suffered burns to 60 percent of her body. She told *Good Weekend* that, like Levi, she had lost her naivety. "Actually there is tragedy everywhere you look," she said. "You can find it very easily in certain countries overseas but even when you look in your own very privileged country, it is there in every family. Whether it's cancer or mental illness or misfortune of some kind. Losing a child. Whatever. It's everywhere. And actually that's the way life is."

Despite spending years in recovery, Cynthia went on to acquire a Master's in International Affairs, then a PhD. She became a respected scholar of political science, publishing two books, and an ambassador for the Sydney Swans. She has married, and had a child. She has lived, and been happy. But the memories of the accident and the days after are still too painful to speak about.

❄

SO, WHAT CAN THE living learn from something that makes no sense? Morgan imprinted people with his joy, in life and in death. Nila told me: "It's funny to think that because of Morgan now I live in a more impulsive way. I mean, if I want to do something, I just do it. [His death] made me think that we never know until when we're going to live here on this planet. I remember that he was always full of life and fun, doing things that he enjoyed doing. So, that was one of the most valuable takeaways for me. That was also one of the reasons why I set up my nonprofit organization in a split-second after having three days of sleepless nights, thinking of kids without access to books. I thought, if not now, then when?"

She is right. What I also learned is that, no matter where you find yourself, whoever you are with, even if that relationship may not always endure, we have a serious duty to honor, treasure and fiercely care for that person. We entrust ourselves with each other, in relationships, and it's a very particular kind of duty: to soften blows, to carry and delight each other, to ease pain and plunder joy.

Oh, boy.

❄

I TOOK THE AFTERNOON of Morgan's funeral off work, walked up to the Cloisters in Washington Heights and sat on a park bench in the snow. I wrote him a letter and waited for my friends to call from the wake. He was loved, respected, fêted, awarded and adored, by many. He had been by my side for years, and I was acutely aware of how lucky I had been. The last time I'd seen him, in the middle of a working day, he had leaned across the lift in our building and kissed my cheek. He comes to me in my dreams, still, and he is always grinning.

Before Icarus fell, he flew.

❄

AFTER MY FRIEND MARTHA left Morgan's funeral, she walked through David Jones on her way home and the piano player was playing "Blue Skies" by Irving Berlin, the brilliant New York composer. She wrote to me and sent me the lyrics, about how the sun shines brighter and the days hurry by when you are in love.

It's true, they fly. Which is why we need to relish the relationships we have, and have had. The astonishing thing to think of is how much of a responsibility we have to guard the moments we do have, and cradle them carefully. We so often have less time than we think; we need to care for each other, deliberately and unrelentingly, when we can.

Chapter 5

"Inhale the World": An Ode to the Fire of Teenage Girls

FROM THE MOMENT YOU first cradle an infant girl in your arms, with her tiny, bunched-up face, balled-up fists and splotchy skin, people start to warn you about the moment when she will defy you. A baby, toddler or small girl being stubborn, angry, or just, say, infantile will draw a response along the lines of: "Ooooooh, just *wait* until she is a teenager." Mixed in with the jesting is a sense of gentle menace, anxiety and warning: the rite of passage between your daughter's morphing from girl to woman will be paved with peril. (Fathers begin to worry, strangely early, about the kinds of boyfriends they might bring home, and how they might need to fight or frighten them, but this is the subject of another discussion.)

No one ever warns me about my son's teen years. Or shows of strength. That's just him being a teenager, or a boy. It's the girls we're told to worry about—girls who rebel, who refuse to accept authority. Can it be anything but a coincidence that the years we are warned about are the years in which girls grow into young women who question us?

My girl, obstinate and bold, drew all manner of warnings. I admit she was a fearsome toddler. When I dared to get pregnant with another child when she was two, her scorn was arctic. For months, she would deal only with her father, and her eyeballs burned contempt when they locked with mine. I found it quite shocking; it felt like I was in high school. As a primary schooler, she instructed my friends on what to wear, doled out relationship advice to them and would look at me sternly, saying things like, "Now, I am going to walk out of this room, and, when I walk back in, I would like you to at least *pretend* to be a normal mother."

Ooooh, look out, she'll be hard work as a teenager!

So, I was ready for the teenage years. Steeled, prepped, armed. I understood the brief. She would be wild and angry, and I would be bereft and ground down. I determined not to take any of it too much to heart.

It all began to happen in primary school—the Instagram problems, the boys, the nonsense. Then the sneaking out at night. One day, when she was thirteen, she turned up on our front doorstep in bright daylight, wearing pajamas, wiping invisible cobwebs out of her face and turning in circles. She looked high, crazed. I inhaled and thought to myself: *Okay, fine, she's experimented with something, I need to put her in the shower and get her to bed.* I would be calm and make sure she was safe. She was calling out "There's a spider on me!" repeatedly. She looked so deranged, and was swiping at empty air, so I took her in my arms, spun her about and told her to walk inside. As I did, I suddenly saw a large black spider, the size of my fist, crawling down her back.

Parties, alcohol and boys aren't really the problems with teenage girls, though. I used to sneak out to clubs myself with my best friend, choke on disgusting cigarettes in parks down the street and drink foul alcoholic concoctions when I shouldn't have. The problem is that teenage girls defy you. After a while, as I watched my daughter grappling with a world of burning forests, fading reefs, political inaction and corruption, with a schooling system that still largely requires that young people sit in classrooms for several hours a day five days a week memorizing curriculum content, and with boys who still call girls sluts as they assault them, I wondered how on earth we expect teenage girls *not* to defy this world. I see them trying to patch together an identity as a kaleidoscope of images undermines them—improbably large Kardashian bottoms, fat puffy lips, filtered bikini shots, models trailing sugar daddies, and blown-up breasts. I watch her friends, all long limbs, tumbling hair, earnest and dark, vulnerable and defiant, dramatic and funny, and want to simultaneously wrap them in soft blankets and launch them to the moon with rocket-fueled self-confidence.

I fought with my elders when I was a teen, so I am probably more likely to be kindly disposed to "difficult young women." I had big fights with my father about politics—our biggest were about who believed Anita Hill (me); about the presence of American soldiers at Pine Gap (I had signed a petition at a march and was correctly accused of naivety); and my insistence, at fifteen, after watching a documentary at school, that socialist economic policies would narrow the yawning wealth disparity in Brazil. I marched, chanted, protested and bore placards aloft; Dad brought me "SOCIALISM SUX" badges from Liberal Party conferences. We grew, we laughed about it, we mellowed, we stayed close. But you can imagine my amusement when my father told me recently that he disapproved of my daughter taking a day off school for the students' climate strike: "Well, Dad, it's lucky I am her mother then, isn't it, because I don't have a problem with it."

There is a hidden joy to parenting teenagers. I am not downplaying the moods, hormones, slammed doors and carrying-on, and I am lucky to be close to my daughter, but I have so relished being at her back, cheering her on, which feels much like participating in the Olympic sport of curling. The competitors who so frantically sweep alongside the stone are trying to create heat to melt lumps on the ice and allow the stone to glide more easily toward its destination on a film of water—a target called "the house." Every ice sheet is unique and must be read by the curlers, who will then know how hard to brush the ice. I won't push my daughter directly myself, but I am madly trying to smooth the ice around her so she can be free to roam, or speed toward her longings and desires. I'll stop sweeping soon, I'll get out of the way, but, *Wow*, I find myself saying when I pause to mop my brow, *look at her go*.

To do this curling requires no small amount of grace. Our relationships with our children are mostly fired by grace—and often at a cost—by the need to constantly love despite any mayhem they bring home; despite any bad temper, ingratitude or meanness about your uncoolness. You'd never date someone who treated you like a teenage kid in peak hormonal blast, all silences and bouts of rage. A rage that, through the lens of grace, is understood as transition when girls unfurl and become women. A rage that parents need to stand in like a howling wind, waiting for it to pass.

❄

AN IMPORTANT PART OF parenting girls is watering their dreams. Which is one reason why we should never tell little girls they will grow up to be heartbreakers: it halts flight, stops them in their tracks. One day I was walking along the beach with my girl, when she was nine, and a man stopped and stared at her: "You're going to break a lot of hearts when you grow up." She stared back, uncomprehending.

Why tell her this? Little girls don't understand heartbreak. They have never loved, never lost, never cried with yearning, never ached with desire. Little girls comb their hair carefully in front of mirrors, arrange dolls under eiderdown blankets, vow eternal friendship, topple off foam surfboards, believe as many as six impossible things before breakfast, and curl up to sleep with stuffed toys. And yet already I could hear what she was being told: You will be desired and, because of that, you will reject and hurt men. And you will be called a name for that. This will occur even if you might be leaving, or avoiding, relationships you might find stifling, oppressive, wrong, imbalanced or exhausting.

The most highly ranked definition for *heartbreaker* on the Urban Dictionary website is: "one who screws you over, is mean to you, and gave you hope but ripped it away either quickly or slowly over a long period of heartbreaking time." It's true that little boys get called heartbreakers, too, sometimes. It's not like heartbreak is gender-specific, as the large crowd of those of us who have experienced it can attest. And yet for men it is most commonly a flattering term meaning a man who conquers. Look up synonyms for heartbreaker: *Casanova, ladies' man, lady-killer, lothario, playboy, rake, Romeo, roué, skirt-chaser, smooth operator*. The female terms are sidelined under the word "flirt": *coquette, siren, vamp, vixen, tease*.

We may applaud young women for youth and prettiness, but we also shame them for the power of it. Little girls who are told they might break hearts just by growing up are effectively being told to carry the weight of the happiness and expectations of others on their own shoulders. Thus begins a lifetime of women feeling responsible for the feelings, happiness and, too often, actions of men around them. We are taught to be guilty about our rebellion, independence or refusals to date or tie ourselves to someone. This was a disaster for me when I was a teenager, trying to leave relationships that made me unhappy. I felt so guilty breaking up with two boys, six months apart, when I was about eighteen, that I began to starve myself, exercise and run for hours. I shouldered the blame and felt a scorching shame, so I punished myself.

I know that random man on the beach meant to compliment my daughter. But I instantly, instinctively, wanted to protect her from this idea: that you will be watched as you bloom and you will hurt people.

So, what would I tell my girl, now a teen? To allow herself to fall but to safeguard her heart. To always go where she feels safe. And to warm her days with the flames of self-respect. This is how I try to show her grace, to allow her to be, to smooth the ice. What I really want to tell her is to honor her own heart, the wellspring of life. I want to tell her to free herself from what others want from, and think of, her. To turn her mind to her own desires and thoughts. To allow herself to want.

For these are the stories we should tell little girls—stories of vaulting desire, not cautionary tales of the impossibility of dreams, of happiness:

A Fable for Little Girls (and Non-Binary Kids Too)
The little boys marched about the playground, being kings, lords and generals.

And the crone sat the girl down on a seat, and pointed to the skyline: "Out there, all you can see, all you desire, all you dream of and crave, can be yours if you work for it. People will tell you, as a girl, to narrow your world, to not dream too big, to remember any triumph will take a toll, any success has a cost, any happiness will be incomplete—like the mermaid who lost her voice to walk on the earth, the film actress who won awards but had no children, and the female politician who won votes but slept alone. But know that this is not about 'having it all'; this is about being human, about imperfection, about life on earth.

"Don't let people make you, as a girl, as a woman, feel guilty for wanting. Desire is a mighty furnace that will fuel you to stride continents, to create art, to tell untold stories. Without ambition, would we engineer soaring bridges, resurrect forgotten languages, jump higher, run faster or compose symphonies that make grown women weep?

"Want everything, reach higher, inhale the world."

Chapter 6

On Being Decent Men

MY SON HAS ALWAYS been a naturally kind, giving kid. At the end of protracted negotiations with his older sister, he'd often agree on terms then throw in a few gifts and extra money for good measure. He'd buy her things to cheer her up. He used to give all his pocket money to buskers, dog pounds and animal-rescue centers. He'd amass big collections of Pokémon cards, or Beyblades, then give them to his friends. He'd buy candy at the supermarket and sell it at school, only to burn up all his profits buying his friends food at the convenience store. For Christmas last year, he asked for a packet of M&Ms—I had bought him a laptop for school during the year, and he said I'd given him enough already. His sister rolled her eyes. "That's so lame! Why do you always try to make me look bad?"

But, in the face of a brutish, often Darwinian world, how do we actually nurture, or expand on, goodness? And how do we instil it? How do we show kids a kind of behavior that goes beyond tit for tat, and sometimes beyond decency, to unwarranted kindness, an extraordinary goodness that benefits others who may not deserve it?

Part of the answer may lie in virtual reality. In 2013, researchers tested the impact of the superpower of flight on sixty men and women who entered a simulator and strapped on goggles. The first group flew like Superman and had their arm movements tracked by sensors on both their wrists and heads, while the second were in a virtual helicopter. Both groups were assigned one of two tasks: to find a missing diabetic child who needed insulin, or tour a virtual city from which people had been evacuated following earthquakes. During the first task, the superheroes heard the following message in their headphones:

There has been an earthquake warning and the city has been evacuated. A child has been unaccounted for and the parents have informed authorities that their child is diabetic and will go into shock without insulin. You have a vial of insulin in your pocket. Your task is to fly through the city to find the child and deliver the insulin, saving the child's life. As soon as you see the child, call out. You must indicate to the experimenter that you've found the child, so please clearly announce that you see the child when the child comes into view. You may now begin your search. Lift your arms above your head to take off from the ground.

A couple of minutes into the experiment, the child would suddenly appear. The participants called out once they sighted them, then were taken by the software to the child, where they were told they had saved them from death.

Back in the real world, those who had flown on their own, like a superhero, were more likely to pick up pens that had spilt onto the ground—from a cup "accidentally" knocked over by the experimenter—than those who had not. They picked up more, and more quickly. The researchers concluded that "having the 'superpower' of flight leads to greater helping behavior in the real world, regardless of how participants used that power. A possible mechanism for this result is that having the power of flight primed concepts and prototypes associated with superheroes (e.g., Superman)."

Stanford professor Jeremy Bailenson told the ScienceDaily website: "It's very clear that if you design games that are violent, people's aggressive behavior increases. If we can identify the mechanism that encourages empathy, then perhaps we can design technology and video games that people will enjoy and that will successfully promote altruistic behavior in the real world." In other words, we need to build on the fact that we are more likely to engage in behavior that we have experienced or seen ourselves.

❋

A GROWING BODY OF research shows us that when we witness someone doing an act that is especially good, loyal, courageous, loving or kind, our heart rate goes up—we are uplifted, and more likely to do similar things in order to both mimic the exemplar and become a better person ourselves. Scientists call this phenomenon "moral elevation," the emotional response to witnessing acts of profound virtue or moral beauty that improve the welfare or well-being of others. Studies have shown that moral elevation makes people more optimistic and altruistic. Those who reported being elevated were also more likely to have a physical response to what they saw, such as warm or "tingly" feelings.

In a study of moral elevation in the workplace, researchers found interpersonal fairness, moral integrity and self-sacrifice to be "powerful elicitors" of elevation when demonstrated by leaders. Witnessing this made employees more committed, altruistic and courteous. In other words, leaders promote "virtuous upward spirals" when they exhibit ethical behavior.

In a study published in 2015, the hearts and brains (specifically their medial prefrontal cortex activity, which is associated with high-level cognitive processes like empathy) of 104 college students were monitored as they were being shown videos of heroic or compassionate acts, or funny situations. The humorous videos did not impact them, but the first two kinds did, arousing both "fight or flight" impulses (from the sympathetic nervous system) and calming, soothing impulses (from the parasympathetic nervous system). The researchers explained that when witnessing moral elevation we become alert to suffering and yet also have the pleasure of seeing that suffering eased. Our stress is then eased, too, and we experience a desire to act in similar ways.

One of the authors of the study, Sarina Saturn from Oregon State University, told UC Berkeley's *Greater Good Magazine* that part of the explanation for our visceral responses lies with oxytocin, the "tend and befriend" hormone. In short, she says, "I think we have a tendency to absorb what we're witnessing and that has an impact on our body and brain. We've found that just showing an inspiring video of people being kind is enough to cause these dramatic events taking place in the body and to allow you to want to pay it forward and be prosocial in turn. . . . It's kind of cool to see that what's happening in your body is an impetus to prosociality and inspires people to give and be kind."

❊

THIS MEANS IT'S NOT only games that can encourage kids to do good, but also seeing good being done. Which is why families, kith and kin can be such excellent sources of deep-rooted grace, of caring for one another, even when we drive each other to distraction. This is why I moved back from the United States when my marriage exploded: I wanted my children to be surrounded by the oak trees of my family members—strong, sturdy, and dependable. I wanted my son to spend more time with his grandfather, who worked for years to get refugees out of detention centers, particularly children; to see how his uncles cared for their families devotedly, lived with purpose, and tried to contribute to the world, working in local communities and aged care, raising money for respite centers for the terminally ill and fighting against human trafficking.

My younger brother, Steve, has always been strongly focused on caring for others. He listens intently and always comes up with an innately decent response. In recent years, he has been working on a global campaign to stamp out slavery, online abuse and the exploitation of children. Asked what motivates him in his fight for justice, he cites our mother, whom he saw "model solidarity with the vulnerable and make powerful decisions to support and express kindness toward those in need. This has always been a true north for me."

My older brother, Mike, is a good man, too, and funny. One of those honorable blokes you could trust with your life, who always tries to do the right thing and who is ethical to his core. He was elected to public office awhile back, so I am used to people telling me he is a grub, corrupt, sinister, a clown, a megalomaniacal power-hungry master of the universe. These charges aren't rooted in fact, but they still spin and wheel through social media feeds, where trolls spit bile.

These trolls have not lain on my couch, fresh from the hospital, and listened as my brother, on his knees on my kitchen floor, cleaned my fridge, stocked it with fresh food and wiped it down. They have not watched him weep with love at his daughter's wedding, with sorrow at the pain of her divorce, with grief at the death of his mother, with concern about the kids in his electorate dying of terminal diseases, with emotion when he spoke at my wedding, long ago now, and with relief when my eyes opened for the first time after my nineteen-hour fourth surgery.

Mike is not in politics anymore, and he took on the job of the head of an aged-care provider, having been made acutely aware of the crucial part such organizations played in looking after our mother, who by the end of her life could not walk, move any of her limbs or talk, and was utterly reliant on the support of family and caregivers. Once every few weeks, he goes out on shifts with workers so he can better understand the work they do. The other day when I called him, he told me he had been vacuuming the room of a woman named Dorothy at a home near Nowra on the New South Wales South Coast, and, as an innately tidy person—the kind who walks around on Christmas Day with a big garbage bag collecting discarded paper as people are unwrapping presents—he admitted he had been "meticulous."

Dorothy, now in her nineties and hooked up to an oxygen machine, had been regaling him with stories about her wedding dress, which had been made out of parachute material. I told him I'd once written a paper on how Christian Dior created his New Look with dresses made of silk from unused World War II parachutes, and he relayed this to her, delightedly.

※

WHEN HAVE WE SEEN grace in public life recently? Its absence can make it harder to show our kids what it looks like. I can think of only a few ready examples. The first was from the former New Zealand prime minister Jacinda Ardern. After she heard the news of the Christchurch mass shooting by a far-right extremist in two mosques, which resulted in fifty-one deaths—including New Zealand citizens as well as nationals from India, Egypt, Afghanistan, Pakistan, Bangladesh and Indonesia—Ardern prepared a statement of compassion and empathy, redefining leadership at a time of fracture. "Many of those who will have been directly affected by this shooting may be migrants to New Zealand, they may even be refugees here," she said. "They have chosen to make New Zealand their home, and it is their home. They are us. The person who has perpetrated this violence against us is not. They have no place in New Zealand." She never said the shooter's name, refused to engage with violent rhetoric, and wore the hijab to express affinity with Muslims, who had long been described as terrorists by other global leaders.

The second example involved the late US senator John McCain, who, as a presidential candidate, refused to exploit some of the darker untruths circulating about his opponent, Democrat Barack Obama. At one of his talks, a supporter told McCain that he was scared of Obama and said he "cohorts with" a domestic terror group. The former US Navy officer, a survivor of torture, responded calmly: "I have to tell you he is a decent person and a person that you do not have to be scared [of] as president of the United States." The crowd booed.

Another woman then stood up and said, "I cannot trust Obama. I have read about him and . . . he is an Arab." McCain shook his head and took the microphone: "No ma'am. He is a decent family-man citizen that I just happen to have disagreements with on fundamental issues and that is what this campaign is all about. He's not. Thank you." There was a smattering of applause.

Then there was the occasion when Obama defended a veteran who was heckling him during a rally for Hillary Clinton on November 4, 2016. After the former US president said you couldn't have a commander-in-chief who insults prisoners of war, an elderly man intervened. When the crowd shouted him down, Obama yelled "HOLD up!" repeatedly, trying to get them to stop, then, "Hey, everybody, listen up! I told you to be focused!"

He asked the crowd to sit down and be quiet for a moment. "You've got an older gentleman who is supporting his candidate. He's not doing nothing, you don't have to worry about him. This is what I mean about folks not being focused. . . . First of all, we live in a country that respects free speech. Second of all, it looks like maybe he might have served in our military and we got to respect that. Third of all, he was elderly, and we got to respect our elders. Fourth of all, don't boo! "Come on now!" I want you to pay attention. Because if we lose focus we could have problems. It's part of what's happened here during this election season. We just get stirred up for all kinds of reasons that are unnecessary."

We still get stirred up, and allow others to stir us up, often forgetting that, all the while, children are watching.

PART III
Our Strangers

Random encounters

"MAIN CHARACTER ENERGY" is, apparently, a desirable trait today. It means someone who puts themselves first, prioritizes their own happiness, knows their value and shapes their own narrative, acting like the star of their own show. On TikTok, #maincharacter trended for months, mostly with young women telling other young women to care for themselves, be bold, respect their own time. One poll found that over half of the Millennial and Gen Z generations believe that if they think of themselves as their main character, it will help them become their best selves. Of course, it can also imply a level of self-involvement, hence headlines like "How to embrace main character energy without being an a-hole."

John Koenig, in his *Dictionary of Obscure Sorrows*, describes main character absorption as being "the star at the center of your unfolding story," and defines its antithesis with a word he coined, "sonder":

Sonder n. the realization that each random passerby is living a life as vivid and complex as your own—

populated with their own ambitions, friends, routines, worries and inherited craziness—an epic story that continues invisibly around you like an anthill sprawling deep underground, with elaborate passageways to thousands of other lives that you'll never know existed, in which you might appear only once, as an extra sipping coffee in the background, as a blur of traffic passing on the highway, as a lighted window at dusk.

We so often underestimate the significance of random encounters with strangers, and how even the briefest of exchanges can have an impact on our lives. As we walk through the world, preoccupied with our own trials and dramas, we should keep in mind the concept of "sonder," and remain aware of our myriad everyday interactions with people we don't, or barely, know. We may be the leading characters in our own shows, in other words, but there are thousands of such shows being aired in the places we live in, every day. Every main character is simultaneously a side character, or extra, in someone else's show.

There have been many times in my own life when strangers have provoked, enraged and soothed me, and even saved my life. Millions of people care for strangers every day, including nurses and paramedics, as well as volunteers and teachers. During the pandemic, we learned to applaud these people, as though finally recognizing that they spend their days improving or saving our lives and often risking their own, but the applause was short-lived. We should not forget, outside health emergencies, the strain others are under, the invisible illnesses many bear, the pain people suffer in silence, and how even the smallest of gestures can have a disproportionate impact, for good or ill.

Chapter 7

Other People's Lives

THOSE WHO ATTENDED THE Sydney Writers' Festival in 2023, held at revamped former railway yards, would have likely walked past a stall called the Poetry Prescription Booth. It was run by the Story Factory, a not-for-profit creative-writing center in Sydney, set up to enable young people aged seven to seventeen from under-resourced communities to explore words, write, and stretch their imaginations like putty. Volunteers and staffers stood at the booth, waiting to prescribe a poem for whatever ills passersby might have been facing, and were bowled over by the enthusiasm of the crowds who lined up, asking for a poem for inspiration, or to provide joy or lift some sadness.

The "poetry pharmacists" listened to a host of concerns, including lacking motivation at work, feeling uninspired or flat, or hurting because a friend had ovarian cancer. (One man spoke at length about the fact that he worried he talked too much and didn't listen to people—partly because he was dependent on a hearing aid—and had too many opinions; he was told that was not a bad thing, and a high-five ensued.) In response, the "pharmacists" would put poems—all written by teenagers who had been part of the Story Factory—into little jars, affix labels and hand them to the needy.

My friend Cath Keenan, the executive director of the Story Factory, showed me some of the poems, and they are beautiful:

There are tree branches calling your name
river banks miss your reflection.
There is nowhere in the world
that considers you foreign.
                    —*BEA*

You can find joy wherever you
look—like stroking your thumb
against the pleasant texture on
the spine of your favorite
book.
                    —*Pious Agyeman*

Know that the grass
will always plant
forehead kisses
while the wind whispers
welcomes when the world
becomes too much.
                    —*Asha Tukuitonga*

It struck me, listening to Cath talking about all the people eagerly lining up for some sustenance, or solace, that this is why so many of us read, and write. To give or find comfort or company, or a still place to think. When booksellers around the country told me they gave my last book, *Phosphorescence*, to the lonely, the grieving, the ill, the wandering, the curious, I was so honored. People wrote to tell me they had read it to dying relatives, spied it in the hospitals, asked to be buried with it. It's an incredible privilege to be with people in some way at those times. It's also a reminder that in every queue we stand in, every crowded auditorium we sit in, every train we rattle along in, there's probably someone next to us who would walk up to a poetry pharmacist and ask for words to act as a balm for some ache, uncertainty, longing or fear, to amplify the gentler whisperings of our hearts and drown out the horrors, just for a little while.

❄

THE PARKING SIGN OUTSIDE my daughter's school read *PICK UP AND DROP OFF*. It was her first day at the local public primary school's kindergarten, and I had cried when I'd dropped her off that morning. The school had handed out little packages to parents that included tissues, and my girl had walked off with her new class, into her new world, as my heart tightened. I was bouncing on my feet with anticipation when I went to pick her up, standing next to my car, when, right behind me, a parking inspector printed out a ticket and slid it under my windscreen wipers. "Wait," I said, "I am just picking up!" She said I needed to be *in* or *on* the car, not next to it. I pleaded for mercy, to no avail.

I recognized she was just doing her job, but later I got irrationally mad about this. It seemed unfair to be so punitive in a pick-up zone, especially on the first day of school, when others were doing the same, all standing next to their cars along the street. For a single-parent household, when I was only working a couple of days a week so I could finish off a book, the cost stung—it was almost a full day's work. Every time I saw that parking inspector around my village, I felt annoyed all over again.

Then, a few months later, I was meeting my father for coffee one day when I noticed a woman sitting alone and sobbing inconsolably in the corner of the café. I went over to her and sat down. It was the parking inspector. I asked her if she was okay, and the story came out: someone had told her that her son was dead, and she had spent the previous two hours calling and trying to find him. It turned out to be untrue, and he called her back, but the shock and anxiety had completely overwhelmed her.

I bought her a brownie and listened to her talk.

❄

SOMETIMES, MOMENTS OF GRACE can be slammed by moments of gravity. Recovering from my last operation was no easy feat: after I first walked up a flight of stairs in the local park with my friend Jock, I vomited into my front garden from the exertion. But slowly I inched my way back into the world outside my home. The operation had winded me, and I couldn't breathe properly for a while—perhaps because the surgeons had scraped my diaphragm?—so I needed to get a lift up and down the hill to the bay to swim. Some of my friends even offered to hire me a decked-out mobility scooter. What a moment it was, when I first slid into the sea again!

I remained a hermit for a while, just tired and shy and feeling quiet, adjusting to changes in my body, trying to eat the right things, trying to sleep. Then a friend asked me to an annual dinner party she throws with her husband in honor of Scottish poet John Keats, where each guest performs a poem and whisky is drunk in volume. I put on a dress and forced myself out the door, telling myself it was time to be social, to be open to new things, clutching a poem by American writer Brad Aaron Modlin. After the readings of some bawdy and some lovely poems, and much laughter, I downed some whisky to prepare for reading mine. I don't know why I needed to; I guess because I didn't know anyone there except the hosts—both delightful people—and was feeling timid. But on I went, after everyone else, standing up and reading "What You Missed That Day You Were Absent from Fourth Grade."

The poem, sweet and whimsical, is about all the things you wished your teacher had told you, such as "how to stand still and listen to the wind," "how peeling potatoes can be a form of prayer," "ways to remember your grandfather's voice," and "that *I am* is a complete sentence." Before I had even sat down, a woman cried out, "That is the biggest load of shit I have ever heard in my life." While other guests tried to calm her, she continued to berate me: "That poem is absolutely fucked," and so on.

Not a big deal. Just a cranky stranger. But I was crying so hard by the time I reached my house that when I sat down on the curb and called my partner, he thought something terrible had happened, and prepared to pack his bags for Sydney—I so rarely cry, usually preferring to bottle tears. Then he started to make out the words "poem" and "shit" in my garble, and he slowly worked out that my children were okay and I was not in the hospital; I had simply read out a poem at a party and someone had been mean. He took it seriously, and talked me down off the cliff, but it's something we laughed about for months.

I don't know why it hit such a nerve; perhaps because I'd been so sheltered in those months, swaddled in the care of my infinitely supportive friends, and then, when I had summoned the nerve to leave the house, I'd come face to face with a living troll. In other circumstances, maybe I'd have applauded her for her candor. She doubtless has her own concerns, and everyone had been drinking, it may have been no more than that. I don't know what was happening in her life, and she had no idea what had happened in mine. The whisky probably didn't help me either. But, having repressed emotion for the better part of a year, I cried in a way I had not when facing surgery, enduring surgery, when gripped with post-pain surgery, when cannulas could not find a vein in my arm and every insertion took several goes and my forearms became more black than pink with bruising.

Maybe this woman was, inadvertently, lancing the boil of feelings that had mounted for a year. Maybe none of us know the state the rest of us are in, how fragile the eggshell skulls.

Chapter 8

The Comfort of Strangers

I WAS EIGHTEEN WHEN I first traveled to Spain. I was on my own, having left my traveling partner in Florence. After a couple of delicious weeks in Barcelona, I headed to Seville. I had dyed my hair red in Paris, and now decided I needed a haircut. I found a hairdresser who knew a few words of English, I indicated how many inches I wanted cut off, and settled down happily with my book (a biography of Oscar Wilde, by Richard Ellmann) as she snipped away. A few minutes later, she held up my fringe and said something in Spanish. I showed her with my thumb and forefinger how much I wanted trimmed—just a few millimeters. I then felt the scissors sliding along my scalp and realized too late that that was how long she thought I wanted my fringe to be.

I looked ridiculous but thanked her, paid and walked out, cursing my stupidity.

A day or two later, I got sick. I didn't know what was wrong, but I hopped on a bus, using the last coins I had, to try to get to a bank (to cash traveler's checks—yes, this was how we had to travel in the Paleolithic age) and then a medical center, only to realize I was going in the wrong direction. I quickly jumped off in an area unknown to me. By then, I was too weak and nauseous to carry my backpack and I did not know what to do. How would I even find the money to get to a bank? Looking pretty crusty with my odd scarlet hair, a vintage matador jacket I had found in Madrid, and cut-off shorts, I sat down on top of my bag, near a park, and, like a grown, independent woman, started to cry. Once I started, I could not stop, and I ignored the stares of passersby.

Then an old woman came up to me, her face riven with lines, hairs sprouting from her chin, and a colorful cap jammed on top of wild gray hair. She paused, looking hard into my face, then leaned in and stroked my head, gently, murmuring in Spanish. I stopped crying and stared back, struck by her bright cornflower-blue eyes. I had no idea what she was saying—it could have been sorrow for the state of my hair, or disdain for my public display of pain—but what it felt like to me, overwhelmingly, was kindness. I understood she was expressing sympathy and comfort, that she was trying to soothe me. A woman who appeared to have little money of her own had taken the time to stand next to a bawling, red-faced, red-maned teenager from Australia, stroke her hair, and say, *It's okay, I am here, this will pass, it's okay.*

That year, when I was young and clueless, I took a lot of stupid risks and relied a lot on the goodwill of strangers, but I have never forgotten the crinkly eyes of the Spanish woman and how much her simple gesture consoled me.

Sometimes, it's the smallest things that help. When my Twitter friend Alisa was trying to get away from a situation of domestic violence, she told me she went to a park, sat down and cried. A stranger stopped, asked if she was all right and gave her a tissue. Alisa said: "A small act for her, but it really was a turning point for me that day and also restored my faith in humanity." When the singer-songwriter Nick Cave went out of his house for the first time after his teenage son died, he went to a local vegetarian takeaway in Brighton. Though the woman who worked there knew him, she refrained from saying anything, or asking prying questions. But when he went to pay for his food, she squeezed his hand silently, "purposefully," and he was immensely moved. In a conversation with Sean O'Hagan, published in the book *Faith, Hope and Carnage*, he described it as "such a quiet act of kindness. The simplest and most articulate of gestures, but, at the same time, it meant more than all that anybody had tried to tell me."

As Maya Angelou said, people may forget what you have said and what you did, but not how you made them feel. Always remember the kind of impact you can have on someone by recognizing, quietly, what they are going through, and, instead of stumbling to say something, just showing, with a simple gesture, that you understand and are there.

❄

INTERACTIONS WITH STRANGERS CAN mark us for a lifetime. Especially as help sometimes comes from the most curious of quarters. For example, twice in my life, completely unexpectedly, a reggae band has saved me from some kind of peril. The first time was in Turkey. I was backpacking with two friends, and, as we were leaving to go to Yugoslavia, I was struck by a terrible bout of food poisoning at the Istanbul train station. I needed to lie down, but the hostel we'd just left was now full, as were several others we called nearby. We were trying to work out what to do as I vomited into a bin on one of the platforms, when a reggae band we had met the day before suddenly materialized. They stopped, concerned, and called the manager of their hotel, who agreed to give us a room.

The next time was more significant. I was in the middle of a two-month trip to Morocco, with my then boyfriend, Morgan, hiking in the Atlas Mountains, exploring major cities and driving through the desert. One day we got caught in a sandstorm, during which we could see less than a foot in front of and behind our car. We were already slightly on edge because two hours earlier we had been disturbed by a van full of men who had stopped our vehicle and asked us where we were going. An hour after that, the same men had approached us again aggressively when we paused for fuel, circling us and peering into our car. We refused to answer their questions and drove off along a remote highway heading further into the desert, anxiously glancing behind. Then we'd watched as a wall of whirling sand had swung in rapidly from the hills, turning everything white and swallowing us whole.

With cars behind and in front of us, we were unable to stop, but we slowed down, put the lights on, rolled the windows up and kept the wipers sliding across the windscreen. After an hour or so of driving at a sloth's pace, we began to worry we would not find our next place to stay. The map was confusing and the turn-off we had marked wasn't where it was supposed to be. We took a guess, turned right onto a remote road and drove down it for some time—before the van appeared again, circling us, the men yelling, menacing and threatening us. We kept driving, trying to steer around the van, but then it pulled to a stop in front of us, forcing us to brake.

Suddenly, another van appeared, containing a friendly, grinning reggae band, who swung their back doors open, assessed the situation, shouted at the men to leave us alone and told us to follow them. Somewhat stunned, we drove behind them closely, very closely, until about half an hour later, as the sandstorm finally cleared, a hotel loomed in front of us like an oasis. I almost cried when they told us they had room for us. That night, at dinner, the band played, and we danced for hours, giddy with relief, struck by our luck, free.

❋

ONE OTHER TIME IN my life, a stranger I wish I could thank saved me from a potentially very ugly episode. I was in India and had just left Delhi, where I had been at the wedding of my dear friends Rohini and Jungbir, which had involved two weeks of hard dancing, drinking and celebrating at a farm on the city outskirts. Eager for more adventure, I headed to Varanasi, also known as Benares, a holy city where Hindu pilgrims go to bathe, to die and to be cremated on pyres by the River Ganges—their scriptures say if they are cremated there, the waters will clean them of sin and they will break the cycle of birth and rebirth and attain liberation, or *moksha*.

At the train station, I met up with a guy—let's call him Curtis—an American executive I had crossed paths with previously in India and with whom I had made a friendly agreement to travel together. We made our way to a hotel near the ghats—the steps leading down to the river, where the bodies are burned. That night, when we went to a music concert at the Monkey Temple, I befriended another woman, from Britain. Chatting away, we went outside the gates of the temple for a quick chai. I had been feeling a little uncomfortable, as Curtis— whom I did not view romantically—had started coming on to me a little strongly and was clearly annoyed that I was talking to someone else. When he found me drinking tea outside, he burned with anger. He grabbed the back of my chair with white knuckles, face reddening as he told me he was going to make his own way home, that I was on my own. I asked him to wait, said it was late, could we please go together, but he turned and stomped off.

It was midnight, and I barely knew the city. I found a rickshaw driver who would take me as far as he could go, but the center of Varanasi is a maze of tiny, labyrinthine alleyways no rickshaw can fully traverse, so he dropped me a kilometer or so away from my hotel, near the main ghat. I exhaled slowly, stepped onto the road and headed down to the river, by which I was hoping to navigate back to my hotel. Embers were glowing on the ghats, bodies were still burning, and rangy, hungry dogs were prowling around the pyres. A large tangle of electricity wires dangling from a rooftop sparked overhead as I walked along the ghats. I inhaled, held my breath and took one step, the next step, one step, the next step, one step, the next step. After about a hundred meters, a group of young men emerged from the shadows, called out to me then surrounded me and began tugging at my dress, a thin green salwar kameez, and pulling on my arms. Terrified, I tried to tug away and keep walking, but they stopped me, one man holding my right arm, another my left, their nails digging into my wrists.

Time paused.

Then, to my left, out of nowhere, appeared a holy man with a shock of white hair, dressed in white and bearing a wooden staff, which he waved in the air as he yelled at the men. They grumbled at him, dropped my arms, then dispersed. The holy man—of the kind known as *sadhus*—asked me where I was staying, then wordlessly turned and started walking toward the hotel, the *thunk, thunk* of his staff hitting the ground matching the thumping in my chest. Keeping his head bent, he looked very determined, only occasionally turning to yell at other men who called out from the shadows.

When we got to the hotel, it was shut and the front gates were padlocked. He hit the door with his staff repeatedly until someone came to let me in. Once he was certain I was safe, he walked off without a word. I went up to my room and lay on my back on the floor, smoking tightly rolled bidi cigarettes and watching the fan spin on the ceiling, shot with adrenaline, furious with Curtis, and unspeakably grateful to my anonymous rescuer.

Curtis returned to his room next door two hours later, spitting with anger. His rickshaw driver would not take him to the hotel, he said—he had clearly, stupidly, forgotten that it would have been physically impossible for the driver to do so. I stared at him in disbelief as he described berating this poor man, then getting into a fistfight in which he said his boxing training had really helped—"I could feel his jaw crack as I hit him." I was disgusted. It did not occur to him to ask how I had got back to the hotel.

I sat rubbing the scratches on my wrist, waiting for the sun to rise. Then I sneaked down to reception. As I was checking out, the hotel manager told me it was very dangerous down by the ghats at night, and that women often got raped there. She shook her head. "We don't know what to do, or how to stop it, and it's only getting worse."

I made my way to the nearest café for a ten-rupee yogurt and banana breakfast (where, happily, I met some funny, warm New Zealanders, with whom I'd subsequently spend a glorious month hiking and rafting through the Himalayas). Over the next few days, I looked everywhere for the holy man but was unable to find him. He hadn't known me, hadn't needed me, hadn't asked for anything. But I owed him so much.

Chapter 9

The Discomfort of Estrangers

"SOME PEOPLE ARE LEG men, some are breast men," said an old boss of mine as he stretched a clammy hand to my head and began to stroke. "I'm a hair man." I sat in my chair, paralyzed. I was nineteen, living in New York at the end of a year spent backpacking, and grateful for the work, which was flexible and well paid. He was the only person in the office, a sole operator, my only boss. I sat still, nauseated, and kept typing.

I often wonder if there were any times in my own life when I failed to give people the benefit of the doubt, some leeway or compassion. But when it comes to cruelty and harassment, again and again I think the best thing to do is walk away and seal the cracks. With bullying, research has shown there are long-term benefits to forgiving—notably, less anxiety and less enduring hurt—but when it comes to short-term strategies, forgiveness is likely to be more stressful than leaving and avoiding the perpetrator.

When this boss reached his hand out again the next day and began to caress my hair, I jumped up and ran downstairs to get a toasted bagel. I did this each time he approached, eventually consuming a mountain of bagels, until I could afford to quit.

Other forms of harassment are more complicated. Take, for example, the behavior of an older colleague at a newspaper where I started as a cadet. I had been made opinion editor at a relatively young age and this had caused some of the older writers, who had previously patronized me, to uncomfortably resist or protest against the fact that I was now managing them. In hindsight, it's staggering how badly they behaved.

I loved columns, reading and writing them, and the discipline of them: the sharp openings, the concise arguments, the (hopefully) original views, all in seven hundred and fifty to a thousand words—all were part of a craft I had admired and studied for a long time. I hungrily read Maureen Dowd, Gail Collins, Barbara Ehrenreich, the late Christopher Hitchens and Paul Krugman, as I still do today, along with Jamelle Bouie, Charles Blow, Frank Bruni, Caitlin Moran and Marina Hyde. The fact I had been given a chance to write my own column the year I'd joined the paper was a dream made real, and I was very serious about it. I labored on my columns, savagely criticized each one of them, over-researched everything and took all feedback personally. These were the tumble-turn years of my life: I also finished my PhD, went to study in the United States on a fellowship, got married and came back to Australia, where I returned to writing newspaper columns and picked up a radio show, then fell pregnant. On top of my weekly Monday op-ed, I was asked to write a weekend column for *Good Weekend* magazine, which was an honor that made me anxious, as it appeared at the front of the magazine, featured a full-page image of me looking uncomfortable (I hate having my photo taken), and needed to be filed three weeks in advance, so was divorced from the news cycle. I experimented with different themes and styles, trying to find a manner that fit.

In the meantime, one of my older male colleagues at the newspaper—let's call him Creepy Man—had unilaterally decided to appoint himself as my mentor. He invited me to lunches and I accepted, thinking it couldn't do any harm to learn from a veteran. Over each meal, Creepy Man would talk to me about writing technique, but his favorite subjects were himself, his disdain for people who couldn't write headlines, and the reasons for his success. He also asked questions about my partner, which made me increasingly uncomfortable. Were we close? Was I happy? Was he a jealous man? Did I ever take an interest in other men? Who did I find attractive?

Soon I began to make excuses, and one day I stayed at home to work, fat-bellied with my first child, instead of spending half of the day traveling to the city to see him. He sent a curt email, telling me how disappointed he was, and that he had things to tell me.

Oh, I responded innocently, like what?

And out it came. He wrote, in part, that my career had been "remarkably successful for someone who hadn't been in journalism all that long." He told me to ask myself if my success was "running ahead of your abilities and experience." Comparing me to the female politicians I had written about for my PhD and first book—which looked at how women MPs were consistently stereotyped and underestimated—he suggested my bosses were building me up "like mad for their own reasons" but would "discover with shocked amazement that you're not as great as they convinced themselves you were" and would then "dump on" me. Cheering.

The problem, he went on, was that journalism was dominated by older men, baby boomers, who needed to attract a "younger, hipper audience." I was Gen X, female and "bright," and men could not "help themselves" around some women. Yet I could soon be "the victim of a reassessment of whether you've got the talent to justify the prominence [in]to which you've been thrust."

He then went on to list the ways in which I lacked talent: I was not "a natural on radio," and I needed to "give highest priority" to my column writing—"no effort could be wasted." It could be "partly about getting better ideas," he said, but "mainly about improving your technique." In some sui generis mansplaining, he told me that when writing columns I needed to make sure I had "something substantial to say" and that I then said it. Which is of course something that had never occurred to me.

He did, however, have a solution to my shortcomings: motherhood. He again explained, as a man who had never given birth, that he understood that being a mother was "about to turn [my] world upside down," far more than I could comprehend, and could even "completely re-order" my "personal priorities." Another surprising revelation. He gave veteran reporter Laura Tingle as an example of this: "the most competitive journo in the press gallery" until she had a baby and then for a while left at 5:30 every night to go home to her child. Our champ wrote: "It convinced me she was human after all and I've liked her a lot more since then. It's the natural, ordinary things of life that are most important and satisfying—the things generations of men and women have done before you—and being a parent is near the top of that list. It would be a great pity to sacrifice such things just to get back to a career."

Finally: the chance to abandon the career I wasn't much chop at anyway. He said I should seize the opportunity motherhood would give me, to give up "a lot of your many commitments"— and not just take a break, but quit them altogether—to dial back on my work and to devote time to analysing my faults and inadequacies.

In later years I would see this as what documentary filmmaking legend Sheila Nevins calls "above-the-neck harassment." It's not the worst kind of harassment, but it's pernicious and it's undocumented, hidden. In the *New York Times*, it was described as "the moments when you get demoralized as a woman in a room when you feel that you are circumvented and that you are not seen or heard, and the boss only thinks it's a good idea if a guy presents it." But it's also much more than that. It includes another specific kind of behavior: bullying by powerful men who reach out to younger, usually female, colleagues, declare they will champion and mentor them, then overstep boundaries. When the objects of their attention demur, they grow angry.

Some "mentors" wreak revenge, some try to destroy confidence by telling their protégés they are talentless or telling them to work elsewhere. Stories of this kind of behavior are legion in the two cities I've spent most of my professional life in, Sydney and New York. It's typical of the under-the-radar structural bullying and bigotry that women, especially women of color, and members of any kind of minority group—whether gay, disabled, trans, young or old, or other people of color—so often have to manage in the workplace, along with the putdowns from colleagues who remain blithely unaware of their own privilege and imply or explicitly state that others are employed only due to a "box-ticking exercise," to fulfill quotas or window dress.

Of course, there are worse dramas, and I survived. I was privileged to be even having that discussion, to have been in that position. But it bothers me because I know others have also been told that they have reached too far, that they were given their positions only because they were women or any other minority and had not earned them through slog and sweat. Others who were told to step down, to shrink, to stay home.

And sometimes the consequences are serious. I know of at least two other women whom this man "mentored" before he took me on. Neither is working as a journalist anymore; both left the profession. Both told me they had registered serious complaints, but I am unaware of the process they followed, the substance of the complaints, or the outcome. At any rate, he remained untouched and the women vanished.

This is the silent toll of harassment and discrimination—when people resign, exhausted, annoyed and sick of being diminished and having to slog for recognition. A Singaporean study found one in two working women quit their jobs after being harassed, and one in four switched careers. Evidence of similar patterns has been found in a range of countries including the United States, Australia and the United Kingdom. It's a quiet exodus, riddled with stories of opportunities lost and income forgone by those wishing to escape bigots.

❄

THIS KIND OF HARASSMENT has existed, of course, across countries, careers and centuries. When reading about the history of scientific thinking for parts of this book, I found myriad examples of the work of women, and other minorities, being dismissed and coopted. In 1925, astronomy student Cecilia Payne turned in her doctoral thesis on the topic of stellar atmospheres, in which she concluded that the sun was very rich in hydrogen and helium, more so than astronomers had thought. She argued that hydrogen was the major constituent of all stars, making hydrogen the most abundant element in the universe.

This may seem like an obvious fact to astronomers today, but at the time Payne's idea was startling. One of her advisers—Henry Norris Russell—disagreed with it and demanded she take it out of her thesis. Later, he decided it was a great idea, published it as his own theory and got the credit for the discovery. Payne continued to work at Harvard, a "stern, chain-smoking presence," but because she was a woman she received very low pay and the classes she taught weren't recognized in the course prospectuses. Regardless, she published five books and more than

150 papers on stellar atmospheres and stellar spectra, established that stars can be classified by their temperatures, and won a raft of awards. Despite facing gender discrimination throughout much of her life, she became the first woman to chair a department at Harvard and is now celebrated as a brilliant and original thinker for her contributions that changed our understanding of the way stars are born, live and die.

❉

I WAS DEVASTATED BY Creepy Man's email. I was also shocked and angered that he would put such an unmitigated slab of patronizing sexism in writing. It wasn't that he was completely lacking in insight, but he was completely lacking in awareness of his own privilege, and entirely wrongheaded in his belief that younger journalists should think and write like him, seek his approval and not challenge his thinking. And in his patronising suggestion that a woman would benefit from taking time off when she had a baby, when he had never had to do the same.

My friends and I tore the email to shreds as we dissected the myriad expressions of his misogyny. Like putting a fellowship awarded by a foreign university on completion of a PhD, which had taken several years of hard, unsalaried slog, down to luck, or men who "couldn't help themselves." He even twisted the arguments of my PhD to argue that I was lacking in ability.

A few months later, I moved to Manhattan to take up a job as a senior editor. In America, my mentors, male and female, told me to stop thinking small when writing, to tackle big subjects, to be bold, to dream. When I began to write regular columns for *Newsweek*, then the *Philadelphia Inquirer,* then the *New York Times*, I raised a fist to that guy, who had tried to shut me up, as he had done to other women.

The grace I will accord him is to bury his name.

Chapter 10

Restlaufzeit: In the Time We Have Left, We Must Dance

INTERVIEWER

Do you still wake happy but aware of your mortality?

JACK GILBERT

Yes, though sometimes I have to have a cup of tea first.

—Paris Review

WHY DO SO MANY people assume being sick makes you wise? It can, sometimes, but not automatically, instantly or on demand. Sick idiots remain, quite often, idiots. Despite this, there can be a hushing and a whispering about those staring down the spinning tunnel of their own mortality that can falsely or presumptuously recast ill health as some kind of knowing. In Lisa Taddeo's novel *Animal*, for example, the narrator, Joan, is dragged by her half-sister, Alice, to a yoga class in Los Angeles that Alice has said "would make everything better," after Joan has discovered she is pregnant by a man she slept with once. Alice tells her the class "will reset your head. It might knock some sense into you."

As the class starts, it begins to dawn on Joan that she does not belong there. The instructor says: "We have a very whetted understanding of time in this room, don't we, and we appreciate that this hour is precious. This is a *special* class. We are a *special* group." Everyone has a life sentence, he says, but there can be a "marvelous freedom in that." HIV/AIDS does not define them; those are "merely letters."

Joan is shocked and afterward challenges Alice for taking her to a class meant for people with HIV/AIDS. Alice responds that when we are sad we should "seek out the dying."

There's something grotesque in this: a lean, beautiful LA yoga instructor—as Alice is—utilizing other people's suffering as a kind of #wellness tool, a mode of therapy. These #inspo suggestions imply we can automatically extract wisdom—lessons in resilience!—from almost anyone who has experienced, or is still in, pain and trauma, for the purposes of our own personal growth. It's odd, and off. And probably why I so often wince at the posting of quotes from those who have truly suffered by people who are mostly complaining of First World problems. It just rings false.

Yet one of the most common assumptions about the chronically or terminally ill remains: that you immediately possess a rare and precious wisdom—and courage. You can, of course, gain insights and perspective, but, when you are really sick, you are mostly just trying to get through, trying to stem tears of acid, trying to stay alive.

Palliative medicine physician Sunita Puri explained in the *New York Times* that "doctors and families alike can shackle those who are dying with gauzy expectations: Perhaps they have newfound wisdom to bestow. Maybe their regrets will remind us what really matters in life. Saccharine fantasies of deathbed reconciliations protect us from the full spectrum of our emotions and those of the people we will lose. But romanticizing the dying strips them of their complexity. They are still human, equally capable of picking fights or making amends. . . . A good death should be defined by how well and honestly we care for the dying, not by their performance on our behalf."

Many people in their final days become agitated and cantankerous. Some with dementia can become aggressive, abusive and mean. Yet still people come to your side in hospital beds, on couches, and open up about their own problems and anxieties, seeking counsel. These conversations are frequently prefaced with "This is nothing compared to what you are dealing with, but . . ." I don't mind this though. I mostly find it relieving to concentrate on something or someone other than myself, and understand that, at the times when I am ill, much of my purpose is to wordlessly provide perspective. Might as well be useful for something, right?

I eventually considered my first surgery, to my surprise, to be an enormous gift, despite the shock and the pain. It changed the way I worked, parented, played and wrote. I lived with an urgency. I even embraced impermanence. I knew that what I had experienced had been profound. But by the time of my fourth surgery—actually, earlier—I was definitely over it. This cancer kept coming back. I had had enough of depth, enough of suffering, and instead yearned for frivolity, nonsense and abandonment. Some of the finest moments I have known have involved sheer abandon and carelessness, and I miss that. My New Year's resolutions have long tried to counter the fact that so many of my years have been spent working hard and carefully, often to the point of exhaustion. In recent times, I have pledged to drink more whisky, or margaritas, and, of course, I easily and happily manage to achieve these goals.

❊

IF WE CAN WADE through the slick clichés and stereotypes about the apparent infinite wisdom of the sick, though, I will concede there is a reason so many books containing lessons from the dying have become bestsellers, such as *The Wisdom of Dying, The Top Five Regrets of the Dying, Die Wise*, and *When Breath Becomes Air*. And that is because in the same way attending funerals can quicken our steps, many of these books contain simple, urgent truths that blowtorch our passivity and complacency about the way we live in our *Restlaufzeit*, a German word meaning "the time we have left in life."

Poet Mary Oliver wrote the poem "The Fourth Sign of the Zodiac" after being diagnosed with lung cancer in 2012. In it, she challenges the oft-expressed sense of shock—one I know well!—that cancer appears by surprise, with stealth, without permission. She wonders why she was so surprised, given that cancer moves like a hunter in the forest, a predatory fox, a snake, quietly and with intent. She asks her readers if we need to be prompted with darkness, reminding us of the English poet John Keats, who died at twenty-five of tuberculosis but wrote sublime poetry, and lived intensely. She writes, too, of having a tenacious desire for more time, for more life.

I know that fierce wanting, I have breathed it.

So, what does darkness teach us? How does it prod us? Is it true to say being close to those who are sick can make you wise? Is it just about thanking your luck, or the whims of fate, or the night stars, that you can still turn the lights on? Or is it about living with a kind of grace, which involves gratitude, a relishing of the senses, an appreciation of breath?

In the last days of his life, British chartered accountant Elliot Dallen, aged thirty-one, wrote a piece in *The Guardian* about what he had learned from facing a terminal diagnosis of adrenocortical carcinoma. He hoped, he wrote, that an impending death granted him "the licence to sound prematurely wise and overly grandiose," because he had had time to think about what really matters. He decided it was gratitude: "A life, if lived well, is long enough." Allowing yourself to be vulnerable, and accepting help from others. Doing something for others. Protecting the planet. Dallen died the night the article was published.

Australian nurse Bronnie Ware's fascinating book *The Top Five Regrets of the Dying*, published in 2011, was based on interviews with patients at the end of their lives. She identified these regrets:

1. I wish I'd had the courage to live a life true to myself, not the life others expected of me. "It is easy to see how many dreams have gone unfulfilled."

2. I wish I hadn't worked so hard. "All of the men I
   nursed deeply regretted spending so much of their lives
   on the treadmill of a work existence."

3. I wish I'd had the courage to express my feelings.
   "Many people suppressed their feelings in order to keep
   peace with others . . . and never became who they were
   truly capable of becoming."

4. I wish I had stayed in touch with my friends. "Everyone
   misses their friends when they are dying."

5. I wish that I had let myself be happier. "When you are
   on your deathbed, what others think of you is a long
   way from your mind."

The only one of these I'd wish to add to, or qualify, is number
two. The treadmill of a work existence, and giving employers
too much of our time and effort to the detriment of the people
and things we love, is to be avoided. But I know that when I am
preparing to commando-roll into the sunset, I will be glad I have
worked hard at things I cared about, and tried to, in even the
smallest of ways, make life better for some people. Glad that I
didn't give up on some of the dreariest projects because I had
vowed to complete them. These things—like working with
purpose—matter.

A decade after Ware published her book, British broadcaster
Georgina Scull, who almost died as a result of a rupture following
an ectopic pregnancy, also interviewed a host of people nearing
the perimeter of their lives—mainly people with terminal illnesses
and the elderly—about how best to live, and published their

answers in *Regrets of the Dying: Stories and Wisdom That Remind Us How to Live.* She summarized what she had learned as including: "We shouldn't worry about the things we can't control . . . You should always follow your heart . . . That we are enough, just the way we are, even though we can't always see it in ourselves . . . Appreciate the everyday moments"—an inoffensive if perhaps obvious mixture of stoicism, grandmotherly good sense and atavistic advice.

Some insights are clearly sharper, more pressing, more immediate than others. But there is, in short, a grace present even, and especially, when one is conscious of the precarity of life. There is a grace in the distilling of wisdom, and the sharing of that wisdom. There is a drumbeat of urgency at every funeral: How are you living your life?

❄

DR. RACHEL NAOMI REMEN, a physician, professor of medicine, and writer, spent decades working with people with cancer and wrote a book called *Final Wisdom: What the Dying Can Teach Us about Living.* She is convinced the ill can be great teachers because of what she sees as the superior clarity of "the view from the edge of life." Asked why it is so hard for so many of us to take life seriously until we slam into the edge of it, Remen, who suffered from Crohn's disease for more than sixty years, answered that we get distracted by false stories that tell us material things will make us happy and safe. People who have experienced difficult things, she says, can be teachers of wisdom: "It's as if the repository of this wisdom [to live well is] the sick people in our culture, the ill people in our culture."

This wisdom is not—and this is very important—about "positive thinking." The oft-touted idea that positive thinking can beat cancer, or other illnesses, is bullshit. A 2007 study of more than a thousand head and neck cancer patients found emotional well-being had zero impact on survival. Three years later, another study—with the same lead researcher, James Coyne— confirmed this finding when examining, among other things, the role of positive factors like a "fighting spirit" in extending the lives of people with cancer. He concluded by urging "positive psychologists to rededicate themselves to a positive psychology based on scientific evidence rather than wishful thinking."

All this "positivity" notion does is make the already sick feel guilty that they were not sufficiently cheerful during, and about, their suffering, and to blame themselves for their own illness, the random mutation of their cells. I remember standing at a sports game, while my kid was out fielding, blinking as a team parent told me she'd wished away her breast cancer through sheer cheer and optimistic thinking. I fell silent, thinking through all the ways I could respond: *You mean, given I am living with this still, I am just not firing up the right neurons? It's my fault? Not only do I need to get through this somehow, I need to be heroically optimistic about it?* Internally, expletives followed.

Psychologists from the University of British Columbia, in a meta-analysis of the impact of depression on disease progression and mortality, also referred to the damage that the "emotional straightjacket" of the positivity myth can do to the mindset of already vulnerable patients. "It has become accepted in popular culture that cancer patients need to maintain a positive attitude to heroically defeat cancer," they wrote. Indeed.

In recent years, a few studies have claimed a slight, or weak, impact of positivity on health outcomes, but these were cohort-based studies, considered by scientists to have significant limitations and confounding variables. In 2015, researchers in Australia carried out the "largest and most methodologically robust prospective study of the relationship between hope, optimism and survival in advanced cancer patients." Along with hope and optimism, they examined associations between anxiety, depression, healthy utility and survival in 429 patients starting first-line chemotherapy for metastatic colorectal cancer. They found that depression, quality of life and health utility (the patient's ranking of the state of their health) affected survival, but not optimism, hope or anxiety. I buck against part of this finding, however, because I cling to hope, and I know that mentally this has been a buoy for me, anchoring me against tides and currents of uncertainty and fear. Perhaps hope prevents depression, perhaps science can't measure some things, but I also know people insisting that just keeping your chin up will dissolve tumors is offensive to those living with them and swallowing poisons to erode them.

Dr. Darren Saunders, cancer researcher and deputy chief scientist of New South Wales, is frequently frustrated by the continual touting of the idea that being an upbeat "warrior" will overcome deadly disease. He says: "The myth of positivity as a way of beating cancer—or a lack of positivity as a possible factor in causing cancer—has been around for a long time. There is no convincing data supporting the idea that maintaining a positive attitude has any effect on disease progression or survival. The appeal of the idea is entirely understandable, but at its core it's a cruel and heartless notion when you think about it."

※

IT DOES RAISE THE question, though, of why we don't take as much stock in the wisdom of the chronically ill as we do in that of the terminally ill, even though the former perpetually inhabit a kind of physical limbo (and I include myself in these ranks). We are much more interested in the cheerfully pained than in the grumpy ones, though surely most sufferers are both. We seem to have little understanding of the nature and extent of chronic pain, and little patience for or interest in those who suffer from it.

So, what would they say if we did? Tamika Woods, a clinical nutritionist who suffered the fall-out from a tropical parasite for ten years, says she has learned that you should: listen to what your body is trying to tell you; take responsibility for your own health; enlist the help of a team you trust; believe you can be better again; and understand that self-care is not negotiable and you are not alone, as many others suffer ongoing health problems.

Freelance writer Christina Ward, who spent years living with nerve pain, learned: to let go; to identify "fair-weather relationships"; to take advantage of her isolation to focus on herself; to "deal wisely with guilt" in a kind of character-building "unburdening"; that "sometimes life removes things from you, forcing you to 'recalculate' and that's okay" (her pain led her back to her writing, her purpose); that speaking your truth forces you to be more honest with people; that "life is too short to face it with a bad attitude"; and that pain will challenge your self-esteem and sense of purpose, and teach you empathy. She ended a piece entitled "The Life Lessons of Chronic Illness–Pain Will Teach You" by acknowledging the pressure on sick people to focus on the "upsides," to wring a "silver lining" from gray pain: "I hope you understand I do not devalue your pain. I have had more tough pain days than I can count. I am sick of Netflix. I am about to move my family to a new house and I can't even pack a box right now. I'm not trying to wash over your suffering with a silver paintbrush."

❄

WHAT HAS PAIN TAUGHT me? I hate the question actually. I'd rather be taught by, say, an English professor, an Indigenous elder, a boat skipper or a professional free diver than by chronic pain. I'm writing this now curled up in a corner of a couch, holding a hot-water bottle to my stomach, having been up since 4:00 a.m. with a burning pain that no drug seems to touch. Still recovering from my last surgery, I've been here all day. I almost cried when my best friend texted me from New Zealand a short while ago, asking if she could call the head nurse at the hospital for me, and saying, "You don't have to deal with this alone. I'm on my way home." Some friends are wrought of gold.

I also try to be "excessively gentle with myself," in the words of a blessing by Irish poet John O'Donohue. I wait for bouts of pain to pass, and either binge TV shows or write my way through it until it fades. I have learned again and again, from small interactions when someone has been rude or mean, or when a member of the public has yelled for some random reason, that the best way to treat people who shadow our paths is to assume that they may be going through some private hell we don't know anything about. This resembles, but goes a little beyond, that golden rule found in several religions—treat others how you would like to be treated—as it adds a phrase: treat others as you would like to be treated, on good days *and* horrific days.

What if that rude man in line next to you has just been told by a doctor that his child has a terminal illness? Or by his wife that she loves someone else? Or by his boss that he is being made redundant? Or by his own demons, quietly, daily, that he is not worth it, doesn't deserve to live? What if the aggressive woman in the car behind you is suffocating under the grip of a coercive boyfriend who keeps threatening to kill her? Or has found out that her crippling endometriosis has not responded to surgery? That her thirteenth round of IVF has failed? Has been made redundant, or can't find a place to live? What if these people were sexually abused as children, raped as adults, beaten because they were gay, left for years in refugee camps or repeatedly discriminated against just because of who they are? Or they suffer excruciating pain, or an invisible illness, that no doctor can fathom?

I know, kid gloves would be quickly worn out if we tried to handle every stranger with such delicacy, but we need to be alert to the smallest of signs that someone might be struggling or overwhelmed and, even if those signs are absent, be respectful, at the least, and obliging.

The converse is true too: What if we were kind to people at the moment they needed it most? As we have seen, the smallest of gestures can change lives. You don't need to pressure yourself to come up with the perfect words when someone you love is in strife or pain; you just need to be there.

Sometimes I wonder how many people on social media platforms like Twitter are experiencing chronic pain, given that so many seem to have a hair-trigger temperament. Chances are, a fair few. *The Lancet* claims almost one in three people worldwide experience chronic pain. The Australian Institute of Health and Welfare reports that chronic pain—which it defines as a "common and complex condition characterized by persistent pain experienced on most days of the week"—affects one in five Australians aged forty-five and over, with the percentage increasing with age. I certainly narrow, grow crankier and am more dismissive of other people's First World problems when in pain. At those times, I wonder why so few people factor in the privilege of health, how they can appear to be so oblivious to their own good fortune.

Like many people with invisible illnesses or disabilities, I tend to measure my days in spoons, with each spoon representing a block of energy I can devote to one task—I can do most things, but not all in one day. Christine Miserandino came up with the "Spoon Theory" in 2003, while sitting in a diner with a friend and explaining how the energy of a person with chronic health conditions—in her case, lupus—is limited and needs to be rationed. Let's say we have ten spoons per day, on a good day. When I first came out of the hospital, taking a shower, for example, would use six spoons, and I'd use the other four on moving from room to room, eating and other basic functioning. Now, a shower requires a fraction of a spoon, but an ocean swim uses one or two spoons. I can clean the house and go to work but can't also go for a long walk. My energy is returning now, but I still need to figure out how to allocate my spoons each day. A lot of the ill don't feel brave, just tired, a lot of the time, just trying to get better and trying to do as much as we can and love as much as we can with all that we have.

Every birthday is a celebration. Can you remember how you felt the moment you first clapped eyes on a gray hair, if you have them? I was covered in dust, having been immersed in old documents and archives for days. I went to the bathroom of the windowless annex I was studying in, washed my hands, wiped my face and saw a glistening silver hair. I stared at it for minutes, annoyed. I was only in my twenties; did I have to feel so old already?

Then, not long ago, in my home bathroom I spied a white hair in my eyebrows. I paused, leaning on the vanity, surprised to feel tears springing to my eyes. I was happy: happy to be growing older, happy to be here for another year, happy to be alive when I thought I might not be, happy to be slowly wrinkling, aging, on this mad, sparkling, spinning planet, with the people I love most. This is, perhaps, the grace of aging: caring less, relishing more.

❊

KEATS WOULD SURELY HAVE been chuffed to know that a poet like Mary Oliver used him as a prod, a reminder of a man so singular in his purpose and mind that he lived a lifetime in twenty-odd years. After being repeatedly mauled by critics (and the pretentious Lord Byron), who looked down on the middle-class poet, Keats grew depressed and asked that his body be placed under an undated tombstone bearing only the words, "Here lies One whose Name was writ in Water." In a letter to his fiancée, Fanny Brawne, in February 1820, Keats, who had eschewed medicine for a literary life, wrote: "I have left no immortal work behind me—nothing to make my friends proud of my memory—but I have lov'd the principle of beauty in all things." This love was apparent in his work, and made it glow.

One thing that upset Keats toward the end of his life was that he could not dance and was too unwell to take out the blue-eyed Brawne, leaving her to socialize instead with army officers and fend off numerous invitations as he fretted jealously at home. I mention dancing because apparently what the dying regret most is that they did not dance more. I learned this from aged-care chaplain Kerry Egan, who, in her wonderful book *On Living*, writes about what preoccupies people in the months before they die, what they care about, what stories they tell and what they long for.

One of her most striking findings was that people are saddened by the way they viewed, and treated, their bodies as problems, or sources of embarrassment, shame, sin and guilt. She writes: "There are many regrets and many unfulfilled wishes that patients have shared with me in the months or weeks before they die. But the time wasted spent hating their bodies, ashamed, abusing it or letting it be abused—the years, decades, or, in some cases, whole lives that people spent not appreciating their body until they were so close to leaving it—are some of the saddest." (I remember once mentally itemizing all the things I considered—or had been told were—defective or wanting about my own body, and the only features left off this list were my ears. This was before surgeons started carving into my body, hollowing me out, slicing into my skin with scalpels, suspending my ribcage from hooks. But that's the way the patriarchy works; to be female is to be flawed, requiring constant, endless remedying and rebuke. It's not the way I want my daughter to think.)

Second in intensity to the regret of hating their bodies, says Egan, was "the wish of the dying that they had appreciated their bodies in the course of their lives." In their final moments, she found, people love to reminisce about their bodies and the best things they did with them: "The feel of the water the first time they went skinny dipping. The smell of their babies' heads. The breeze on their skin that time they made love outside." One woman told her that, although she would never admit it to her husband and kids, what she would miss most of all was her own physical self: "This body that danced and swam and had sex and made babies. It's amazing to think about it. This body actually made my children. It carried me through this world."

But not dancing enough was what people regretted most of all. They spoke of losing their bodies in sound and finding them in rhythm. Of the sheer, too often underrated pleasure of moving limbs to music until thoughts fade, your muscles ache and you are drenched in sweat and joy. Egan writes: "I can't count the hundreds of times people—more men than women—have closed their eyes and said, when describing [armed forces] dances during World War II, or shagging at South Carolina beach houses, or long, exuberant nights dancing at roadhouses and discos and barns and wherever else there were bodies and music, 'If I had only known, I would have danced more.'"

This makes me happy because I remember, a few years ago, my friend Jock and I wondering if we had danced too much in our teens, twenties, and much of our thirties, if we had spent too much time jumping about on dance floors when we could have been doing . . . something more constructive? We decided we could have danced even more: in the rain, in the car, in dance-party halls, clubs, friends' homes, coastal pubs, warehouses, our faces blurred under laser lights, lost in the sounds, soaring with the beats, grinning with the joy, weaving in and out of jostling crowds with a linked line of friends, holding hands so we wouldn't lose each other, hobbling home with blistered feet and buckled shoes, skin crisscrossed with fishnet imprints, legs weary, hearts full. There is a very particular bliss that comes with losing yourself in a kind of flashing, pulsing oblivion with your friends, dancing until you can barely walk, because you love them and love life and love music—a grace of motion, elevation, sublimity.

So, there it is: gravity and grace. Our bodies—our misshapen, lumpy, wobbly, birth-marked, uneven, scarred, imperfect bodies—are our vessels. If only we were more gracious toward them. They won't last forever, they will eventually grow frail, and we will miss the strength and vigor of our younger selves. But, for now, when alive, when upright, when walking through days with purpose, without pain, they are vessels for adventure, for sleep, for song, for dance, and a place where we experience joy.

And, surely, the less we worry about them, the more we will dance, whenever and however we can.

PART IV
Our Sins

Forgive us our sins

THE SUN IS A PERFECTLY SHAPED SPHERE. A neat, round, glowing ball of light that has confounded scientists with its precision. But there is a violence at its core. The giant ball of glowing, hot plasma on which our lives depend, that warms our faces, kisses our skin and favors our crops, that drags beauty across our skies twice daily, is a noisy, violent star, fueled by chaos.

Instead of the flames our ancestors imagined leaping from its surface, the source of the sun's light is the motion of nuclear fusion, where light particles constantly, relentlessly smash into each other like bumper cars, sticking together and releasing energy and heat. In other words, the sun does not burn hydrogen, it fuses it, into helium. The light spreads from the core—which has a temperature of about 15 million degrees Celsius—to the edges and makes the sun incandescent.

The sun also screams. Scientists say if we could hear the noise the sun makes, we would be deafened by its sheer volume. Heliophysicist Craig DeForest estimates that if the laws of physics could somehow be adapted to permit sound waves to travel through space (and I am so glad it can't), the sun would sound like "ten thousand Earths covered in police sirens, all screaming." On top of this, in 2007, astronomers presented research showing that violent solar storms carrying charged gas "let out a thunderous scream" before they hurl radiation storms into Earth's magnetic field.

The sun, in other words, is not settled, static, benign or gently glowing. It is constantly moving, rattling, flaring, smashing and, as my grandmother would say, carrying on like a pork chop spitting oil on a hot pan.

In this way, the sun is much like grace. Our lives are fueled by grace, by the undeserved gift of existence and entry to the natural world, by second chances and the unmerited forgiveness of flaws and fuck-ups, and we are fed by its warmth. But we often forget, too often, that grace is also hard fought, hard won, hard to give. It can take immense effort to execute. There is a swirling, violent chaos at the heart of grace—the chaos of being human, of wanting to take an eye for an eye, to seek revenge, to win, to crush our enemies or bury them. Sometimes we can rise above this chaos to offer forgiveness.

Forgiveness is usually made possible by some expression of remorse, by regret, by justice and by a moment of recognition of another person's humanity and our capacity to fail and to hurt. When it does occur, the person who caused the harm is allowed the possibility of redemption, and the victim the possibility of freedom from what someone else did to them, to be a survivor who leaves their "suitcase of grievances" at the foot of the person who created them, as one person I interviewed put it.

This section is about the times we can do this, and the times we cannot.

Sometimes the only way we can protect ourselves is by walking away. Sometimes the expectation of forgiveness is a burden. And sometimes choosing to focus on healing ourselves, telling our story and educating others shows another kind of grace. To be able to do this takes true grit.

Grace is about forgiving, but not necessarily about forgetting. To understand forgiveness, we need to understand the ways cultures have historically weighed harms, which ones are dismissed and which ones are punished. As the next chapter shows, history tells us forgetting is often a privilege accorded to the few, and expected of the many.

Chapter 11

Napoleon's Penis: What We Choose to Remember

"HISTORY IS A SET of lies that people have agreed upon," said Napoleon, seemingly certain that he somehow would determine how he was remembered. "Even when I am gone, I shall remain in people's minds the star of their rights, my name will be the war-cry of their efforts, the motto of their hopes." I wonder how he might feel if he knew one of the best preserved relics of his life is his penis, a wizened, two-century-old phallus passed like a baton between collectors since an English surgeon secretly removed it from his body during an autopsy.

Napoleon Bonaparte had been exiled on the island of St. Helena for several years, gardening and chafing at his imprisonment after fighting sixty-odd battles in two decades and winning all but seven. The British had long lampooned him as "Bone-a-part" and, in effect, this is what they did to him when he died in 1821.

Napoleon's member was smuggled to Corsica by a priest and sold to booksellers in London and then Philadelphia, before being snapped up by John K. Lattimer, an American collector of "strange relics." A urologist who had treated top-ranking Nazis at the Nuremberg trials and worked on the autopsy of John F. Kennedy, Lattimer was protective of Napoleon's manhood. He bought it because "fun was being poked at it . . . it was an object of derision," and he refused all requests to see the penis, instead placing it in a suitcase and putting it under his bed.

This may have been for the best for those intent on preserving the dignity of the first emperor of France. When displayed in New York City in 1927, the penis was described as "like a piece of leather or a shriveled eel," or "a bit like beef jerky." A *TIME* reporter likened it to a "maltreated strip of buckskin shoelace." The French government refused a chance to purchase it, and wouldn't even acknowledge its existence. After Lattimer died in 2007, author Tony Perrottet was given a rare viewing, reporting it to be "very small, very shrivelled, about an inch and a half long . . . like a little baby's finger." Lattimer's curious collection of memorabilia was auctioned in 2016; it is suspected that Napoleon's appendage was scooped up by an unnamed Argentinian collector, along with a number of Nazi relics. The man who declared he would remain in people's minds as "the star of their rights" and is considered one of the greatest military generals would doubtless object to being reduced to a piece of jerky.

In contrast, the object claimed to be the penis of Russian mystic Grigori Rasputin, now displayed in St. Petersburg, is massive, some twelve inches long. It appears, though, that this daunting horse-size apparition is unlikely to be that of the man known as the Mad Monk, despite the claims by those who wish to firm up his legend as a sexually voracious guru.

Other significant body parts of the famous have been preserved for posterity: Galileo's middle finger, pointing at the heavens or perhaps flipping the bird to the scientific establishment he outsmarted (since joined at the Museo Galileo in Florence by an index finger, thumb and tooth); parts of Beethoven's skull; Albert Einstein's brain; one of Buddha's teeth; a portion of Mussolini's brain; some shattered bone fragments belonging to Abraham Lincoln; my personal favorite, the last breath of inventor Thomas Edison; and, of course, shamefully, countless skulls of Indigenous people who bore the blunt end of colonialism's indifferent rapaciousness. John Lennon's decaying tooth has been listed for sale, as have Winston Churchill's dentures. I have not found similar artifacts from female bodies—say, the clitoris of Catherine the Great or the frontal lobes of Marie Curie—but I suspect they'd be grateful for the oversight.

❄

EVEN THE MOST PROMINENT of us will be buried with some secrets. Enthusiasts can hoard withered body parts, and imagine, but we will likely never know the darkest or most ignorant thoughts of powerful people, even if biographers near-expire in piles of diaries and documents trying to discover or guess at them.

But I'd argue all scraps matter. The fullest, most detailed studies of a person, and their time, can have incredible value, providing new perspectives on the complexity and messiness of someone's aspirations and behavior over a lifetime. Having spent several years wrangling a century or so of archival history into a biography of Queen Victoria, I am convinced that the best antidote for the most extreme and unforgiving elements of what is loosely called "cancel culture" is history (and biography), which shows that people can be incredibly complicated and are usually able to change (for better or worse). They can simultaneously house beauty and ugliness, generosity and meanness, darkness and light. They are capable of greatness, horrific acts and mediocrity all at once, across years or in a single day. Queen Victoria was, like most people, complicated: tender and savage, kind and selfish, clear-eyed and histrionic. She failed to intervene in the English handling of the Irish potato famine, she was the avatar of the empire during the atrocious, rapacious "grab for Africa," was rude to her children and brutally cold to at least one prime minister, yet still inspired millions.

History shows us that forgiveness has a cultural context: what we consider sinful and shameful changes over time, and the possessors of power are most likely to grant themselves forgiveness, and assume they are entitled to it from others. The powerful and privileged tend to insist their good deeds be remembered, and their bad attitudes—or the odd genocide, invasion or political prejudice—be whitewashed, cast in the gentlest light. This is important to understand when examining current debates— to remember who is most likely to be forgiven, and for what. Colonialism has long been trumpeted, racism excused and violence against women accepted—all as simply part of life, mere "domestic strife" or the natural exercise of male lust.

But I want to be clear here that impunity is not grace. Nor is censoring, concealment or suppression. Shutting people up, closing down uncomfortable truths and sidelining the already marginalized is not either. Believing that racism, sexism and violence are acceptable is the opposite of grace, which is naturally entwined with an impulse for freedom and the fight for justice. Condemning bad attitudes or bad behavior is about reckoning with the truths of our past and the flaws, or humanity, of our public figures; there will always be debates about which flaws we accept and which we punish.

The most important task for a historian is not to forgive, or judge, but to provide a fuller understanding of individuals and events, of context and accuracy. Understanding means knowing the noblest of humans have feet of clay—or at least a couple of toes. We all think and say stupid things and reflect the prejudices and progressions of our times. Some surpass them, and, if we wish to join their ranks, we should figure out why, and how, this happens. We are also more likely to have empathy for, or show grace to, people we understand.

Reading history involves endless questions of interpretation of the sepia tones of the past. Should this person have known better about gender, eugenics, race, homophobia and colonialism, or do they represent their time? Were they given an opportunity to recognize privilege and erase bias, but refused it? If they achieved great work and yet harbored ugly attitudes, how harshly should we judge them? If tremendous leaders were terrible fathers, or mothers, how much does it matter? And why have so many been quick to shrug off evidence of domestic abuse, racism or anti-Semitism in relation to figures of the past?

This is where we learn how public forgiveness is taken for granted, or exploited.

❅

WHAT WE CHOOSE TO bury is as revealing as what we choose to remember. The "genius" of men, for example, has rarely been permanently tarnished by evidence of violence or misogyny. Consider these widely lauded names: Norman Mailer, William Burroughs, James Brown, Don McLean. Mailer wrote more than forty novels and won two Pulitzers. He also headbutted people at parties, beat women and nearly killed his second wife, Adele Morales, with whom he had two children. He later told one he had "let God down" when he'd stabbed their mother with a penknife at a party in their Manhattan apartment in November 1960. He would marry four more times, but said on a talk show that women were "low, sloppy beasts" who "should be kept in cages" and argued that hipsters understood the "artistry" of rape. Still, he is considered "one of the most original and powerful writers of the twentieth century," his personal life held far apart from his work.

One man Mailer deeply admired was William Burroughs; he described him in 1962 as "the only American novelist living today who may conceivably be possessed by genius." This alleged genius did not prevent Burroughs from killing his first wife. At a party in Mexico in 1951 the author shot Joan Vollmer in the head, in the presence of their four-year-old son. Although his story changed over time, Burroughs at first said he asked the twenty-eight-year-old Vollmer to balance a glass on her head during a "William Tell act." The cause listed on her death certificate was "bullet wound penetrating cranium." Burroughs was given a light slap—a two-year suspended sentence for manslaughter. He was convinced he'd been possessed by something he called "the Ugly Spirit" on that night, and in 1954 wrote to fellow Beat Generation scribe Allen Ginsberg, saying it was "as if the brain drew the bullet toward it." Typical woman, drawing bullets with her brain.

In truth, we rarely care about violence against women, so foundational it is to our culture. We have long shown leniency toward influential men, and throughout history we see acts of violence committed against women and people of color with impunity. This violence is normalized and glorified, in opera, theater, cinema, popular music and literature. Great writers kill wives and their reputations remain pretty much intact. Violent actions like John Lennon's physical abuse of his wife Cynthia are quietly forgotten. Actors like Charlie Sheen slam the heads of women they profess to love onto marble floors, and continue to act, work and, often, beat their partners.

The #metoo movement, powerful in its torrential rage and rapid global contagion, dented this ancient entitlement, but the backlash came swiftly. And women still end up dead. One woman a week dies in Australia at the hands of an intimate partner. One a week, every week. In America, it's three women or girls a day. Globally, one woman or girl is killed by someone in her family every eleven minutes. According to the United Nations Office on

Drugs and Crime, in 2020, forty-seven thousand women were killed by intimate partners or family members. While in Europe the average number of gender-based killings went down by 13 percent over the past decade, in the Americas it went up by 9 percent. Coinciding with the COVID pandemic, in North America alone, the number went up by 8 percent during 2019–20. Despite some drops in homicide rates over the past decade, the "magnitude of such gender-related killings remains largely unchanged."

James Brown, the "Godfather of Soul," subjected his wives to years of cruelty and violent abuse—firing guns and wielding iron pipes—and was arrested repeatedly on charges of domestic violence. His daughter Yamma Brown wrote that the sound of his second wife, her mother, being thrown against the walls was "like thunder rolling through the house." "During those fights," she wrote in *Vulture*, "I could feel the whole house shake with my father's crazy rage." She saw her mother pinned down and punched, blood spurting from her face. Brown himself had grown up with violence—he was four when his mother left, after his father threatened to kill her—and he repeated it.

And yet his talent as a singer, songwriter, producer and dancer was so phenomenal and unquestionable, critics say, that he deserves our forgiveness. "Regardless of what went on in his personal life, his legacy is secure," wrote Rick Rubin in *Rolling Stone*. "He certainly did things along the way where you can't help wondering, 'What's going on?' But the good stuff comes from these one-of-a-kind people. These people are just touched by God. They are special. And James Brown is one of them. His legend will loom large, because the rhythm of life is in there."

It's true, and it has, and yet, and yet—do we care about these women?

Don McLean's "American Pie," a much-covered song of coded lyrics and nostalgia, was voted one of the Songs of the Century by the National Endowment for the Arts. He still travels the world performing it, in his seventies. (It's a song I will always love. My parents listened to it when I was growing up. I sing it with my kids as a ritual on every road trip to the New South Wales South Coast. As we turn off the highway and head to the small village perched on a beach, I play it and we sing along with full lungs, full hearts.) But as McLean basked in the fame that song brought him, he terrorized his wife, Patrisha, and daughter, Jackie. Now an indie rock musician, Jackie told *Rolling Stone*: "There was a constant state of fear in the house about the slightest thing [that] would make my dad turn into a crazy person." They eventually fell out over his "furious" objection to her dating a Black man. Patrisha, married to him for twenty-nine years, said: "Our survival in the home was dependent on making sure he was happy, managing his moods, hypervigilant. . . . He had complete control over every furnishing; over every single thing that was in that house."

McLean admitted: "I would snap sometimes; I did have a temper." In 2016, Patrisha called 911 after an altercation. McLean was arrested on six charges, including domestic violence and assault. He pleaded guilty to four of them, though the assault charge was later dismissed, and he paid fines for the others. In a statement to the court, Patrisha said Don had been physically abusive throughout their marriage and had recently threatened to kill her with a gun. "My husband has a violent temper," she said. "His rage was unfathomably deep and very scary."

Divorce ensued. Patrisha obtained a ten-year restraining order against McLean, and founded a grass-roots organization helping survivors of domestic abuse, called Finding Our Voices. McLean, meanwhile, is now dating a *Playboy* model who is forty-eight years younger than him. While stating that he had only pleaded guilty in order to "provide closure for his family," McLean told a reporter, "I can truly say that my ex-wife is the worst person I ever knew." He sounds like a truly horrible man. I would not go to see him perform, but I still like his song.

※

THEN THERE ARE THE men who seduced teenagers. Jerry Lee Lewis married his third of seven wives when he was twenty-two and she was thirteen. Myra Gale Brown was his first cousin once removed, and he had not yet divorced his previous wife. This scandal led to a canceled tour and a blacklisting on radio playlists, injuring his career, but little notice was taken of the *state* of the marriage. Thirteen years later, Myra filed for divorce on the grounds of abuse and adultery, claiming she had been "subject to every type of physical and mental abuse imaginable." In the months beforehand, she'd called the police after Lewis had threatened to murder her if she left him, and knocked her to the floor. His infidelity was the final straw.

Chuck Berry, the man dubbed "The Father of Rock and Roll," served two years in prison for taking a fourteen-year-old girl across state lines "for immoral purposes" (though some believe this law was being weaponized on racial grounds). In 1990, a lawsuit brought by fifty-nine women accused him of installing cameras in his restaurant's female bathroom and filming hundreds of women without their consent. Protesting he was just trying to catch a thieving employee, he settled.

Elvis Presley called underage girls "cherries," and met his wife, Priscilla, when she was fourteen; she was living with him in Graceland by the time she was seventeen. He lost interest in her after they had a baby, telling her he did not desire women who had given birth. He fired a pistol into the bedroom of another lover when she refused to bring him yogurt. Countless other rockstars, such as David Bowie and Jimmy Page, have slept with young groupies, many underage, with nary a whisper of scandal. Consent is assumed.

In 1975, Aerosmith singer Steven Tyler, then twenty-seven, convinced the parents of sixteen-year-old Julia Holcomb, to make him her guardian so she could cohabit with him in Boston. Now known as Julia Misley, almost fifty years later she is suing Tyler for sexual assault, sexual battery and intentional infliction of emotional distress. Tyler has insisted she consented to the sexual relationship and he had immunity as her legal guardian.

One of the saddest stories, to me, is that of the abuse of thirteen-year-old Mandy Smith by the former bassist for the Rolling Stones, Bill Wyman. Smith says they first had sex when she was fourteen, before marrying when she was eighteen. She had a rare, striking beauty, all long limbs and tumbling curls; he had power and fame. But she was a child when she first came under his influence, and her family fell for his grooming. The marriage lasted a bit over a year, until she began to unravel, physically and psychologically. As an older woman, she worked as a counselor to abuse victims and spoke of the relationship with regret. In 2010, she called for a higher age of consent: "It's not about being physically mature. It's emotional maturity that matters. I don't think most sixteen-year-olds are ready. I think the age of consent should be raised to eighteen at a minimum."

Wyman had a different view. He wrote in his 1990 autobiography: "She took my breath away . . . she was a woman at thirteen." Which would make him properly geriatric at forty-seven. When, after years of innuendo, Jimmy Savile's grotesque pedophiliac behavior was finally revealed to a revolted British public, a guilty Wyman said he went to the Metropolitan police to see if the public prosecutor wanted to talk to him about Smith. They said no. Smith did not press charges because she said she carried some of the blame for falling in love with him. But in 1993—the year of her divorce from Wyman—she dedicated her autobiography to "every woman and girl who has suffered abuse—sexual, emotional and psychological—at the hands of a man."

Despite some recent social media backlash, can you imagine someone suggesting we shouldn't listen to the Rolling Stones' music? Sleeping with underage girls was part of their schtick. Check out the lyrics to "Stray Cat Blues," for example. Even the merchandise sold during the 1994 Voodoo Lounge tour bore the legend: "Stones Withstand Divorce, Slander, Rip-Offs, Slagging, Under-Age Sex, Alcohol, Drugs." The groupie culture has changed, but the stories continue to abound. The Red Hot Chili Peppers' Anthony Kiedis boasted about bedding a fourteen-year-old girl—the inspiration for their song "Catholic School Girls Rule"—only to hastily return her home once he discovered her father was a chief of police. No one blinked.

Tolerance has long leaned toward the powerful.

❄

WHAT WE TOLERATE IN a musician is different from what we tolerate in a politician or partner, or a neighbor, nurse or teacher. I would not vote for a man who beat his wife or disrespected people of color. I would not marry, but would vote for, a man who cheated on his wife, because it doesn't usually affect the job he does. I would not vote for anyone who vilified any part of the LGBTQI community. I would vote for someone who had a track record of supporting LGBTQI rights but had said something ignorant ten years ago and regretted it. People can evolve, and should be given second chances and, often, the benefit of the doubt. Public figures can have moments of both great grace and deep nastiness, like the rest of us. Winston Churchill and Mahatma Gandhi are two examples.

Churchill, a great wartime leader and fervent believer in British superiority, opposed Indian nationalism in the 1930s. He once called Indians "a beastly people with a beastly religion," according to a cabinet minister. He ridiculed Mahatma Gandhi, then garnering global support for his campaign of civil disobedience to free India from British rule, as a "malignant subversive fanatic" and "a seditious Middle Temple lawyer, now posing as a fakir of a type well known in the East, striding half-naked up the steps of the Viceregal palace." He called Chinese people "chinks," said "I hate people with slit eyes and pigtails," and reportedly did not think "Black people were as capable or as efficient as white people." Scholars have argued his views on race were "deeply retrograde even for his time." When Churchill refused to provide famine relief to Bengal in 1943, the colonial secretary Leo Amery said: "On the subject of India, Winston is not quite sane. . . . I didn't see much difference between his outlook and Hitler's."

Being racist does not mean Churchill was not a great war leader. But his prejudices influenced his policies and blinded him to suffering caused by colonialism, and for this he should be held to account.

When Gandhi was fatally shot three times in the stomach by a Hindu fanatic in January 1948, Churchill's silence was deafening. There was no acknowledgment, either in public or private, of his widely admired rival's passing.

※

GANDHI FACES HIS OWN charges of racism. For decades, the anti-violence leader and lawyer has been revered. The first Black president of the United States, Barack Obama, hung a painting of Gandhi on the wall behind his desk when he became a senator. More recently, however, Gandhi's legacy has been challenged because of what he said and wrote about Black South Africans as a young man.

Black people, Gandhi said in 1903, were "troublesome, very dirty and live like animals." He called them "kaffirs"—a derogatory term—and said he considered Indians "infinitely superior." He took the side of the British Empire when the Zulus rebelled in 1906. In their 2015 book, *The South African Gandhi: Stretcher-Bearer of Empire*, South African academics Ashwin Desai and Goolam Vahed called Gandhi a racist and apologist for empire. Desai told the BBC: "Gandhi believed in the Aryan brotherhood. This involved whites and Indians higher up than Africans on the civilized scale. To that extent he was a racist."

Some tell another story here, of growth and enlightenment. Gandhi's biographer Ramachandra Guha told NPR that Gandhi reflected, then discarded, the prejudices of his age: "He thought in his twenties that Europeans were the most civilized. Indians were almost as civilized, and Africans were uncivilized. However, he outgrew his racism quite decisively, and for most of his life as a public figure, he was an antiracist, talking for an end to discrimination of all kinds."

Others have questioned Gandhi's practice, in his seventies, of sleeping unclothed next to naked young women, including his teenage grandnieces and his private doctor, ostensibly to test his self-discipline in abstinence. His personal secretary, R.P. Parasuram, wrote him a furious letter: "I object to your having massage done by girls. . . . Those people who know that you are naked during massage time say that you could at least put a cover over it." Several staff resigned in protest, but the press ignored the story.

How you might view these failings could depend on whether you are or were Black, white, Indian, female, male, his niece or wife or political opponent. What if Gandhi had been canceled as a young man as he is being canceled by some now? How different would Indian history be?

If we deify any human beings without reckoning with or at least acknowledging their failures, then we will be unable to fathom or accept the behavior of any human being, let alone know when, how, or what to forgive.

❄

AS WE TRY TO conduct archival digs into the hearts of people from the past, we still hang on to physical remnants to remind us that people were made of flesh and blood. In 2012, a soiled pair of briefs worn by Elvis were (unsuccessfully) put up for auction, and in 2019, an "anonymous UK telephone bidder" paid £3700 for a pair of used pink silk underpants belonging to Hitler's long-time companion Eva Braun. How grotesque it is that Nazi memorabilia are sold for profit, instead of placed in museums, if merited or wanted. Such history should be public, not privatized.

It's strange, isn't it, the things we hang on to from the past? What is recorded and remembered, what is written, taught and revised as history is often arbitrary, and usually infected by spin, propaganda and politics. It is difficult to control. We are much more likely to remember things done, said and possessed by white men, and some white women, even to the point of absurdity. The British wanted to prove Napoleon had a small dick (leaving it to air-dry instead of, say, preserving it in formaldehyde); some Russians wanted to prove Rasputin's member was impressive. Others just like to collect odd things.

What really changes the way we view powerful figures from the past is the testimony of those they have bruised, and the dogged work of archivists, journalists and historians in uncovering evidence and stories not meant to be told. We need to know the history of what has been forgotten, excused or allowed to fester in full sight, if we are to understand why so many people refuse to forgive today, with good reason.

Chapter 12

When You Can't Forgive

Heav'n has no rage, like love to hatred turn'd,
nor Hell a fury like a woman scorn'd

—William Congreve, *The Mourning Bride*, 1697

THE WORD "UNFORGIVING" MEANS harsh, hostile. In its definitions, the *Cambridge Dictionary* includes "not willing to forgive people for things they do wrong" and "unpleasant or difficult to deal with," and gives as an example "an unforgiving fabric or item of clothing can make you look fat." In one of its definitions, the *Collins English Dictionary* explains that "if you describe a situation or activity as unforgiving, you mean that it causes a lot of people to experience great difficulty or failure, even people who deserve to succeed."

In other words, not good. Tough. Unrelenting.

The assumption often tends to be that it's good to forgive. Even that you *must* forgive. Even if, in many cases, forgiveness can be poison for the abused. Forgiveness can too often be mistaken for submission, obedience and compliance—forgive your abuser, forgive your rapist, forgive the partner who cheats and treats you like dirt, forgive the boss who shouts at you in the office, forgive the entire patriarchal, white colonialist system for insisting pain and suffering is part of your lot.

A woman who refuses to forgive is countercultural, and her rage is painted as extreme, pathological. Hence the oft-repeated saying "Hell hath no fury like a woman scorned," which is often misattributed to Shakespeare or the Bible, but derives from the lines quoted at the start of this chapter, from William Congreve's late seventeenth-century play *The Mourning Bride*. Funny since, as we have seen in Chapter 11, it is men who kill the women who leave them and not the other way around. I'm not saying women skip down the street giving flowers to strangers if they are betrayed, but statistics show they don't tend to shoot their exes dead as payback.

So why has that phrase been in currency for more than three centuries? Because the world has long been oiled by female forgiveness, female long-suffering. A woman who hasn't forgiven, softened or erased bad behavior is slammed as somehow demented, as bitter, twisted, obsessed or mad. A twisted concept of forgiveness has been used, in short, to gaslight women—and many men too.

Abuse survivors often fret that they are unable to forgive, and that because of this there must be something wrong with them. But who benefits from this? Salma Hayek wrote in the *New York Times* that she had been proud of her "capacity for forgiveness" in not reporting the sleazy behavior of Harvey Weinstein toward her, only to later realize she was yet to come to terms with the abuse, which had "hurt deeply."

I nearly drowned in forgiveness studies while researching this book. I became a bit dubious about some of the academic approaches, because many of the authors didn't seem to take trauma into account, or to prioritize the long-term needs of the victim. I'm wary of those who preach an easy forgiveness, for the same reasons. There are varying, competing definitions of forgiveness; the ones that concern me seem to place a further burden on the victim. Academics usually define forgiveness along the lines of: "a process of reducing negative thoughts, feelings, and behaviors toward a transgressor, which might be accompanied by evoking positive thoughts, feelings, and actions toward the harm-doer. Thus, forgiveness occurs via shift in beliefs, affects, and motives."

British philosophy professor Joanna North argued in her article "Wrongdoing and Forgiveness" that "the value of forgiveness lies in the fact that it essentially requires a recognition of the wrongdoer's responsibility for his action, and secondly that forgiveness typically involves an effort on the part of the one wronged: a conscious attempt to improve oneself in relation to the wrongdoer." And herein lies the problem: the effort of the one wronged. Is there really a need to "improve oneself" when you have been harmed? Isn't forgiveness then a burden?

The idea of forgiveness as some kind of gift to the person who wronged you seems to be prevalent. Professor Bob Enright, a psychologist at the University of Wisconsin–Madison, known as the "father of forgiveness" for his three decades of research on the subject, thinks it is more than moving past something, forgetting about it, or—as the meaningless cliché goes—"moving on."

Enright, the cofounder of the International Forgiveness Institute, argues it is also about expressing something positive, "some kind of goodness" to the person or people who harmed you, whether it is compassion, empathy, or understanding. He says forgiveness is a moral virtue, that "lives side by side with seeking fairness," and should not be confused with reconciliation. I understand why he says this, but simultaneously buck against it—it still seems to me to place a burden on the victim.

I am writing this as someone whose natural instinct is to forgive. It's baked in, probably because of my mother's fierce insistence on it. My friends regularly pull me up for cutting jerks slack, for always seeing the best or the potential for the best in people, even, sometimes, when they hurt me. I spend a lot of time wondering why someone did something, why they were mean or cruel. Then I try to move on. Sometimes I do this too quickly and too soon, and I internalize what should be anger as sadness, something Lucia Osborne-Crowley wrote about elegantly in *Meanjin*, arguing that women are "taught that it is our responsibility to keep relationships alive and intact, and that anger is destructive." But suppressing anger is also not good for your health, or your rights.

There is a reason many religious groups teach women to submit to men—and why, in the Christian tradition, some heavily emphasize Bible verses instructing women to be quiet while ignoring the verses that tell slaves to obey their masters. Male control is central to these doctrines, and often perilously so. American author Jude Ellison Sady Doyle, who grew up in the Catholic Church, wrote in the *New York Review of Books* in

2018: "Women in the Church were pressured to forgive men constantly, and rarely for good reason. Sexual violence was something women and girls in my church were sometimes asked to forgive. So was domestic violence, and child abuse, and so was a husband who cheated on you, or talked down to you. . . . 'Even if they don't repent, we still have to forgive,' [American evangelical group] Focus on the Family tells us, in its marriage-counseling section. Women were expected to do the work of forgiveness so that men did not have to do the work of change."

The Fundamentalist Church of Jesus Christ of Latter-day Saints, the polygamist cult that is an offshoot of the mainstream Mormon church, has told women to "keep it sweet," which former member Rachel Jeffs says means to not express anger, and not feel anger, resentment or frustration. Former church president Rulon Jeffs, Rachel's grandfather, told women that their approach to their husbands should be "keep sweet, pray and obey," as documented in the Netflix series named after this advice. The women dressed in long, loose-fitting, pale-colored dresses, puffed up their hair in French braids and, as teenagers, were married to far older men. The highest-ranking senior men had dozens of wives in what they called "plural marriage." Imagine being told to pray away discomfort and rage as a girl married to an eighty-five-year-old man. The current leader of the church, Warren Jeffs, who is in jail after being convicted of sexual assault, had seventy-eight wives, twenty-four of whom were under seventeen when he was arrested in 2011.

The 2022 film *Women Talking*, adapted from Miriam Toews's book of the same name based on the true story of an incident in a Bolivian Mennonite community, explored how difficult it is for women in faith communities to expose abuse and seek justice, given the pressure to forgive. It tells of mass serial rapes carried out by a group of men who gassed entire households with a veterinary sedative sprayed through windows and doors at night. Many rapes went unreported, and many girls and women—aged between three and sixty-five—were raped numerous times. Victims would wake in the morning with bloodied, dirty sheets, grass in their hair, ropes around their wrists, semen on their bodies, and debilitating headaches. This went on for several years until two men were caught breaking into a house and named others. In a culture where women are silenced, the dangers are obvious. The women in the Mennonite colony were told to submit, were not allowed to be ministers or vote for ministers, and were, and still are, encouraged to forgive rape and incest—amid calls to release the perpetrators from jail.

A polygamous cult and mass rapes are extreme examples, but in thousands of religious communities around the world, women are taught to be docile and submit to men, that challenging male authority is a sign of sin, and that forgiveness should be automatically bestowed upon abusers. Awareness of these injustices is growing, and some incremental changes are occurring, but not nearly quickly enough, and deep, fundamental inequalities remain. As I found in my years of investigating domestic violence in faith communities for ABC with my colleague Hayley Gleeson, abusers and faith leaders can often demand forgiveness and capitulation to male control so quickly and so often that faith communities inadvertently become shelters for abusers, sometimes fatally.

❋

FORGIVENESS CAN BE WEAPONIZED by the families of abusers, as well as abusers, as Sydney-based lawyer and author Amani Haydar found. After years of controlling behavior, Haydar's father killed her mother in her kitchen, stabbing her more than thirty times, while yelling "slut" in Arabic. All through her father's trial, Haydar's phone flashed with messages and missed calls from unidentified numbers—"some of Dad's overseas relations berating me, victim-blaming and slandering Mom. They said Allah would punish me some day because I was a dishonest daughter in breach of religious obligations to her father." She added: "Some of Dad's nieces and nephews—some of whom never even lived in the same country as Dad—lamented that my father had been a good person and was now being judged based on one 'incident.'" The lack of compassion shown by her family, who continually insisted she forgive her father without him even expressing any remorse, was genuinely jaw-dropping.

Haydar had hoped that when she delivered her victim impact statement—in which she said goodbye to a mother who had grown cold and was lying "on a metal refrigerator bed"—these relations would finally recognize her suffering. But the abuse continued. "One person commented that my dad was a 'great father' and that the murder was just a 'tragedy.' When I deleted the comment, the same person rang and abused me, concerned that the family had been dragged into the limelight: 'YOU'RE JUST A LITTLE SHIT, YOU KNOW THAT! YOU JUST WANT PUBLICITY!'"

❄

HAYDAR'S AWARD-WINNING, ELEGANTLY crafted book is called *The Mother Wound*, a title that refers to the theory that the relationship between mothers and daughters is affected by unhealed traumatic experiences passed down matriarchal lines in both ancient and modern worlds, as a male-run society denies women access to "ongoing matrilineal knowledge and structures."

Over a cup of tea in a Parramatta café, not far from the studio in which she creates her striking artworks, Haydar told me that in classical Islamic jurisprudence forgiveness is seen as a spiritual, personal matter, entirely separate from justice. Yet she was constantly pushed to forgive, even though she is someone who walks through the world with grace, creating beautiful art and speaking the truth about abuse in the hope of shining light into shadowed corners. Her mother, she says, gave her the courage to speak and taught her to pray: "I read somewhere that if trauma can be inherited then so can strength, resilience and joy." She and her sisters have raised a significant amount of money for cancer research, and her advocacy for victims of domestic violence has been tireless. Can Haydar lift the burden from her heart by fighting for a different world? Sometimes abusers are so wily and manipulative that the best way to manage them is to seal every crack, to close the windows, to lock them out. To eschew their darkness and find the light elsewhere.

Today, high school students ask Haydar if she feels bad for cutting her father out of her life: "They are captivated by these declarations because no one has ever told them that it is okay to unapologetically remove men from your life. No one ever told me. Some of the girls nod in agreement and others appear frozen in thought. Maybe even disgusted. I don't mind. I've been there."

✳

RESEARCH SHOWS HAYDAR'S EXPERIENCE is not singular. When women experience intimate partner or family violence, it dents their desire to forgive. A study of 572 college students from a large Midwestern university found such women were less likely to forgive themselves or others, and generally had lower levels of benevolence. This reluctance to forgive is also self-protective: one longitudinal study found partners who were more forgiving of psychological and physical abuse were more likely to be the subjects of that same aggression.

Another complicating factor is that many perpetrators of domestic abuse see themselves as victims; it's part of their modus operandi. A 2020 study, based on in-depth interviews with fifteen partners who had been together between four and thirty years, found that "the male batterers perceived forgiveness confusingly out of their dual self-perception as both perpetrator and victim. However, whether as perpetrator or victim, they clung to the position of forgiver . . . the issue of forgiveness preserved the status quo."

Forgiveness, in other words, can result in impunity. James McNulty from the University of Tennessee conducted a longitudinal study of newlywed couples that identified, as the title of his published article put it, the "Dark Side of Forgiveness." He found that the tendency to express forgiveness "may lead offenders to feel free to offend again by removing unwanted consequences for their behavior (e.g., anger, criticism, rejection, loneliness) that would otherwise discourage reoffending." The study revealed a positive association between spouses' reports of their own tendencies to express forgiveness to their partners and those partners' reports of psychological and physical aggression. This meant that "although spouses who reported being relatively more forgiving experienced psychological and physical aggression that remained stable over the first four years of marriage, spouses who reported being relatively less forgiving experienced declines in both forms of aggression over time."

To prompt forgiveness, remorse is usually required, along with justice. But how can we forgive in a culture of no consequence? If a tiny fraction of sexual assaults are reported, and a tiny fraction of those end up in court, and a tiny fraction of those charged end up convicted, an entire system is weighted against victims, and militates against their ability to forgive. We have a culture that often pressures victims to forgive, but allows abusers to fly free.

❄

IT SEEMS REASONABLE, THEN, to argue that forgiveness can be, at times, bad for you. If it exposes you to abuse, if it forces you to keep enduring abuse, then it will compromise your physical and mental health. Intimate partner violence leads to anxiety, depression and a host of negative physical health outcomes, including heart, immunity and sexual health issues, and survivors are generally less likely to trust others. Women who have been abused are more likely to have abnormal pap results and be diagnosed later with cancer, and less likely to survive cancer. A 2006 study found women with breast, ovarian, endometrial, and ovarian cancer were 2.6 times more likely to present with cancer at later stages if they had a history of family violence. Another study from 2014 found the prevalence of cervical cancer reported by abused women was ten times higher than the general population. A meta-analysis from 2018 confirmed a significant, positive relationship between violence and cancer diagnoses, particularly for cervical cancer.

A cross-sectional study of 14,100 middle-aged Australian women underlined the link between domestic abuse and physical ill-health, including the following conditions: allergies or breathing problems, pain or fatigue, bowel problems, eyesight and hearing problems, low iron, asthma, bronchitis or emphysema, and cervical cancer.

❋

PART OF THE PROBLEM is how we define forgiveness. What is commonly agreed is that ill-will is replaced with some form of goodwill, changing a negative to a positive. Must the positive benefit the abuser or the perpetrator? Or can the positive be redefined as an *absence* of ill-will, as in "I will not seek vengeance (though I will seek justice) and I will not allow you to tarnish my capacity for good, my ability to love"?

One definition is "refraining from mentally holding a grudge against that person [who harms you] in order to free up your mental space." Can we free ourselves mentally without forgiving? Or without expressing any kind of goodwill, just a kind of neutrality, or turning away? We too often assume forgiveness takes a single moment, rather than ongoing, daily hard work.

Ijeoma Oluo, author of the bestselling *So You Want to Talk About Race*, says that as a survivor of sexual assault, and an advocate for other victims, she is often lectured on the need for forgiveness. She also hears about it from survivors of physical, sexual and emotional abuse who write to ask her how to forgive, and about why they can't forgive. "Instead of focusing on healing and comfort," she says, "many survivors find themselves obsessing with forgiveness, trying to will away their trauma in order to 'move on.' When they can't do this, not only are they judged by those closest to them, they judge themselves as weak and trapped. The shame of being unable to forgive compounds the pain of the original hurt." She continues: "Far too often, the pressure to forgive brings the focus back to the perpetrator and keeps harmful people in your life or on your mind, while pushing your feelings and your healing to the bottom of your priority list."

PTSD expert Anastasia Pollock says she does not use the word "forgiveness" in trauma therapy. Instead, she uses the word "unburdening," meaning a letting go. "Even if the intention is coming from a good place," she says, "trying to get someone who has been violated to forgive can [make them] feel like [they are] being victimized all over again." Pastor Nadia Bolz-Weber refers to forgiveness as "a way of wielding boltcutters and snapping the chain that links us" to "assholes," thereby freeing us from them. This makes sense to me.

Often, the moment abusive, illegal behavior is exposed, people almost immediately ask how quickly the perpetrator can be redeemed. The question is, who benefits when abusers, usually powerful men, face no consequences and are instantly forgiven and folded back into the empathetic breast of society? Whose pain is minimized, whose lives are trashed? And who isn't forgiven or excused? How can a victim of sexual abuse at the hands of the Catholic Church forgive an institution that disbelieved, silenced and ignored them, and trashed their reputations then sued them, as pedophile priests moved from parish to parish unimpeded? Has a sufficient reckoning been had now, with reparations still being fought and victim suicides still a regular occurrence?

❄

WHAT WE NEED IS an understanding of forgiveness that is not divorced from social context, and not crudely imposed on wounded people. One that does not mean pardon, erasure or a kind of reconciliation.

While researching her book *Triumph of the Heart*, author Megan Feldman Bettencourt interviewed several women who had forgiven perpetrators of sexual assault. She found the primary reason they forgave was "their own self-preservation—their drive to not only survive but to also enjoy a quality of life that hatred would never give them." She argues that "the very act of speaking up, being heard, and getting some degree of justice—without pressure to reconcile—eases the way for forgiveness." She also insists: "The more we view forgiveness as a process of releasing resentment, rather than an abdication of justice that implies silence or reconciliation, the better equipped we'll be to help survivors."

This is what forgiveness is *not*: condoning, excusing, pardoning, justifying, erasing, absolving. It is *not* suggesting justice be shrugged off, or consequences forgotten. It is extremely difficult to forgive in a culture of no consequences.

Chapter 13

The Stolen Generations: What Does Forgiveness Mean?

HAZEL WALGAR WAS SLICING into some fresh, home-baked bread as her husband, Gavin, boiled a tin pot over a fire to make us tea. She asked for two bags—"I like my tea like I like my men: strong, and Black"—as Gavin smiled to himself. Then she pointed to the horizon: "Look there, the humpback whales, can you see them?" A regular appearance of creatures highly respected by the traditional owners.

As we sat on the hill overlooking Cardabia Station, a 2,000-square-kilometer property on the Ningaloo/Nyinggulu Coast in far northwestern Australia, which was purchased by the Indigenous Land Corporation in 1997, I looked out to the whales crashing into the blue as a kangaroo wandered around us. The Bayungu (or Baiyungu) people, the traditional owners, now run the property. To the south stretches Coral Bay, and to the north lies the former US submarine base at Exmouth, but there were no houses within sight. All you could hear was the songs of the robins and cicadas that dwell among the large red termite mounds dotted on the hills like tents. It's one of the remotest parts of the country, singular in its beauty, an unspoilt wilderness edging onto bustling Ningaloo/Nyinggulu Reef, where turtles, rays and starfish mill about in a vibrant underwater world and every year thousands of humpback whales and whale sharks migrate along the shore.

This is where Hazel can heal. "I like coming up here, Julia," she told me. "It gives me peace." Two years ago, her eldest son died by suicide: "It ripped me apart." When Gavin went to work, she would be curled up in bed, unable to move, and when he returned, she would still be there, mute and inconsolable. It was not until a spiritual healer came to town, and spent three days with Hazel on country, she said, that she was able to move through the world again, although "the pain is always with me, it's always there."

When she was just six, Hazel was stolen from her parents. She was sent against her will to the Churches of Christ Carnarvon Mission with other local Aboriginal children, including her sister and other young relatives, and stayed there for six years. The children were made to do domestic work and only speak English, in a system akin to child labor.

"We went in there fluent speakers," said Hazel, "and the punishment we got for speaking our language was out of control: beatings with belts, rinsing our mouths out with chemical stuff, soap and . . . My sister was four years older than me. . . . She died

190

two years ago from throat cancer, and this is a woman who never drank alcohol or smoked cigarettes. . . . I sometimes think, Was it that treatment we got in the bloody mission? We used to use a cleaning substance called Trusol; they would make us swallow it. It was poisoning."

Hazel is a member of the Stolen Generations, the term used to refer to the thousands of Aboriginal children forcibly removed from families under the guise of "protection" and assimilation, between the 1920s and 1970s, by government agents and church missions. The impulse for this cruel and devastating policy, the traumatic impacts of which are still real and tangible today, came from racist, paternalistic beliefs that young Aboriginal kids would be better off in institutions, away from their culture and kin, where they could be somehow "cleaned up" and integrated into white society.

Hazel left the mission when she was twelve and found her parents were struggling. "Mom and Dad had to move; they took the people off the country, there were no jobs, reserves were set up, and housing. By the time [I'd had] that big gap of missing them, my mom and dad, their health [had] deteriorated, they['d] had bad diabetes and had to adapt to Western life. I feel I was robbed of being around Mom and Dad; they were both gone when I was eighteen. I was then in a very violent relationship at a young age; I thought it was normal. I had little boys, Mom and Dad gone. But Dad always told me, 'One day, my baby daughter, you are going to find a husband who will marry you and look after you,' and that's him there." Gavin, sitting on a crate playing a game on his phone as the sun set behind him, looked up and grinned.

Still, Hazel invites white people onto her country and tells them about her ancestors, her spiritual connection with the land, her life's work—all despite the fact that white people tore her from her parents, and forced her and her sister to gargle poison to stop the sound of their own words, their own tongue, coming out of their mouths. As a traditional owner of the Ningaloo Coast, she is now also a joint manager of the area with the WA Department of Biodiversity, Conservation and Attractions.

While camped on these ancient grounds, Hazel's ancestors watched the reef grow over thousands of years and witnessed the retreat and advance of the sea. But her language, Bayungu, is now close to extinction, despite her best efforts to record it for future generations, including studying linguistics at university.

When I asked if forgiveness had any relevance to her experience, Hazel's face shifted, dropped. You never move past an experience like she had at the mission, she said, which makes sense. How could you? Trauma like that is in your bones, your blood, your mouth. It is in your thoughts as you bury your sister, and your oldest son.

❋

IN 2008, THE AUSTRALIAN Prime Minister, Kevin Rudd, finally apologized to First Nations people for the fact that many thousands of children were taken from their families. Rudd chose to deliver this apology on National Sorry Day, which, since 1988, has been held annually on May 26 to commemorate the Stolen Generations and has become a sacred, profound occasion. It is a day when white Australia needs to listen, and reckon, and try to understand how the actions of their forebears still live on in the houses, skins and minds of Australian Aboriginal people. And how those scars are borne by people who are disproportionately living in poverty, in prison, in pain.

When former prime minister Scott Morrison stood in the federal parliament fourteen years after the Rudd government issued the Apology to Australia's Indigenous Peoples, he made a stunningly obtuse remark, saying forgiveness should follow an apology, thus placing the onus on First Nations people to forgive. I want to quote his remarks at length because Morrison states he was drawing on a tradition of his Christian faith, which urges forgiveness of the undeserving. But his focus should have been on what his government could do, not what Indigenous people should do in response to oppression:

Forgiveness is never earned or deserved. . . . It's an act of grace. It's an act of courage. And it is a gift that only those who have been wounded, damaged and destroyed can offer.

I also said fourteen years ago, "Sorry is not the hardest word to say, the hardest is 'I forgive you.'" But I do know that such a path of forgiveness does lead to healing. It does open up a new opportunity. It does offer up release from the bondage of pain and suffering that no simple apology on its own can achieve. And nor do I believe that such forgiveness is a corporate matter. It can only begin with the individual. And forgiveness does not mean forgetting. Nor does it mean that there are not consequences for actions, and the need for redress and restitution.

The response of the First Peoples' Assembly of Victoria, which is currently working on shaping a treaty with the state government, was blunt: "Get in the bin." The co-chair, Bangerang and Wiradjuri elder Geraldine Atkinson, tweeted: "I'm horrified."

Academic and elder Marcia Langton, a former Northern Territory co-commissioner, on the inquiry into the Stolen Generations, told reporters that the direction to forgive was not Morrison's to give: "If people have been severely traumatized, it is very damaging to them to be told how to behave. You can't make traumatized people play by parlor game rules. With all due respect to the Prime Minister and his Christian belief in forgiveness, and knowing about these cases as I do from working as the assistant commissioner in the NT, I'd have to say that one must be very respectful of the victims and their capacity to navigate their way through very severe intergenerational trauma. There just is no easy route and I think it is completely the wrong approach to suggest to them how they should conduct themselves. It's entirely inappropriate."

Pastor Ray Minniecon, who spent his childhood living in fear of being snatched by the authorities, told Marina Cantacuzino of the Forgiveness Project that forgiveness was something he struggles with because it's hard to forgive when you still have an open wound. The apology from Prime Minister Rudd was a "turning point," he said. "It pricked the conscience of a nation." He continued: "Rape of the soul is so profound—and particularly for the Stolen Generations who were forcibly removed from their parents, communities and culture. You can't put a Band-Aid on that. For these people, the concept of healing, and the concept of forgiveness, is difficult. Reconciliation only happens when you're restored in your own spirit. That's why we prefer to talk about emotional and psychological well-being. If you fix the psyche and restore well-being through a process of reconnection and reconstruction of identity, then you have a platform for someone to deal with intergenerational pain and be a human being again. Only then can someone have an opportunity to receive or express forgiveness."

Still, Minniecon practices forgiveness every day to "relieve my bitterness . . . It's a moment by moment thing because I can walk into a shop and have a person do racist acts without even knowing they are racist. And when that happens I have to walk away and deal with my rage and anger, and learn to say, 'Okay Ray, forgive that person.' If I didn't forgive, then the past would always be present."

As Anglican scholar and priest Geoff Broughton reminded me, in the original Greek, forgiveness means "release."

How can you forgive attempts at systematic erasure, genocide and wholesale theft of children from their parents, which in many cases amounted to slavery, especially when those same people are still dying younger and being locked up at greater rates than white Australians? How can you forgive the violence that has endured and is ongoing today? Isn't the point of saying sorry to stop the behavior that you needed to apologize for and atone for it? Not to say, *And now you need to get over it.*

❄

ELLA HISCOCKS, A TALL white woman with gray hair, became the matron of the Cootamundra Home for Aboriginal Girls in 1945, as a recent widow, and stayed in the position for twenty years. When she eventually adopted a young child herself, one who had been removed from her parents at just five months old, she developed a very particular night-time ritual. She would sit with the girl, then about five, every night, and, as the girl said later, "stroke my nose down the side saying it would make it straight." She tried, every night before the girl climbed into her bed, to erase her culture, her race, her face. To make her white.

The Cootamundra Home for Aboriginal Girls, which operated for several decades, is notorious among First Nations people in Australia. Ella Hiscocks was known for both odd bouts of tenderness and a regime of severity, one for which she was awarded an MBE. She urged the misnamed Aboriginal Protection Board for more resources for a better life for the hundreds of Aboriginal girls brought to her after being taken from their parents, and saw her role as their champion, "surrogate mother," and humane protector, but still employed emotional abuse, deprivations and rigid rules to control her charges.

When Aunty Lorraine Peeters was taken to the Cootamundra home in 1943 at the age of four, her head was shaved and her clothes and belongings were burned. She says Hiscocks improved things marginally, but the fundamental degradation remained. She soon shut down as a result of grief and trauma, from "being told every day you must be white, you must dress white, you must speak white, you must do everything that you're told—otherwise you'd be punished with a huge whip they walked around with. . . . You were there specifically to be trained as a domestic for white families; you were taught in [an]other's culture, forced to forget your own. It got a bit better as the staff changed, but it was very strict in my time."

Sexual abuse was rife, she says, which is why, until a couple of years ago, she could not recall two years of her childhood. One night she was sitting at home with her husband watching *Revelation*, a documentary on ABC about criminal Catholic priests grooming children, and the dam that had contained repressed pain for decades burst. She told her husband, Harry, "That's what happened to us," and she was overwhelmed with anguish, as her husband, adult daughter Shaan, and granddaughter Meagan looked on. "So I went back to Coota," she said, "got my four-year-old self and brought her home with me. That's a key in healing. She is with me now, I am complete."

In order to heal, Aunty Lorraine had to spend time mourning "for that little person and what that little person went through." She said if she hadn't addressed it, she would "always [have gone] back to that room forever." The most important part of healing, she says, is spiritual well-being, "the core of our being for us mob."

When people ask her whether she forgives the people responsible for the darkness of her childhood, Peeters says: "No, what have I got to forgive for? I am the survivor here, a survivor of horrific abuse as a four-year-old. I am the one who has had the damage done to me. If you let that worry you and you turn that inwardly into anger or vengeance, that's bad [for] you. No, *they* have to own that shit, that's not my shit, what they done to me."

It is easy to forget for how long, and how vehemently, in the 2000s, the experience of the Stolen Generation was dismissed as a "myth"—partly due to ignorance, partly due to bias, partly due to poor historical record-keeping, and partly due to culture warriors who make sport of selective history-telling and fact-spinning, one calling the idea of the Stolen Generations a "giant intellectual fraud." "We are all evidence of the wrong that was done," says Aunty Lorraine, "the harm done through removal, and evidence of the slavery that people are in denial about. Some people haven't been through it, and don't know."

Without some kind of truth-telling commission—a moral reckoning at a local level whereby white people can "own that shit"—and while so much racism is endemic and entrenched, the question of forgiveness is not one that can be asked here. It is also, simply, completely wrong for a powerful white man to tell Indigenous people it's time for them to forgive.

As Martha Minow writes, this was also the experience at South Africa's Truth and Reconciliation Commission, set up in 1996 to investigate the crimes of the apartheid system. It allowed for a carefully planned and structured period of confession, during which people admitted to having committed terrible acts of violence, sexual assault and financial abuse. There was an acceptance of responsibility and recognition of wrongdoing. Yet while many victims indicated they were prepared to forgive or reconcile with police or government officials from the apartheid regime, they did not want forgiveness to be assumed, and would "recoil" when perpetrators came to them with open arms and outstretched hands. Minow writes: "A survivor may think, 'Should you not wait for me to stretch out my hand to you, when I'm ready, when I've established what is right?' Forgiveness is a power held by the victimized, not a right to be claimed. The ability to dispense, but also to withhold, forgiveness is an ennobling capacity and part of the dignity to be reclaimed by those who survive the wrongdoing. Even an individual survivor who chooses to forgive cannot, properly, forgive in the name of other victims." The expectation of forgiveness, Minow argues, "is to heap yet another burden" on victims.

AUNTY LORRAINE IS A gentle, tenacious soul. She laughs easily and speaks generously. Her role in traditional Aboriginal culture would have been as a healer and perhaps a teacher, she told me. She stresses she cannot speak for others; forgiveness is an individual thing. But she has taken hundreds of people—Aboriginal and non-Aboriginal—through her healing and education programs and runs booked-out sessions in Victorian prisons. She exudes a kind of stoic tender-heartedness. She has understood pain and seeks to lift it, to help others heal, connect to their spirits and be unafraid.

The grace, in this instance, comes not from a forced forgiveness, but from the fact that First Nations people, despite everything, after all the trauma and hurt, asked other Australians to join them in a makarrata—a coming-together after a struggle. "We invite you to walk with us in a movement of the Australian people for a better future," says the *Uluru Statement from the Heart*, in a makarrata that "captures our aspirations for a fair and truthful relationship with the people of Australia and a better future for our children based on justice and self-determination." The generosity of this act is striking.

※

OTHER COUNTRIES HAVE FACED similar reckonings, calls for reparations and apologies for brutality. Pope Francis apologized to the Indigenous communities of Canada for the role of the Catholic Church during decades of "evil" mistreatment of Indigenous children at "catastrophic" residential schools, which saw 150,000 removed from their families and exposed to sexual violence, starvation and indoctrination in order to strip their heritage from them and "turn them white." He asked for forgiveness "for the ways in which many members of the church and of religious communities cooperated, not least through their indifference, in projects of cultural destruction and forced assimilation promoted by the governments of that time, which culminated in the system of residential schools."

Australia's First Nations people wondered why they did not receive the same apology.

World leaders have made varying apologies also, some fulsome and genuine, others tempered or tepid. Though too many to list, they include Japanese Prime Minister Tomiichi Murayama's apology for crimes committed and suffering inflicted during World War II; British Prime Minister Tony Blair's acknowledgment that the UK government had stood by as a crop failure turned into the devastating potato famine in Ireland in 1845–51 (his words fell short of a full apology); and the Belgian government's apology for kidnapping thousands of children from African colonies. Public recognitions are vital first steps in reckoning with the past, even if many of these efforts can be shrugged off as toothless platitudes.

The "comfort women" of Japan, for example, are still seeking accountability for the horrors they endured as sex slaves during World War II. When I visited the Women's Active Museum on War and Peace in Tokyo, I was shocked to discover how difficult it was to find, and how sparse their resources were. The refusal of the Japanese government to fully or collectively apologize and take responsibility for, to recognize, investigate or teach the truth about what happened to these women has been the source of immense grief and controversy. The museum administrator, Ayano Kasajima, told me forgiveness cannot occur without reparations and remorse, "but by keeping records we can hold onto the hope that one day things will change."

Where such acknowledgments have not occurred, grace can mostly be found in endurance and resilience, in a desire for reconciliation, in calls for justice, and in the work of education, healing and spiritual strengthening. It can also be invited, by ensuring we see the faces and hear the stories of those who have been told to be quiet and move on from the horrors of the past.

Chapter 14

"We Will Wear You Down with Our Love"

FOR THE 2023 NATIONAL SORRY DAY commemoration, the relatives of the now elderly Cootamundra Girls (see Chapter 13) organized an event with music, stalls and celebrations in Sydney's Botanic Gardens. I arrived at lunchtime, fresh off the plane from Hobart, dragging a large neon-green suitcase, exhausted after a few long days of filming. Behind the canvas tents, the harbor glittered in the sunshine as ferries carved a path to Circular Quay. Parked at the entrance was a bus with *UNLOCKING OUR PAST TO FREE OUR FUTURE* painted on the side, containing information about the Kinchela Boys' Home. Sitting inside were men who were sent to the home as boys, who told me of being taken from their families and put in a home where pedophiles had full rein, tying the boys to a tree outside with chains and "doing what they liked" as night fell. They spoke to me of their own children struggling with their mental health, of lifetimes of erasure and little understanding of what it means to lose your family, culture and community as a kid, to feel unmoored forever.

I wandered around looking for Aunty Lorraine Peeters; she saw me and enveloped me with a hug before being dragged off for another interview. Her granddaughter Meagan had organized the event and she was in hot demand. But Aunty Lorraine was worried about something else that day: Australia's most prominent Aboriginal broadcaster, Stan Grant, a respected anchor and celebrated author, had just taken leave from his job at ABC because of an overwhelming volley of visceral, racist attacks, and, he said, the failure of management to publicly defend him following his comments, during coverage of the coronation of King Charles III, on the British royal family's role in the dispossession of Indigenous Australians. Grant's great-aunt had been a Coota Girl: Eunice Josephine Grant, known as "Number 658."

❇

EARLIER THAT WEEK, ON a cold Melbourne morning, I had crept into a conference room on Lygon Street, Carlton. I found myself sitting at the top of a rectangle of desks, next to Aunty Lorraine and her daughter Shaan, who were leading this workshop, called the Marumali Program—*marumali* being a Gamilaroi word meaning "to put back together"—about the intergenerational trauma of the Stolen Generations. When Aunty Lorraine had told me that if I really wanted to understand what she did, from beginning to end, I needed to attend one of her workshops, I couldn't say no. How could I pretend that a partial or shallow understanding was enough?

The workshop participants were mostly white people who work with Aboriginal people on reparations, mental health and counseling, and in various bureaucratic positions for which an understanding of deep trauma is required. Much of the workshop was about empathy, asking us to put ourselves in the shoes of people taken away from their parents. How would we feel at the time? Ten years later? Fifty?

We were trying to better understand a history we have been robbed of, and reckon with it. When I flicked back through my high school history books, I was shocked to discover the first reference to Aboriginal people was under the headline "Problems for Squatters." For many years now, I have been trying to shed that ignorance I was fed, gather knowledge about our true history and grasp how that history is embedded in our present. I wanted to listen, to know how to recognize trauma and how to be a respectful ally, to shoulder some of the load, without blundering in where I wasn't wanted or needed.

Aunty Lorraine told her own story of forcible removal and said, "My story is everybody's story." She alternated speaking with Shaan, who has a quietly authoritative presence and gives the impression of a woman who has seen a lot of shit and isn't particularly keen to put up with anymore. We spoke about cultural myths and the history of Aboriginal people being likened to flora and fauna, dispossessed, treated like animals, placed in holding pens and stripped of their hair, names, religion and family, no matter whether their mob came from salt water, fresh water, desert or rainforest, all in an attempt to "breed the Black out." Of how, at children's homes, any changes in skin color were monitored, girls were bought and sold to stockmen, liberties lost and liberties taken. We heard about the many times when, on refusing food, a kid would be beaten, stripped naked, locked in a dark room for hours and abused physically, psychologically and sexually, and how memories of those experiences might be triggered by noises, smells and places like hospitals. Of people being asked to prove their Aboriginality: *You took me because I'm Black, and now you're asking me to prove it?* We heard about the forms that trauma takes and how to normalize it, respond to it, remind people of their strength, ensure they are not alone.

We all discussed, too, the effects of that history, breaking into groups and writing words and phrases on whiteboards: *trauma, disconnection, anger, lack of trust, shame, guilt, disorientation about identity, harm to self and others, poverty, ability to show love, lack of parenting role models, grief, frustration, incarceration, addiction or self-medication, suicide, chronic illness, anxiety attacks, inability to establish healthy relationships, mental health issues, a lack of a sense of belonging.* We were encouraged to think about the difference between mental illness and spiritual illness, and about our own histories, and we all sat quietly in a kind of grief and sorrow.

I felt very . . . white. I kept thinking of my own kids, and how unbearable it would be to be parted from them even for a year, let alone a lifetime. Of how accepting the kidnapping of your offspring howls in the face of every biological instinct. Of the enduring racism that frames people who speak of Aboriginal history—or a full account of Australian history—as killjoys, "problems," downers, when it's just a factual family history. Of how hard it would be to gain a sense of myself growing up in a strange building, surrounded by strangers, disciplined by strangers, without love or community or security. How that might shape a life. Of how little we understand trauma. Of, despite it all, how gentle Aunty Lorraine was, how kind her eyes.

All the while, my phone was constantly flashing. Intent on listening to the others, I flipped it face down then back up again, trying not to get distracted but also concerned I'd miss some vital development in the Stan Grant controversy—one in which I was deeply embroiled, as I had hosted ABC's coverage of the coronation.

❄

IT HAD BEEN AN insane few weeks. Just a few days before the broadcast was due to take place, I had been pulled in to copresent with the delightful Jeremy Fernandez. It was my first time back on air since having further treatment, which included surgery and chemotherapy. My clothes hung loose on my scrawny frame, and more than half my head of hair had fallen out (my hairdresser estimated I lost about four-fifths of it; it streamed out so much I was afraid to wash or comb it). So there were many things rattling through my brain before I even made it to my first editorial meeting: Could I make it through four hours on air? Would I look weird? Did I have any clothes that fit properly? Returning to work after being ill is often an anxious experience.

But what mattered most of all, of course, were the stories we were going to tell. We had so much to cover: the legal, cultural and religious significance of the occasion; the protests; the decline in popularity of the monarchy in Britain as well as Australia; the attempts of the new king to modernize the ceremony; the kind of king and queen Charles and Camilla might be; the moves toward a republic in many countries in the Commonwealth; the crowns, the jewels, the thrones, the orb and the sceptre and all the pomp and paraphernalia.

There can be few better illustrations of the fact that history is a complicated, contested, living beast than the coronation of a monarch. When young Elizabeth II was crowned on a wave of postwar hope, the popularity of the royal family was stellar, the sheen on the imperial crown largely untarnished. By the end of her seven-decade reign, the queen's personal standing remained high, but support for the monarchy had dimmed, and an interrogation of the destructive impacts of the British Empire had been flaring across the globe. Reportedly, when Prime Minister Anthony Albanese had raised the issue of King Charles III visiting Australia, the king had asked: "But will I be welcome?"

Would it, we wondered, be rude to mention this, a lèse majesté? Or would it be accurate and refreshingly candid? And given that we were working for a public broadcasting organization tasked with representing diverse views and voices in our country, should we focus only on how jolly the coronation would be, how pretty the jewels, how solemn the occasion, or did we have a duty to include the perspectives of First Nations people, migrants and others so often excluded?

Three hours before the coronation began, as the first people were trickling into Westminster Abbey in pressed pants and fancy hats, we held a live panel discussion about the meaning of the monarchy for Australians, its history here, and its future.

"The Crown is not above politics to us," said Grant, "because the symbol of that Crown . . . represented the invasion, the theft of land, and, in our case, the exterminating war, which next year will mark two hundred years. In the name of that Crown, martial law was declared on my people." On the panel with him were Wiradjuri lawyer Teela Reid, monarchist MP Julian Leeser and the head of the Australian Republic Movement, Craig Foster. Grant spoke of the dispossession of his people not as an abstract matter of the past, but as trauma that endures. He said: "Let's not imagine that we can just look at this ceremony tonight and see this as something that is distant, that is just ceremonial and doesn't hold weight. It is scars, it is broken bones and it is too many damaged souls and we need to heal."

AFTER THE BROADCAST, WE were wired with adrenaline. I raced off to a friend's fiftieth across town, then crawled into bed as Jeremy prepared to host the national budget coverage. On Sunday afternoon, a conservative commentator sent me a curt text: *Julia. WTF. Stop being an activist. . . . What's got into you and your leftie mates. I'm very disappointed in you mate.* I didn't respond, but, sensing the beginnings of a concerted campaign, I did message Stan to see how he was. Unfortunately, this text was a sign of more ugliness to come, a bellwether of emotional, visceral and unhinged reactions.

A few days later, after receiving physical threats online—for which a man has since been charged—and what he says was a lack of public support from ABC, Grant said he had decided to step away from his job for a time (he has since resigned). ABC apologized and announced a review into how ABC responds to racism against staff.

Aunty Lorraine was watching, worried. Stan Grant had spoken truth on behalf of so many First Nations people, and so many were being affected by the attacks on him, including the elders, who were still being wounded at the same time as they were trying to heal.

"All the aunties love him," she said.

※

SO, WHAT HAPPENED DURING that broadcast, exactly, that was so offensive? No critic cited any particular comment as insulting, or incorrect. Just the simple fact of having the discussion at all, hours before a coronation, seemed to be regarded as intrusive and impolite. Radio host Neil Mitchell said the discussion—forty-five minutes in eight hours of coverage—"soured the mood [with] all this bitterness about our Indigenous history." It was also called a "hate-fest," "race-obsessed" and a "woke bin-fire of self-loathing." On Sky News, former conservative politician Cory Bernardi declared Grant was the night's "whiner in chief" and likened the discussion to "propaganda." These critics, Grant wrote later, "tried to depict me as hate-filled . . . accused me of maligning Australia."

The problem, according to two commentators writing in *The Australian* newspaper, is that Grant's words reflected "a growing mood among academics and schoolteachers that Australia's British heritage is to be regarded with shame." This argument is a well-worn trope, disregarding the efforts scholars have made to correct whitewashed accounts of "rescued" Indigenous people with the facts of massacres and other deliberate attempts to exterminate Indigenous populations, and implying that to attempt to teach a full account of history is somehow shameful, when in fact the shame lies in concealment.

Solemnity does not require obsequiousness. And discomfort is core to any inclusive, honest, cultural reckoning. For decades, women and people of color have been routinely excluded from public discussions of history, and portrayed as rude, negative, ungrateful and aggrieved when they do speak, as if getting in the way of true, positive stories of war and conquest. In the years prior to the coronation, in books, podcasts, pubs and university halls around the world, discussions were being had about the dark side of colonialism, including in Britain, India and Australia, while Jamaica called for both independence and slavery reparations. The truth is that Indigenous people have been dispossessed. As Teela Reid says, "The Crown dishonored their own rule of law, failing to seek the consent of First Nations people, declaring martial law—these are the facts and the facts matter."

Just a month before the coronation, Buckingham Palace gave unprecedented support to a research project looking at the monarchy's centuries-long involvement in the transatlantic slave trade, following the publication of a document showing that money was transferred to William III from slave traders. It was also shown that King Charles's ancestors had owned slave plantations in Virginia.

What intellectual honesty demands—as I discovered as a royal biographer—is to recognize that, along with orchestrating publicity, the royal family have controlled and censored history for centuries; if there is any propaganda, it comes from those who demand we pay obeisance to an unblemished, unproblematic monarchy and a Boy's Own adventure story of imperial conquest. When the Royal Archives tried to stop me from publishing material I had found in the house of Queen Victoria's doctor's descendants, I became aware of how opaque and unaccountable they were, of how little we still know, and how much has been burned and destroyed.

The question is, as always, who gets to write the complicated, nuanced history of this country? Who gets to even speak it? Here, two Indigenous people, an author/broadcaster and a lawyer were powerfully, articulately, accurately speaking of the past, saying they did so "with love," but their words were not just ignored, they were distorted and sensationalized, and ultimately went unheard in a roar of backlash. Jeremy and I, and ABC, were criticized for platforming such "truth-telling."

Once I became aware of the range of complaints about our program, I quickly understood that the most important issue was not the timing of the conversation about our colonial history— and present—but the nature of the abuse. In an era of trolling, and concerted online campaigns, we need to be able to distinguish between genuine complaints and racist heckling.

Critics reported that there were an "unprecedented" 1,700 to 1,800 complaints about our coverage. But according to ABC, while there were "around 1,832 audience contacts, more than 1,100 of those were either racist or abusive content, or did not raise a substantive issue, and are not considered good-faith complaints." So, if one of those contacts says they just don't want to see Aboriginal people on the television, or is abusive, is that a complaint? Or a spitball of venom?

Craig Foster, the head of the Australian Republic Movement, who was also on the panel, pointed out afterward on Instagram that he had not been vilified for the views he expressed. He said, "Australians have been taught that the Crown is beyond approach and immune to accountability," and that "when a First Nations person enters that conversation, just like for the last 235 years, they are flogged, massacred."

A report from the ABC Ombudsman found there was no breach of editorial standards, there were no errors, and that the discussions were "legitimate and newsworthy." Only sixty-one complaints queried editorial policies. The portrayal of this feedback as a deluge only fed the ugliness that slithered onto online forums. As did the false claims that people turned off their televisions.

The speech Grant made a few days later, when he withdrew from ABC at the end of the show he hosted, *Q&A*, was telling and powerful. He invited the nation to live and think a different way, according to the Wiradjuri concept of *yindyamarra winhanganha*, "the wisdom to live with respect in a world worth living in":

To those who have abused me and my family, I would just say if your aim was to hurt me, well, you've succeeded, and I'm sorry. I'm sorry that I must have given you so much cause to hate me so much, to target me and my family and to make threats against me. I'm sorry.

And that's what yindyamarra means. It means I am not just responsible for what I do, but for what you do. It is not just a word. It is sacred. It is what it means to be Wiradjuri. It is the core of my being. It is respect. It is respect that comes from the earth we are born into. From God, Baiame. If I break that, then I lose who I am.

I am down right now. But I will get back up. And you can come at me again, and I will meet you with the love of my people. My people can teach the world to love. As Martin Luther King Jr. said of his struggle, "We will wear you down with our capacity to love." Don't mistake our love for weakness, it is our strength. We have never stopped loving and fighting for justice and truth, the hard truths to speak in our land.

That, right there, is grace. It exists even alongside, and in the thick of, trauma. Sunlight piercing a cloud.

Chapter 15

The Callus: On Restorative Justice

DEBBIE MCGRATH WAS TWENTY-FOUR and eight months pregnant when she was woken in the middle of the night by a phone call. It was March 7, 1991. She checked the clock—2:00 a.m.— and swung her legs out of bed, hoisting up her large belly, and walked to the lounge room. It was her father, who asked to speak to her husband. She was sitting on the couch when she heard her husband say, "I can't tell her, I just can't." He handed the phone back to her and her father told her that her twenty-year-old brother Michael was dead.

She gasped, "What happened?"

The next sentence he spoke, she said, "changed everything [I had] in my life and had believed in." Glen, her brother's close friend, had taken a double-barreled shotgun to Michael's house and shot him dead.

After having a bath, Debbie sat on the back steps of her two-bedroom house in Wagga Wagga, looking out into the trees in the backyard, and waited for the sun to rise. Her two-year-old daughter's clothes hung on the Hills Hoist clothesline, pale against the blackness. In the world outside, oil fields were burning in Kuwait, Rwanda was embroiled in a civil war, the Soviet Union was crumbling, Bob Hawke was the Australian Prime Minister, George H. W. Bush was president of the United States—where a video of Rodney King being beaten by police had just been released—and Mariah Carey was the queen of the charts. Debbie sat there, holding the phone in her hand, unmoving, waiting for her father to call and say it had all been a terrible mistake.

The whole thing was senseless: the two men had been friends ever since Michael had pulled his car over to the side of the road to pick up Glen, who was hitchhiking. They'd gone on holidays together, gone camping, fished together and tinkered with cars, and just that night had played darts at the pub, in a competition Michael had won. There was no reason for violence, and no reason has ever been given. In a statement, all Glen said was that it was an accident.

Debbie went with her family to view her little brother's body at the local Catholic church and sat down next to his coffin. She held his hand, and spoke words of love, "things I should have said when he was alive." She thought he looked like he was sleeping, until she noticed the dried blood around his ears, and the way his hand held on to his crucifix, and realized his right arm was missing. "I promised my brother right there that that piece of feces would pay for what he had done. I just never realized how that promise would consume me and affect me for the next eleven years of my life."

Sitting through the trial was punishing. Debbie and her sister had both given birth in the months prior, so they spent their nights caring for infants and their days in court, incensed by the lack of concern for the victim, the passing around of photos of Michael's body by the jury "like they were holiday snaps," and the pausing of the trial so they could watch the Melbourne Cup. There were no opportunities to provide victim impact statements for those who had lost a brother or a son, a boy who had set his alarm early every Saturday so he could ride his bike, only to regularly sleep through it and have it wake up everyone else. A boy who had a large nose, pimples and a beautiful smile. Who disliked vegetables and liked country music, who was loyal to his friends, who drank and smoked and drove his car too fast.

Glen was sentenced to sixteen years in jail, with a non-parole period of twelve years. Nevertheless, Debbie became slowly consumed with hatred, obsessively ruminating about Glen and what she could do to him, how she'd like to infect him with HIV/AIDS, for example, chain him to a bull ants' nest, or torture and kill him. She felt broken and lost, as though everything she had ever believed in had crumbled. "I went into a world that I never knew existed and never wanted to be a part of," she said. "Everything was foreign to me. I was experiencing thoughts and emotions that were so intense that they frightened me and took over my life. I had no idea how to stop them." She "hated, really hated," for the first time in her life. "I lost my laughter. My trust in people had been taken away from me. I could not be in a crowd without having a panic attack. The fear that took over my body was enormous. I would check the windows and doors constantly, day and night, to make sure they were locked. My innocence was gone, and evil was introduced to me." Her life was leached of joy and beauty, and she found herself plotting murder while staring at sunsets.

Perhaps worst of all, she struggled to love her baby boy, because she was afraid of loss. "I was terrified that something could happen to him, and that, if it did, I would not survive that pain again."

❋

THE ADVICE DEBBIE WAS given, when she sought help, was to forgive, and move on. Her local priest said she'd be fine if she forgave Glen. She saw a series of grief counselors, one of whom airily told her to forgive and forget, but apparently Debbie told her "where her forgiveness and her memory loss could go." She wrote Glen a letter, but then was furious when he responded with what she saw as insincere sentiments. Her parents grew worried. When Glen appealed against his sentence, Debbie and her mother went to court, and Debbie found a scream erupted from "the bottom of my toes": "You are not going to get away with this, I won't allow it. You are not going to get away with this. He was your friend." She tried to visit Glen in prison but was refused access.

Nothing worked, nothing made her feel better. Then she saw a powerful documentary about restorative justice conferencing, in which the mother of Michael Marslew, an eighteen-year-old killed when he was working at a pizza shop, spoke to his murderers, and something in Debbie clicked.

❄

ELEVEN YEARS AFTER HER brother died, Debbie found herself sitting in a bare room in a high-security facility surrounded by bush, with her mother and sister alongside her, waiting for Glen to appear. She had one rule: she did not want to hear him say sorry. As it happened, it was the first thing he said.

She had decided she needed "nothing from him," but wanted to tell him how his actions had demolished her life. Then, she says: "I looked up and I saw him walk past a window on his way into our conference. He was there. My nightmare was walking into the room and was now sitting opposite me. My heart was beating a hundred miles an hour, I felt sick, I had butterflies. The overwhelming emotions were rising up my body. I sat there and just stared at him. He was still the same ugly weasel that I had remembered. He looked nervous and worried, and so he should [have been]; he was sitting opposite me, and he had read my letters."

It was her turn, now, finally, to speak. Debbie told her brother's murderer how after what he'd done she'd been too scared to love her son. She spoke of the panic attacks that struck her at the supermarket, her constant anxiety about the safety of her children. She spoke also of how the grief had impacted her health: she'd started sleepwalking, had put on 30 kilograms, contracted acute dermatitis, been diagnosed with lupus, and was tormented by constant nightmares. She told him how her father had started drinking, which had exacerbated his diabetes and led to the amputation of parts of his body. And that Michael's son—just nineteen months old when his father died—had had a difficult childhood.

Murder was now at the center of their family's story. Debbie showed Glen a photo of Michael's grave, where the family gathered for birthdays and anniversaries and on Christmas morning. She spoke of "watching the light go out of your mom's eyes and never see[ing] it return, and then hearing your mom say that she'd thought of killing herself for a split second after Michael's murder." She explained that "to watch your family crumple into a thousand pieces and never recover, the pain is indescribable."

Then, about halfway through the appointment, Debbie felt an enormous weight lift from her body. She looked around in surprise to see if someone was behind her, as she had felt herself physically lighten. She had given Glen Ainsworth what she called her "suitcase"—her hatred, pain, anger and obsession. "I left it at his feet," she said. "It now belonged to him, to haunt him for the rest of his days."

She still struggles to find words for what happened to her that day, but she says it changed her life. "I don't know if it was forgiveness, but it was definitely peace." She began to heal, stopped hating and stopped thinking about Glen. She still shakes her head at the irony, that the man who caused her the greatest pain also somehow enabled her healing.

✳

I LOVE THE USE of the word "knit" to describe the magical process of broken bones becoming whole again. In the days after a bone fractures, a blood clot forms around the break to protect it, before a kind of healing tissue or soft bone known as the callus—the knitting wool, if you like—wraps around the bone. The callus then becomes bony and cartilaginous, holding the broken parts of the bone together as they slowly harden. On an X-ray, the callus appears as a mist, which gradually becomes thicker, then solid. The callus holds us in place until our strength returns.

This to me seems much like the process of restorative justice for some people—it can, in the right circumstances and with the right preparation and guidance, aid in healing. It seems like madness, sitting down with the source of your greatest pain, instead of simply walking away. In some cases, it probably is. Debbie McGrath says people tell her all the time that she was crazy, and struggle to understand why she did it, or how it changed her.

What's fascinating about restorative justice, experts say, is that the loudest calls for it are coming from survivors, who are pushing for alternatives to a justice system that too often revictimizes and fails the people who have been harmed. Typically, restorative justice works alongside—not in place of—the legal process, and involves bringing victims together with perpetrators in a facilitated environment where they can seek accountability, information and an opportunity to speak some truths. It aims to give victims a voice, usually denied in court, where they may only get to answer questions or, in some rare cases, when there has been a conviction, give a witness statement. Victims usually want to be heard and believed, and to be sure the person won't reoffend.

Restorative justice has been used with great effect for decades in juvenile justice, with victims of motoring accidents, and in dealing with a range of other offences, in myriad ways, in Canada, New Zealand, Norway, Northern Ireland, Belgium and the US state of Arizona, and among Navajo, Maori and Aboriginal and Torres Strait Islander communities. There is growing momentum globally for the expansion of restorative justice programs, but they are still poorly resourced in many places and not yet widely available.

There are strict rules in place to scaffold the encounter. Offenders need to accept responsibility, acknowledge what happened and admit guilt. Both sides must be ready and willing to meet, and must refrain from attacking or retraumatizing people. The role of the facilitator is crucial in ensuring the needs of the victims are met. The focus is not what can be proved and which laws have been broken, says former criminal defense lawyer Nareeda Lewers, now the manager of Open Circle, a restorative justice program that forms part of the RMIT Centre for Innovative Justice, but "who has been harmed and how can we respond to that in a way that recognizes their experience and is beneficial to them."

Participants who have been harmed may want different things, says Associate Professor Jane Bolitho, chair of Restorative Justice at Victoria University of Wellington. Some may ask the offender to do something, such as write a letter expressing remorse or agree to do something that might prevent the reoffending, such as making a commitment to find work, get an education or sign up for counseling; others may seek particular information, like what their victim's last words were; yet others may want the person who caused harm to simply accept responsibility, or to just tell them how their actions impacted their lives. As a concept, Bolitho says, restorative justice "never, ever requires or expects forgiveness to transpire."

The director of the ACT's Restorative Justice Unit, Richard Dening, says there are a lot of myths around about restorative justice, including that it simply means people sitting down, someone apologizing, then another person needing to forgive them (which ignores the many months of careful, expert preparation). Forgiveness, he says, only comes up if it is important to the person who has been harmed—it can never be pressed upon them.

"The perpetrator might ask for forgiveness, but we would need to explore that with everyone before the conference; it could be really damaging if the person felt pressure to forgive." There are many meanings of forgiveness, too, Dening says: "In some environments it is offering atonement and release, a virtue or a gift they genuinely want to offer; for others it's about letting go of the past—'it's not going to control me in that way'—and maybe they even feel the need to communicate about that [and it becomes] an act to tie a loose end."

It's not about excusing moral culpability, he says, but sometimes forgiveness is more of a "de-burdening of yourself in some way . . . we see a lot of that; restorative justice is not just about restoring people to the relationship they had before but about setting relations right," which might mean there is no further contact, or strict boundaries are put in place. After a conference, sometimes there can be "real euphoria," he says, for people who know they have just completed something incredibly challenging.

At the core of it is "the creation of a space that opens up possibility and therefore hope," says Jane Bolitho. "Restorative justice offers an optimistic lens for connection." She visibly brightens when she talks about the times when the process really works, when huge burdens springing from trauma are lifted, as Debbie experienced, or when there is a moment that is hard to replicate or describe, when victim and perpetrator speak, or listen to each other. At its core, she says it is about recognizing humanity, where two people can navigate incredibly complex emotional terrain with the help of skilled convenors.

"Restorative justice is not therapeutic but seems to have a therapeutic impact on people," she says, especially after violent crime. "You don't have to embrace the person [the perpetrator is], but you might see a glimmer of humanity." She pauses, reaching for words: "There is something extra to what is in the room—you get this sense of ritual. It's effervescent, it's like a symphony by an orchestra—it lifts off, when people are given dignity and accountability. There is an unquantifiable element that you can really feel."

This echoes the experience of the parents of Georgia Larsen, who was fifteen when the car her boyfriend, Joshua Lewis, was driving veered off a gravel road and slammed into a tree. She died a few hours later in the hospital. Eighteen-year-old Lewis, who had lied about having his license, was sentenced to four years in a juvenile justice center. The sentence meant "nothing" to Georgia's parents, Tracey and Shannon. They visited him in prison just under two years later, after having been through an extensive preparation with restorative justice experts at RMIT's Open Circle. The moment Shannon saw Josh, he hugged him, "[something] I will never, ever forget," says Tracey. They spoke to him for more than two hours, asking questions, telling him about the impact of the loss of their daughter, listening to his apology, his guilt.

Tracey told ABC News that the fact they knew Lewis made it harder to "keep onto that hatred, but it does eat away at you, that hatred for another person—it's such a bad feeling inside." Meeting him, she said, did not take away from the guilt and pain "but it allowed some growth and I think some forgiveness. I'm not going to say closure because that's a crappy word that people use when they haven't actually been through it—because it's not closure, there's never a time when you say, 'Okay, that's done now, we're all good with it.' But it allows you and the perpetrator, I suppose, a chance to say what you need to say, understand each other's feelings but also come to a position where you're much more comfortable in that forgiveness and that realization. It was really, for my husband and myself, probably one of the most therapeutic things that we'd done."

What is clear is that conventional versions of forgiveness don't apply to these models of repair, but the ideas of an "unburdening," a loosening of ties and an attempt to understand another person's motivations and mistakes do. Meredith Rossner, professor of Criminology at the Australian National University, writes that expressions of forgiveness can occur on a continuum, and may not be verbal. It's not a question of saying, "Oh, you're right, mate, no worries, it's all water under the bridge now." It is rarely dramatic and often delicate and nuanced—and practical, in that people can reach an agreement about how to offer some repair for the harm caused.

Even more subtly, other researchers see forgiveness as a shift in energy, moving from the past to the offense and then the future. One study found that forgiveness was rarely articulated, but was manifested in recognition of the offense, nodding, shaking hands or even the offer of a hug. Rossner, too, writes: "Participants and practitioners told me about the importance of turning points and the subtle cues that represent symbolic reparation and forgiveness, such as smiling, touching, laughing, or making small talk over tea after the formal end to the conference." She calls this a "subtle energy of forgiveness" and adds: "While apologies can restore, forgiveness can transform."

❊

THERE ARE SOME CRITICISMS of restorative justice, however. The jury is out, for example, on whether it has any impact on reoffending (though there is evidence that so-called circle sentencing—whereby a magistrate works with elders as well as victims and the family of the offenders to decide on an appropriate sentence—leads to lower rates of imprisonment and recidivism in Aboriginal communities). Some worry that people will be revictimized, while others say that the best result for a victim is a long prison sentence. Some argue that restorative justice is "soft" on crime. That it tends to preserve and amplify power relations, especially in sexual assault and domestic violence cases. That it absolves traditional legal institutions—the law, the courts, the police, the jails—of responsibility, makes them less accountable.

But after jail, what next? What happens when people return to the community? And what if a victim decides not to press charges? What about all of the victims who feel silenced, sidelined and unheard by judges, jurors and perpetrators? Why not make those who caused harm bear witness to the pain they caused, really understand what trauma does to someone's life, family, body and soul? Once people begin to grapple with the impact of their behavior, lives can be transformed. Convenors, experts and survivors alike all told me stories of serial killers with heads hanging in shame, of rapists finally comprehending the impact of their actions, of pennies dropped.

Nareeda Lewers says she has observed how many people have a need "to recognize the humanity in the person who wronged them." On one level, it's a generous act. On another, it redistributes fear. For a person who was robbed, meeting the thief changed her view of him as a "shapeless, all-powerful demon." Another sexual assault survivor found that her mental image of her perpetrator shrank from a terrifying, powerful "monster" to an ordinary person sitting in a chair.

There's something else, too, Lewers says. There's something about "people wanting to connect with the other in a way that opens possibilities for them, something about generosity of spirit: my healing is bound up with your healing."

❆

I AM ACUTELY AWARE that some people will be reading this with one eyebrow raised, thinking, "Yeah, right, if someone came and hurt someone in my family I'd want serious consequences, not a chat." But forgiveness, or unburdening, or finding peace, is separate from justice. Declan Roche, a former lecturer in Law at the London School of Economics and author of the book *Accountability in Restorative Justice*, told me about a time when he was visiting a restorative justice program in Texas for the families of homicide victims, which arranged meetings between the families and the offenders, who were on death row. One survivor said after meeting the man who had murdered her family member, "I forgave him, and now I want him to die."

Think of how heavily incarcerated our community is now, and how few victims feel satisfied by the court process, let alone protected. Making more evidence-based options available to victims so that they can speak and mend is surely a good thing, especially given that survivors are asking for it. Lewers is well aware of how cynical people can be about the process. But, time after time, when she engages with an offender, she discovers a genuine desire "to make something better for the person harmed." Accountability is a gift, she says, a hard and unpleasant one, but one that some people who have hurt someone else say can ultimately help them. One woman she worked with agreed to the process because, she said, "I feel like because of what I had done my soul is tainted and I want to atone for that."

Roche attributes much of the success of restorative justice to the power of storytelling, and the fact it offers a forum for stories: "Offenders to hear stories from victims, and vice versa, and the stories that victims and offenders tell themselves." What Debbie was doing, he says, was "creating a new narrative, in which she was no longer powerless . . . or defined by what had happened to her."

What about that moment that Bolitho speaks of? Lewers says such connections are hard to define or identify but occur when "there's a recognition between people. . . . We talk about it all the time. We are so lucky to do this work because we get to see that and participate in that moment—it's so affirming. You see people are capable of so much more than we dare to imagine; this work is teaching me that all the time. When you create the space, people can be bigger, and want to engage with the other [party] in a way that wants the best for everyone." As a lawyer, she finds it awkward to speak about restorative justice as it sits outside a neat legal framework, "but so many times I have been lucky to see that [connection] happen. For example, with [a conference involving] a driver responsible for the death of a man's wife, the two men met and when they saw each other they hugged. We cry all the time when we facilitate these things."

Renee Handsaker agrees. The principal restorative justice facilitator at RMIT's Open Circle, who has done a lot of work with institutions that have perpetrated harm, says it is very common for people to say to her, "For the first time in twenty-five years, I have had my dignity and hope restored." Again, it's undefinable: "Often you feel something has happened in that conversation and something is different on the other side." What can free people is the sense of being "deeply acknowledged."

✳

IN HIS EXCELLENT TED TALK, "The Neuroscience of Restorative Justice," Dan Reisel argues that our brains are far more capable of change in adulthood than we realize. Whereas once we thought no new brain cells grew in adults, scientists have shown there is some evidence of the birth of new brain cells in the adult mammalian brain. If we applied this thinking to the criminal justice system, which has been static in its punitive approach for a long time, then we might invest more in alternative pathways like restorative justice, in the hopes of stimulating the amygdala of the incarcerated and allowing for the possibility of change.

TODAY DEBBIE MCGRATH IS a fierce, passionate advocate for restorative justice. She said to me repeatedly, "I do not know where I would be today if the conference had never gone ahead." Now a social worker, she would love to be able to go into prisons and tell people who have committed horrendous crimes that they still might be able to give a gift no one else can, "not closure, I don't believe in that, but peace, even a tiny speck of something." Nearly thirty-three years after his death, Debbie still grieves for her brother every day, but she no longer grieves for herself. She's a grandmother now, and loves her grandchildren, which she had feared she would not be able to do. A return of love to a cracked heart is almost in the realm of the impossible.

Chapter 16

"A Broken Place": People Who Have Forgiven

AT THE AGE OF TEN, Chris Carrier was a happy kid. He liked to ride his bicycle, climb trees, shoot hoops with his friends and spend hours quietly drawing. In photographs, he has a sweet smile, big eyes and a mop of thick brown hair. Innocence in sepia. Then, one afternoon, he left his school in Miami and caught the bus home. On the way home, he met a man who told him he was planning a party for Carrier's father and needed help with decorations. The man lured him into his car, took him to his motor home and stabbed him with an ice pick. He then drove to a remote place in the Everglades and shot Carrier in the back of his head.

Six days later, the day after Christmas in 1974, a farmer found the young boy bruised, bloodied, blinded in the right eye and his skin pocked with cigarette burns, presumably from people trying to figure out if he was still alive. He spent his first week in the hospital not knowing what had happened; all the adults in his life assumed someone else had told him.

Peace was elusive. Even though police guarded his family's house around the clock for a time, Carrier wondered if the man who'd shot him, David McAllister, was going to come back to finish the job. McAllister was never charged; although he was a prime suspect, there was not enough physical evidence to convict him, and Carrier could not identify him in a line-up.

People touted him as a miracle child, Carrier said, but "I didn't want to be singled out because when I looked in the mirror all I saw was broken, disqualified from all the things my friends would have been doing, all the sports. I was very limited." Due to his head injury, he had to avoid contact sports. For about three years, he says, "honestly everything that moved or creaked or made a noise would have me running to the edge of my parents' bed to sleep."

As the years passed, Carrier married, had two daughters and worked as a youth pastor. He attributes his ability to move past the trauma to his supportive, close-tied family and community, and the strong faith he found at thirteen. Then, in 1996 he received a phone call from the detective who had run his case decades earlier. McAllister, now in a nursing home and seventy-seven years old, had confessed to involvement in the crime. Would Carrier like to accept that confession? "Absolutely."

Walking in was "the definition of awkward," he said. He had no idea what he was going to see or feel, and he took a friend along for back-up. "But I walked into that room and what I saw was a seventy-seven-year-old man who weighed roughly 60 pounds [27 kilograms]. He was all alone, he had no family or friends with him, he was in a nursing home, he was blind from glaucoma. . . . It took a New York second for me to realize I would despise being in his situation. He had no energy to get up or out of bed, no ability to see what was going on around him. His two coping mechanisms of smoking and drinking he couldn't access, [and he couldn't] get out. He didn't have family and friends to visit him and on top of all that he was not a prisoner in a jail cell but a prisoner in his own limitations. He was a man who was resigned or reduced to lying in bed and living in his own thoughts, regrets and memories of what he had done.

"And I think he had probably spent many years wondering if my father would be catching up to him or if I grew up with a sense of vengeance. So, the opportunity to walk into that room overwhelmed me with a sense of just sheer compassion, not out of a sense of love or kindness [but] almost of sympathy, of saying, 'Nobody deserves to be reduced to such a humiliating . . . end of life, and the only thing you have are regrets and hurts and there's just no one offering an olive branch or a sense of hope.'"

After initial defensiveness, the old man admitted he had left a young boy to die in the woods, and he began to cry. Carrier's friend Danny leaned over and asked, "Did you ever wish that you could have told that young boy that you were sorry?" The man wept and said yes. Danny said, "Well, the young man on the other side of the bed from me is that very boy."

McAllister turned to him and said sorry.

"From that moment," continues Carrier, "it was absolutely easy for me to say, 'Look, we're in good stead now. I want you to know that I forgive you. I don't want to hold you in that regard anymore, in fear or in anger. I want to establish a new relationship with you.'"

Over the next three weeks, Carrier went to visit McAllister every other day, taking him his favorite treats of smoked amberjack, reading to him, praying with him, caring for him. In the third week, McAllister passed away. Carrier was his only friend.

❉

TODAY, CARRIER HAS A gentle, genial, earnest presence. He speaks slowly, deliberately and politely. The scars on his eye are testament to his childhood trauma, but he has spent his life pondering forgiveness, and touting its power. The font of his forgiveness is his faith. He grew up in a strong, loving clan of people who told him to respond in kind and think of himself not as the victim of a crime but a survivor.

Like Carrier, Father Michael Lapsley, who lost both his hands decades ago to a letter bomb sent by pro-apartheid forces who were targeting him for his activism, believes that "all people are capable of being perpetrators or victims, and sometimes both." By ridding himself of hatred and vengeance, he has gone "from victim to survivor, to victor." When you forgive, you don't release them as much as release yourself from what they did to you.

Still, acts of forgiveness can be genuinely hard to fathom. It seems wild that Carrier would consider forgiving such a grievous act. He wishes McAllister had done jail time, but he says the sorrow of the old man was crucial. Forgiveness is like a gift, he says—two parties must be involved. One person has to take ownership of what happened, no matter the intent or circumstance, then repent and express gratitude for the victim's willingness to forgive. If we think about it just in terms of justice, he says, it makes no sense. "I am not going to say I forgive you if you are going to turn around and shoot me again. . . . I'm a firm believer that the objective of forgiveness is not the removal of consequences. It is for the healing of those who have been hurt, for the discipline of those who have offended. . . . If we are so focused on 'an eye for an eye, and a tooth for a tooth,' we end up always trying to one-up the last one and we never really take into consideration the health of our relationships and finding hope again and being restored. It's a way for us to turn the tables on a culture that just attacks, whether in court or in protests."

I'd hazard a guess few of us would deliberately shoot a child in the head, but fundamentally Carrier thinks we must acknowledge the fact that "this [world] is a broken place, we've all been broken, we've all essentially taken part in it." Today, Carrier, who has worked as an educator for many years, often gives talks in prisons about forgiveness, and finds that many of the incarcerated struggle to forgive themselves. He is adamant that "we have all been hurt and we have all taken part in hurting somebody somehow. [I don't want to] strip my family and friends of the idea that there is hope for redemption, there is a chance to grow through it, learn from it and rejoice in the fact there can be relationships and there can be life again. To me it is truly life-changing."

✳

THERE IS A REASON major religions value forgiveness. I'd argue, too, that a humanist idea of forgiveness as a moral virtue has its roots in a similar idea: a reckoning that we are all flawed and that sometimes circumstances—deep childhood trauma, violence, addiction, mental illness, pain—can shoehorn people into narrow options and lead to dark places and stupid decisions. If Christians believe they forgive because they were first forgiven, that all are sinful, and that sins can be wiped away, this should result in a compassionate view of other people. In Islam, too, and Buddhism, forgiveness is highly esteemed.

For those in abusive relationships, as already discussed, forgiveness can be fraught, and even dangerous. Law graduate and founder of Muslim fashion platform Modest Fashion Australia, Aisha Novakovich, was in a physically and emotionally abusive marriage, which became violent when she was six months pregnant with her first son—her husband left her while she was pregnant with her second. She has wrestled with the idea of forgiveness ever since. While adjusting to life as a single mother and spending years in drawn-out court cases, Novakovich saw psychologists and life coaches, did workshops and women's leadership courses, volunteered in the community, earned a black belt in tae kwon do and practiced salsa dancing for four years, "for healing and to restore trust in men."

Her eventual decision to forgive her ex-husband was a result of her religion and values, she says. Her Islamic faith is rooted in the belief that "the Creator is the most kind and merciful and forgiving. In Arabic terms, it is much more beautiful and rich, with mercy that is infinite, and knows no bounds, that

God created mercy in one hundred parts and saved one part for this world—the rest is for the hereafter. In order to receive that mercy, we ourselves should be merciful to ourselves, animals, creation, everyone in the universe."

When Novakovich was first learning about forgiveness as a teenager, she said she was skeptical: "I thought what does that mean—you just allow people to hurt you and forget about it? We are taught [that if] God forgives us when we do something wrong he wipes that off our records as if it never even existed—[but] as humans sometimes it is dangerous to do that, especially if in an abusive relationship." Novakovich knew this herself. "In fact, my practice of forgiveness is what kept me entangled in domestic violence, because I thought that was the Islamic thing to do. But an Islamic scholar told me, 'No, your Islamic duty was to leave your husband because he was hurting you and your children.' So one principle sometimes overrides another." (She told me later that she now knows that "forgiveness isn't about letting a perpetrator impinge on your your boundaries. Islam promotes forgiveness but is also strict about accountability for harm done to others.") I have spoken to dozens of women in faith communities who have had similar experiences.

Within this idea, of forgiving others because we ourselves are imperfect beings that require forgiveness, is a kernel of grace. Psychologist Julie Juola Exline, from Case Western Reserve University in Cleveland, Ohio, conducted seven studies related to forgiveness between 1998 and 2005 with more than 1,400 college students. She found men more likely to seek vengeance, but that "people of both genders are more forgiving when they see themselves as capable of committing a similar action to the offender's; it tends to make the offense seem smaller. Seeing capability also increases empathic understanding of the offense and causes people to feel more similar to the offenders." All of these factors predict more forgiving attitudes.

There are many exemplary examples of modern forgiveness, some overtly rooted in faith. In 2017, Maha Al-Shennag, a volunteer teacher, charity worker and widowed mother of four, was dropping children off at a Sydney kindergarten when, after a water bottle fell onto the floor of her car, she bent to pick it up, then confused the accelerator with the brake and ploughed into a classroom. Two boys, aged eight and nine, died after becoming stuck under the wheels of the car, and three other kids were injured. The judge described it as "tragic" and a "freakish accident." Al-Shennag was shattered, paralyzed with guilt and self-recrimination, and became a recluse as angry parents and community members bombarded the school with complaints.

But the parents of the eight-year-old, Jihad, tried to cauterize the abuse. After a ceremony at Lakemba Mosque, the father, Raede, a fruit-seller, drove his son's casket to Rookwood Cemetery with a friend, Ahmad Hraichie. On the way, they recorded a live dash-cam video (streamed on Facebook but since taken down), in which Raede spoke Arabic and Hraichie translated, and the child's bright green coffin appeared in the back of the hearse behind them. Hraichie explained: "The father says, all this stuff happening about the threats to this lady and the abuse is not from them. No retaliation is coming from the family of the boy. They have forgiven—if anything they want to sit with this lady and tell her, 'We forgive you.' When all of this is over, she is welcome to come and sit with the family, have a meal and talk about how they can move forward. This was an accident. The lady has four children herself at school, she's got a child at the school, she has a child with a disability, she suffers from mental illness. We have to forgive and not carry on with this behavior."

At a court hearing in 2021, it was revealed Al-Shennag was suffering from guilt, flashbacks and PTSD and wished she had died in the crash. A letter submitted by her adult daughter was read out loud: "I believe the guilt and self-blame my mother feels every day [are] greater than any jail sentence—and she will never forgive herself." In response, Jihad's family said: "We have suffered a tragedy that has completely torn at the heart of our family. But, within this heart, we find the space to forgive Ms. Al-Shennag and we respectfully ask that [the court] take into consideration any possible alternative consequences to a jail sentence."

A tearful Al-Shennag said her life had been a "nightmare" since the crash. She was given a three-year sentence, to be served in the community. Afterward, she apologized "with all of my heart."

❋

THE ABDALLAH FAMILY FORGAVE a less sympathetic wrongdoer. They faced unthinkable agony when three of their children and a cousin were killed on February 1, 2020, by a drunk driver when they went out to get ice cream one night. The man at the wheel was three times over the legal limit for blood alcohol, and reportedly also had cocaine and MDMA in his system. Still, the parents, Danny and Leila Abdallah, both Christian, said they felt "total forgiveness" for him. "Forgiveness is more for the forgiver than the forgiven," Danny says. "When you forgive the other person, you start to heal. [But] forgiveness is not a single action in one moment; it has been more than two years and I must choose to forgive myself and the driver every day—to not retreat into hatred."

After a lone, terrorist gunman entered two mosques in Christchurch in New Zealand on March 15, 2019, and fired at worshippers, murdering fifty-one and injuring forty, Janna Ezat, whose son Hussein was among the dead, told the gunman in court: "I have decided to forgive you because I don't have hate. I don't have revenge. In our Muslim faith we say . . . we are able to forgive, forgive. I forgive you. Damage was done and Hussein will never be here, so I have only one choice: to forgive you." In what was reported as his only show of emotion that day, the gunman nodded, blinked repeatedly and wiped his eyes.

I am not suggesting that true forgiveness comes only from faith. Rather, I am pointing to the fact that much forgiveness comes from a recognition of other people's frailties, and humanity, as well as your own. Take the view of physician Michelle Johnston, who tells me she sees grace as intertwined with forgiveness, for self and for others, and has witnessed this in intensive care units: "Emergency medicine is so fast-paced, so transparent. Decisions are made so rapidly and with limited information, that they are not always right, and with obvious, conspicuous consequences.

Grace is the understanding that this is human, and that those making those decisions did so with honorable intentions." This reminds me of my dear friend Caitlin, who has such an innately kind disposition, and who, when she is hurt, always sighs and says, "I try to think of their intentions." She is forever giving people the benefit of the doubt. For years, I have watched her forgive other people in small and big ways, and seen how, by doing so, she sheds darkness, grudges and hours that might have been wasted ruminating on how she was wronged. I admire her so much, and it's always sunny around her.

RESEARCH SHOWS THE BENEFITS of forgiveness are broad, particularly when it comes to mental health, as it is linked to lower levels of anxiety, depression and hostility and to higher life satisfaction. There is also some evidence linking forgiveness with less substance abuse and reduced nicotine addiction. In one experiment, published in *Psychological Science*, participants were asked to think about times people had hurt, insulted or lied to them, and then asked to consider forgiving those same people. During both scenarios, the scientists studied what happened in the participants' bodies, by measuring their heart rate, blood pressure, sweat-gland activity and facial muscle tension. When the subjects were thinking about how they had been wronged, and nursing a grudge, their heart rates and blood pressure rose; they sweated, and grew anxious and angry. When they tried to ruminate on forgiveness, their physical symptoms of stress dropped; they calmed.

"A lack of forgiveness is like leprosy of the insides," says Anne Lamott, "and left untreated, it can take out tissue, equilibrium, soul, sense of self." There is some truth in this; we all know people whose resentment against someone who wronged them has obsessed or gnawed at them, calcifying over the years so there is no hope of reconciliation—siblings who haven't spoken for decades, parents who disown offspring, friends who perch alone on self-righteous paths. The editors of the book *Forgiveness and Health*, Loren Toussaint, Everett Worthington and David Williams, argue that the most significant reason that forgiveness improves health is because it reduces stress. Toussaint conducted a study that assessed the risk and resilience factors that affected the health, lifetime stress-exposure histories, dispositional forgiveness levels, and mental and physical health of 148 adults. His team found that those with the most severe lifetime stress and lower levels of forgiveness had worse mental and physical health. Toussaint told the American Psychological Association, "We thought forgiveness would knock something off the relationship [between stress and psychological distress], but we didn't expect it to zero it out." Toussaint also conducted a study over a five-week period and confirmed that when participants reported being more forgiving, they also reported being less stressed, and had a greater sense of well-being.

Toussaint recommends practicing empathy, putting yourself in another's shoes, and being patient. Forgiveness can take time, and grit. The mental decision might be over in an instant, but it can take years to live it, zigzagging slowly downward from high plains of anger to lower altitudes of calm. We may forgive, then revert, forgive, then revert, and go through the whole process again. Professor Frederic Luskin, a senior consultant in health promotion at Stanford University, says the two hallmarks of forgiveness are that, when you speak about what happened to you, you no longer get upset, and that you experience a sense of peace.

Evidence shows that global forgiveness therapy groups have had significant results in schools and prisons, and with emotionally abused women, the substance dependent, incest survivors and people with PTSD. Bob Enright's forgiveness therapy process model takes participants through four cognitive exercises: working through bad feelings about what happened, deciding whether to forgive, trying to understand the person who caused hurt or offense, and trying to establish some kind of empathy and compassion for this person. Through this process, says Enright, the participants "begin to see the other person as a wounded human being, as opposed to stereotyping them and defining them by their hurtful actions."

❆

SOME DECISIONS TO FORGIVE certainly seem to defy reason, or can seem too simple or glib, ignoring the pain of others affected by the crime. Along with her twin sister, Miriam, Romanian-born American Eva Mozes Kor was the subject of diabolical medical experiments in Auschwitz for years during World War II. The research was conducted on Jews and Roma by the Nazi doctor Josef Mengele, known as the "Angel of Death."

It included sterilizing subjects, and wounding and infecting them with diseases, and often left them maimed or dead. Twins were of particular interest to Mengele, and every inch of their bodies was monitored and measured. Nazi doctors took pint after pint of blood from their fingers and arteries and sometimes just murdered them in order to dissect their bodies. Mengele would bring the children chocolates before wielding his syringes.

Eva Kor survived. So did Miriam, until the damage done to her body eventually took her life. Kor has never seen her medical files, never learned what she was injected with, what was done to her. For many years, she stayed quiet. In 1993, she gave a public lecture alongside a Nazi doctor named Hans Munch, then went home, and wrote him a letter of forgiveness. It was a gift for her as well as him, she said, as she realized she was no longer a "hopeless, powerless victim." In a bid to heal herself, she then wrote letter after letter to those responsible for her pain—even the by then long-deceased Mengele. She was lambasted for this until she died in 2019, but she claimed this made her happier and more at peace, and felt she was free of even Mengele, and "no longer a victim of Auschwitz or a prisoner of my tragic past."

In Kor's view, forgiveness could be a unilateral act, and in this sense is different from reconciliation. "Forgiveness is an act of self-healing, self-liberation and self-empowerment," she said. "I do not need anybody's approval or acceptance. Reconciliation takes two people; this is why it is so difficult. I also call forgiveness the best revenge against the perpetrator. . . . Some Holocaust survivors do not like this and some call me a traitor. I have been told that in the Jewish tradition, the perpetrator must repent and ask forgiveness. . . . I forgave the Nazis, not because they deserve it, but because I deserve it."

It is true that in Judaism, forgiveness occurs when people genuinely try to make amends in words or actions, with repentance, remorse, and recompense. You have to recognize your sins and resolve to part from them, which makes extending any kind of forgiveness to people like former Nazis incredibly difficult, especially if they are lacking in remorse. In an article on repentance and forgiveness after the Shoah, Professor Michael Dobkowski, chair of Holocaust Studies at Hobart and William Smith Colleges in New York, noted that in Judaism God forgives "only when human beings sincerely seek to make amends in both mind and deed," acknowledging wrongs and vowing to depart from sin. "Moreover, inner contrition must be followed by the outward acts of ceasing to do evil and then, in its place, doing good." The most crucial component of repentance, he says, is remorse.

Still, Dobkowski says forgiveness is fundamental. "In a world without forgiveness, evil begets evil, harm generates harm and there is no way short of sheer exhaustion or forgetfulness of breaking the cycle. Forgiveness breaks the chain. . . . It answers hate with a refusal to hate, animosity with generosity. Few more daring ideas have ever entered the human situation. Forgiveness means that we are not destined endlessly to replay the grievances of the past. It is the ability to live with the past without being held captive by the past." Carrying feelings of resentment and hate is to be weighed down by "a great burden . . . They stop us from thinking of anything else. That is why it is no exaggeration to say that forgiveness is the most compelling testimony to human freedom. It is the refusal to be defined by and enslaved by the past. It represents our ability to change course, reframe the narrative of the past and create a new set of possibilities for the future."

What about the Nazis? Dobkowski concludes, "There may be sins so heinous that even partial forgiveness is precluded. . . . It remains an open question."

Another open question Kor raises is who forgiveness is for. Icelandic journalist Thordis Elva, who wrote a book called *South of Forgiveness* with her former boyfriend, Tom Stranger, who raped her when she was sixteen, has thought hard about this question. She urges people to try to understand those who have caused them harm, and hold them to account. "Once someone has been branded a rapist, it's that much easier to call him a monster—inhuman," she said in a TED talk. "But how will we understand what it is in human societies that produces violence if we refuse to recognize the humanity of those who commit it?" Elva had no legal options—in Iceland what happened was then considered "sexual misconduct," and it took her some time to realize it was rape. Later she arranged to meet Stranger, who then lived in Australia, halfway between their countries, in South Africa, because she wanted to find a way out of shame and anger.

Ultimately, says Elva, her act of forgiveness was something she did for herself: "Many people feel that forgiveness has got to be something that you're giving the perpetrator, that you're laying your blessing over the hurt—it's quite the opposite for me. It's an act of self-interest, and it freed me from some of the self-blame that I'd taken on, and it set me free from a lot of negative emotions that were weighing me down and robbing me of my quality of life."

When her plane landed in Cape Town, she remembers thinking, "Why didn't I just get myself a bottle of vodka like a normal person would do?" But she left with the "victorious feeling that light could triumph over darkness, that something constructive could be built out of the ruins."

Some people, like banksia trees, flower after fire. Some find themselves capable of the most astounding acts when they are broken, suffering or grieving.

❋

MANY OF THE STORIES I have told here are monstrous and dramatic—of murder, abuse, domestic violence, genocide, sexual slavery—and are particular burdens others can't prescribe how to manage or resolve. Most of us contend with forgiveness on a smaller scale: forgiving bullying parents, narcissistic partners, arrogant work colleagues, rude acquaintances, the thousands of deep pains and shallow slights that make up our days. There is no simple equation about forgiving, about how or why, only the strong sense that those who somehow unburden themselves can heal, and live better, and that true remorse, along with just consequences and a recognition of another's humanity, can allow all of these things to happen. Forgiveness can't be forced, it can't be separated from justice, it can take myriad forms, and yet it can be astonishing.

Forgiveness allows for the possibility of redemption. Black civil rights leader John Lewis argued for the forgiveness of even the likes of George Wallace, the staunchly segregationist Alabama politician who had "used the language of race and hate to rise to power," because he had changed, he had "acknowledged his bigotry and assumed responsibility for the harm he had caused."

It's not about understanding in order to forgive, writes Marilynne Robinson in *Home*, but, that forgiveness opens the way to understanding: "If you forgive you may indeed still not understand, but you will be ready to understand, and that is the posture of grace." In her essay "Grace and Beauty," Robinson describes grace as an ethical "understanding of the wholeness of a situation." This means that "everyone is understood in her humanity" and it's also understood that "any moment [is] a thing that can bless time to come or poison it."

PART V
Our Senses

Flukeprint

We're the only things—
leaving religion out of it—
we're the only things in the world
that know spring is coming.

—Jack Gilbert

I LEARNED HOW TO drive a boat while writing this book.
After scans showed the cancer had returned again, I went
back to see the surgeon who had known me since I was first
diagnosed. Following some discussion with her team, she
said she would operate. My brothers and my friend Jock
came with me to see her, and we sat in a solemn little row as
she spoke about cutting out organs, potential dangers and
the chance that she might open me up and have to just sew
me shut again, if it was too advanced. We all stared at little
diagrams she made of my torso and innards, with cut marks
and tubes and varying scenarios. She also told me I would
have to be fed through a tube inserted straight into my veins,

a procedure called TPN—total parenteral nutrition—which takes several hours a day. We got stuck on this point, because I realized this might mean I would not be able to swim. I asked for other options, for a different kind of port, one that could be accessed and de-accessed, even just occasionally, so I could get into the water.

She said: "You are just going to have to find another kind of exercise."

I said: "It's not exercise! It's the *ocean*."

She shrugged.

I made it clear, before going into surgery, that if there was any option at all, I would really like a port that might allow even occasional bodily immersion in water. Anyone who knows me, or who has crossed my path, knows how much I love the ocean, and how much strength I draw from it. In the meantime, I needed another plan, other ways to be on or around water. I fanged around the Gold Coast on jetskis with my kids and loved the speed. Then I hired little motorboats, studied the waterways manuals, and went to get my boat license, with my fourteen-year-old son. To my delight, we both passed, and a new world opened up to us, albeit with a host of new codes, currents and signals. I began dreaming of skipping across waves, curling around little inlets, dropping anchor at tiny beaches. I learned the correct title for the person driving a boat is "Master" or "Skipper," and decided that it suited me.

❄

IN OCTOBER 2022, THE SURGEON went in again. I was scared this time, but so used to the beeps and trolleys of hospital life that I was also calm and quietly looking forward to the anesthetic, to the plastic cone being placed over my face and losing consciousness. Weird, isn't it, to look forward to that, but when you have a crowded head and jostling fears, it's a relief. My greatest concern was that it would all be over quickly, that the sheer volume of disease would overwhelm my body, but my surgeon miraculously managed to clear all of the tumor from my abdomen in a grueling nineteen-hour operation.

I woke sometime later in the ICU, in a darkened room, with a nurse quietly tapping on a computer, lights blinking, and tubes coming out of my neck, mouth, stomach and arms. The drugs had me still floating painlessly somewhere in the ether. I tried to focus my eyes and turned to see my older brother sitting there, his elbows on his knees, hands knotted under his chin, looking at me earnestly. His face lit up when I turned to him: "Jules! You can swim!"

The sweetest thing: I could swim.

I'm not sure what happened in the world around me, when I was curled up tight, trying to heal my insides so I could stand up again. Probably some politicians were corrupt and evasive, and some people were mean and lazy, and culture warriors fired at each other with Nerf guns, and, despite them, many people kept trying to put the world right. Inside my cocoon, the thin layer of silk let in the sun and I was vulnerable like a newborn, trying to adjust my eyes to the light and move through the pain, faintly aware of the figures around me, who were moving in a dance of care, placing blankets over me.

I spent a month in the hospital, with moments of horror interspersed with moments of humor; nurses who were impressively competent and often tender, aside from a couple who were a bit cranky, and visits from family. It became my daily task to first stand, then walk, then circle the ward, and, finally, sit up in a chair for a while. I was weak, dizzy and breathless, until I received some blood transfusions. From my chair, I had a view of a jacaranda tree and I stared at it for hours before I was able to read books again.

The doctors told me to eat jellies and drink sports drinks, which was confusing, but I complied. Shift after shift, the nurses continued to care. I can only remember a couple of their names now, but I tried to thank them at the time, tried to show them how important their work is, how much it mattered to me. I hobbled down to the gift store as soon as I was able to, and brought back chocolates a few times, but they always seemed paltry compared to what these fellow humans were giving me, every day.

Eventually I returned home, where Jock and her wife, Josie, cared for me for weeks—with weekend visits from my partner—before I was ready to look after myself again. Josie, a marvelous cook, read countless nutrition guides to find out what would be best for my stomach, and labored over flavorsome meals packed with protein and goodness, which put steel back in my bones, bit by bit. One day, Jock and I slipped down to the sea, and, on my very first day back in the water, we saw a little cuttlefish. It was astonishing, the joy that creature gave me that day. And the joy the love of those around me gave me.

This is where grace lies: in love and in nature. Which is, I think, why we crave the natural world when we are unwell. Why my friend at the Salvation Army Hall was "really into waterfalls." Sometimes we need to do as the Bayungu people of Western Australia do, and "*jamba nyinayi*"—sit for a little while. It is through solitude, wrote Anne Morrow Lindbergh, that we find our true cores, "the inner spring," the "inner stillness." I often feel the same. So did the poet May Sarton, who wrote the superbly dry and candid *Journal of a Solitude*. Sarton described loneliness as "poverty of self" and solitude as "richness of self." A crucial difference, given how sad loneliness can make us, and how much it can sabotage our health, causing us to sleep poorly and lose immunity, and heighten sensitivity to pain.

I have been so stupidly, hungrily busy for so much of my life, partly because I like working hard, love being stretched and get a buzz from hyperproductivity, partly because I've been trying to make sure, as a single mother, that I can support my children, and partly because I've never been great at allowing myself to just do nothing. My illness has forced me to rest, and the ocean has taught me how, and now I understand that sometimes we need to sit for a little while to comprehend the immensity of the world we live in, and its beauty and fragility—as well as our own. And sometimes we need to acknowledge that being in the natural world is a kind of grace, unearned and complete.

Sarton's advice to imitate trees is wise. "I think of the trees and how simply they let go, let fall the riches of a season, how without grief (it seems) they can let go and go deep into their roots for renewal and sleep," she writes. "Imitate the trees. Learn to lose in order to recover, and remember that nothing stays the same for long, not even pain, psychic pain. Sit it out. Let it all pass."

Such a place of stillness after chaos is much like the "flukeprint" a whale's tail leaves on the water, so beautifully defined in a poem by Australian artist Samuel Leighton-Dore:

A FLUKEPRINT
Is the patch of calm
    left in choppy seas
      after a whale deep dives
That moment of silence
    after a hard cry the
   red on your back after
the kind of hug that
    shakes

That's what nature does. It creates flukeprints in our lives.

Chapter 17

Fever Dreams

grace NOUN *elegance and beauty of movement,*
form, expression, or proportion

— Collins English Dictionary

"I HAVE DECIDED," SAID my son, shortly after falling into a prickly plant, "that I don't like the bush very much." I looked at him with impatience and disbelief. We had flown across the country to the most astonishingly beautiful, remote land in Western Australia, one that had set my insides on fire the moment I saw it. The red ranges sweep down to the turquoise-colored sea, the land is dotted with grasses and 2-meter-high termite mounds, eagles swoop overhead and humpback whales breach the waters on the horizon. The reef is right off the beach: you simply need to wade out and stick your head under the water to hear the corals ticking and see them teeming with life, including bioluminescent fish grazing, rays sweeping past and starfish clambering over purple-tipped branches. Indeed, the reef is so full of life that, as you float along it, the ticking sometimes sounds like tinkling, like wind chimes.

All of which was fine, apparently, but there was no Wi-Fi in our camp, and my two kids had been pestering me about this ever since I'd warned them that this would be the case back in Sydney. Their eyes were locked on the bars on their phones as we drove out of Exmouth blasting vengeful break-up music (my teenage daughter had just split from her boyfriend), while I was loudly marveling at the unspoilt beauty around us.

"Okay that's IT!" my daughter said dramatically as the bars faded. "No more Wi-Fi!" She recorded a final, emotional farewell to her friends on Snapchat, wailing that she would no longer exist in the virtual world for at least four days, before pressing send.

Then she paused. "Wait, Mom, does yours still work?"

As we turned onto the Yardie Creek road, to cross the isthmus and head back down the coast along the other side, they both craned their necks to peer at the cluster of thirteen communications towers that rose high out of the dirt, clearly wondering why these weren't bumping up their reception. I only discovered later that the towers were part of a thousand-acre naval communications center on the North West Cape, established as part of an agreement with the US government in 1963, allowing the United States to plug a gap in its global communications network during the Cold War. The middle tower is 389 meters high and appears to still be used today. For some odd reason, the US Naval Communication Station North West Cape was renamed the Naval Communication Station Harold E. Holt in 1968, after the prime minister who had disappeared while swimming off a Victorian beach the previous year. The logic of this escapes me; I can only hope someone had a sense of humor.

But even these towers could not help the kids, who continued to claim they were losing touch with the world, with all of their sources of information, with their reason for living. My daughter had made all her friends promise they would keep diaries of the doubtless fascinating minutiae of their lives for her to read once she got back to the bars. My son was worried about losing his daily streaks—points you earn for logging in daily—on Snapchat and Pokémon. When he learned that his sister had arranged for her friend Lily to log in on her behalf to maintain her streaks, he sat looking regretful and glum, while trying to stop us from thieving the hot chips I had bought for him at the Exmouth service station.

A hawk swooped alongside the car. We passed a couple of campers, and a handful of caravan sites, but otherwise it was remarkably uncrowded. By the time we reached our campground, I was itching to jump in the water. The name of the coast and reef here, Ningaloo, or Nyinggulu, means "deep water" or "promontory" in the language of the local Yinigurdira people, and sacred sites are scattered throughout the area, including burial grounds, middens and ancient fish traps. Recently, the remains of a thylacine—the now-extinct Tasmanian tiger— were found on the property Hazel Walgar lives on at Cardabia Station. When you turn your eyes to the rugged cliffs or sink into the primordial ocean here, the sense of history is so strong it blows you backward. The reef itself spans 260 kilometers of the coast, from Exmouth (where warnings not to feed dingoes are signposted throughout the town, and emus roam freely) to Quobba Station north of Carnarvon.

It was just after we found our tent—canvas over a sturdy wooden platform, set back along a path near the beach—and before we walked back down to get some food that my son fell into the bushes and declared his opposition to all things wild. I had been saving for this trip for years—it was the one thing I had planned and paid for during COVID, and it was costly—and I was suddenly worried that all of this raw beauty would be wasted on my Wi-Fi-generation offspring. How could you not be thunderstruck by it, on seeing something so rare and fragile and ancient? Yet even before we had left for the trip, my son had asked if he could skip our pre-booked swim with whale sharks, as there was a Pokémon battle on that very day and he was keen to gain some points.

ON OUR SECOND DAY, we found ourselves sitting on the back of a boat, with wetsuits on, listening to a marine biologist named Tash tell us how to move alongside a whale shark: with caution, keeping a respectful distance of about 4 meters, and always swimming behind its pectoral fins. To my deep regret, I was terribly hungover, having taken full advantage of an open bar and a chance to socialize with new friends the night before. My son was green with ocean sickness, and I was hoping the tablets I'd given him would work. My daughter was focused: the Indian Ocean suddenly beckoned.

As Tash spoke to us, spotting planes called the skipper of our boat with the coordinates of sharks. Water whipped our faces as the vessel accelerated and we scrambled into masks and flippers. We pushed off the back and Tash called out to us: "Right here, put your faces in the water now!" Beneath us an enormous whale shark was gliding through the ocean, its bluish-gray skin spotted with starry splotches, its sides trailed by little fish, its bearing ancient and unfussed. We slid into the sea, gazed into the blue, and gasped.

When swimming alongside the whale sharks, as we did seven times that day, I kept up a strong, steady rhythm until the others peeled away and it felt like it was just me, the whale shark and the ocean, in a silent reverence, in total peace. It was like observing a dinosaur in the sea, one completely untroubled by the little fish traveling beside it.

A few times, I dove down to swim behind the tail, which swept from side to side in a graceful arc, a mesmeric metronome of the sea. My kids were near me most of the time, snorkeling with a borrowed GoPro camera. Again and again, they pushed themselves off the boat and into the water, and my heart quietly puffed in my chest. I don't force them to do all that much, but I will force them to experience awe, dammit. The awe that had sustained me through the most physically and mentally grueling times of my life, and was still sustaining me. And what could be more awesome than swimming alongside the world's largest fish, albeit a gentle filter-feeder, which can grow to 18 meters, weigh as much as a school bus and live for more than a century?

As we sat on the boat, panting, recovering, dumbfounded, suddenly a humpback whale swam alongside with its calf, rolling and exposing its white belly. Thousands of humpbacks come here each year on their migrations, and rest with their young offspring before heading to the Antarctic. After that, a bright yellow sea snake wriggled past, and the fin of a leopard shark sliced through the water.

We returned to our base on a high, feasted and drank, and later I lay in bed, feeling like I was swaying as I thought back over the day's events. Swimming with those outsize creatures had felt like a fever dream, largely because of the contrast between the silence, strangeness and majesty of the underwater world, and the noise and bustle of the scene above the water. Once immersed in the ocean, we could have been swimming many thousands of years ago, in an entirely different world, observing megafauna that had swung their tails along these coasts for millennia.

"Yeah, I know I wanted to play Pokémon," my son said later on when I teased him, "but that's because I didn't know what swimming with whale sharks was actually like."

❉

SHORTLY AFTER WE ARRIVED back in Sydney, I spun on my heels and flew to Ningaloo again. I was so drawn to that coastline and knew I had more to do there. I was also facing another round of surgery, and I needed to gather strength. This round would be more brutal than the last, which was genuinely hard to imagine. I wanted to write my book, and I wanted to listen to country as best I could. I wanted to shed myself, and the grief, fear and pain that were giving me fretful, sleepless nights. I wanted to be reminded of a world, an ocean, far bigger than my steroid-inflated face and cancer-riddled gut. I also wanted to get voices of doubt out of the way so I could set down on paper the words I had been straining to say. And I wanted to spend hours just watching the life on the reef, an infinite reel of wonder.

My arrival was not smooth. The airline lost my luggage, it rained for two days and referred pains grew sharper in my shoulder and neck. My face was swollen from a daily dose of corticosteroids, as was my neck, thanks to an accurately named syndrome called buffalo hump, whereby fat pads accumulate at the top of your spine, like a hump, which hurt as my alignment was thrown out. A buffalo was not an animal I had particularly hoped to resemble in my middle years. I walked quickly past mirrors.

Messages were still filling my inbox: I had not been sitting in my usual chair, hosting the TV show *The Drum* for a while, and my face had been puffy the last time—was everything okay? I tiptoed around these inquiries, but one in particular struck me. A woman named Susan had been worried on my behalf and, as a result, had dreamt about me undergoing a curette. She said a mask was being put over my face as someone yelled, *BUT LIFE STILL LOVES YOU!* Yes, and I still love life, and on we roll.

❉

ONCE THE RAIN CLEARED and the sun appeared, I grabbed a double dirty chai from my new favorite takeaway, and drove to

Turquoise Bay in Ningaloo Marine Park. The water was warm, translucent blue, bordered by reef. I walked to the section called The Drift, where you can enter the water at the south end of the beach and allow the current to carry you right up to the north end; in the final stages, you're moving so fast over the coral that it's like flying across an underwater forest. The moment I padded out, I was gripped and I became so excited I caught myself balling my fists with anticipation. Soon I was soaring across corals of many shapes and hues—big, bulging yellow brain-like structures, green forests, pale corrugated saucers. Sea slugs and massive fish swung below me, chased each other, chewed on the coral, fossicked in the sand with their whiskers, and darted about looking pretty, even glowing.

Hours later, just as I was diving down between two large lumps of coral, a reef shark swam past and I turned to follow it. Not long after, a huge hawksbill turtle swayed through the water ahead of me then banged clumsily into the reef before coming to rest on the ocean floor, under a shelf. Its front flippers were marked with white stripes; they looked like angel's wings. I stayed for a while to see if it would emerge, then took off again with the current, only to almost bump into a massive green turtle that was as long and wide as me, with a hard, thick domed shell. It seemed hungry, plunging its face into the coral and tearing off parts of it before moving on again. It rose to the surface, took three breaths, then went back for more food as I followed it at a distance, delighted to be allowed briefly into its world, a world that would indelibly change me. As May Sarton said, "Whatever peace I know rests in the natural world, in feeling myself part of it."

Back on the shore, I dried myself off, drove back across the national park to Exmouth, grabbed a fish burger and a bottle of wine, sat down in my room and began to write, about grace. I wrote and wrote and wrote, all the while aware that although these glimpses of awe among the curious, colorful creatures of the reef were saving me and distracting me from my pain, it was in fact this world, their world, that needed protecting.

❄

IN THE 1980S, THE SLOGAN "Save the Whales" was widely used to mock environmental activists—much like the term "tree-hugger" is used today. Whale conservation was considered the most left-wing of "bleeding-heart" causes, something malodorous hippies went on about.

Given this, it's easy to forget how spectacularly successful the Save the Whales campaign was. The 1980s were a time of reckoning for the commercial whale trade, which had seen thousands of whales slaughtered and global populations dwindle, or drop precipitously, over a century. More than two million whales (of all species) were killed between 1900 and 1978. But the Save the Whales campaign shifted opinion. Many nations that had previously hunted whales began supporting activist groups like Greenpeace, and a worldwide moratorium against commercial hunting was put in place in 1986. However, some countries continued to hunt whales within their own Exclusive Economic Zones, where sovereign states have special rights.

Today, nearly eighty thousand humpbacks glide along Australia's shores, up from maybe fewer than five thousand at the peak of whaling in the early 1960s—a remarkable story of renewal given how close this ancient, singing species came to extinction. The humpback whale has been removed from the endangered species list, a rare conservation success.

And what about whale sharks? Marine scientist Brad Norman found that, globally, their numbers have declined by more than 50 percent in seventy-five years. In 2016, the International Union for Conservation of Nature changed the status of whale sharks from vulnerable to endangered because of the impacts of boat strike, fisheries, by-catch and pollution.

In Australia, whale sharks are protected, but in other countries, especially China, they are fished in large numbers, often for abominably wasteful shark-fin soup—where the fin is used and the rest of the fish is discarded. Successful conservation campaigns have led to the end of mass fishing of these beasts in countries like India, the Philippines, and Taiwan. To save them we need concerted global action, Norman says.

✳

ONE DAY, I BOOKED a seat on an aerial tour in a tiny plane. Below us, the ravines, gullies and gorges rippled like corrugated iron. We crossed the isthmus then swept across the reef in search of whale sharks, whose migration had just passed its peak. It was several days since the spotter planes had sighted any, and they were wheeling and swooping, trying to find even just one to satisfy the boatloads of neoprene-clad tourists waiting on the reef. When a whale shark was finally sighted, the group of local pilots communicating over CB radio congratulated the bloke responsible. He said: "Well, sometimes you just get lucky, eh?"

What was astounding, though, was the number of humpback whales we then saw—several dozen, slowly flicking their tails as they journeyed along the reef, some with calves, some on their own, some traveling in pairs, some breaching and spurting. The pilot told us that forty thousand humpbacks travel along the Ningaloo Coast each season, and it's almost impossible to gaze at an expanse of blue without it being broken by a tail, arched dark back or water spout. The humpbacks usually travel right next to the reef, which drops off quickly into the continental shelf, shifting abruptly from turquoise speckled with coral to a deep blue.

From the beach, the water looks as clear as gin. In many ways, the relatively unsullied character of the reef and its crystal-clear, desert-fringed lagoons is a testament to how muscular, vocal, dedicated communities can fight to protect, and replenish, what they love. In 1987 the Ningaloo Coast was declared a marine park in a bid to protect its astonishing wildlife, and this was extended in 2004 to the entire reef. Well-funded local and Western Australian activists, including the author Tim Winton, managed to stymie plans for proposed developments encroaching on the reef and, as a result, in 2011 the Ningaloo Coast was added to the World Heritage List. Environmental scientist and local Jon Biesse tells me: "There is nowhere else on the planet that has the diversity and abundance of megafauna that Ningaloo has. It's the Serengeti of the ocean, except the Serengeti has thirty-four species of megafauna and Ningaloo has sixty-six!"

But Exmouth Gulf, on the other side of the isthmus, has not been protected, and a range of industrial developments, from a salt project to a port, are being planned, leaving marine scientists and conservationists deeply concerned about the impact industrialization might have on the sensitive ecosystem and the migratory patterns of the region's megafauna. It's a curious oversight, like applying sunscreen to one side of your body, and not the other: the protection is partial. Which is why it is so important that Ningaloo Marine Park is now comanaged by the traditional owners—the Bayungu, Thalanyji and Yinigurdira people; if this cooperation were extended to the gulf as well, Hazel Walgar might fulfill her dream of "healing the oceans" and protecting it from further threats.

How can we luxuriate and delight in the natural world if we don't protect it? Why do we act as greedy landlords and rapacious tenants instead of gentle, respectful and fierce custodians, like the traditional owners? Why don't we listen to country when we sicken and poison it? Why not do everything we can to safeguard this magical land?

Because even being able to swim in these waters, alongside animals we have hunted and killed, animals that could destroy us with a swing of a muscular tail, seems a bestowal of grace, somehow, an unmerited pass to a glowing underworld.

❃

THERE'S GRACE EVERYWHERE IN the natural world. In ecosystems where each part aids the whole. In the root systems of trees that communicate with each other and share nutrients. In the sculptural whorls of shells. In sun rays that burst through clouds, fingers of light reaching to earth. Birds singing at sunset, calling to each other in melodies. The singular crystal shapes of snowflakes. On inland islands in Japan, cleaned of toxic chemicals, now bursting with art and blossoms. In emperor penguins sitting still for months at a time, warming their eggs. In the suck and flow of the tides—water pulled by the moon—that shape the days of many millions of people. In the consistency, dependability and glory of a sunrise. The smooth patch of a flukeprint. The cacophony of sound in a rainforest. In the simple fact that butterflies, Silkie chickens and platypuses exist at all.

There is a "grand laughter" in grace, says Marilynne Robinson, in this mad life in which absurdity and love coexist. Look at the Venezuelan poodle moth, the *Glaucus atlanticus* blue sea slug, the dumbo octopus and the pink fairy armadillo. All crawling, inching, rippling along their paths, all connected, in some way, to each other, to us.

Chapter 18

A Grace Note

Amazing grace! how sweet the sound,
That saved a wretch like me!
I once was lost, but now am found,
Was blind, but now I see.

. . .

When we've been there ten thousand years,
Bright shining as the sun

—from the hymn "Amazing Grace"

WHEN WORDS SEEM PALTRY, people often sing of grace. For example, when former US president Barack Obama was invited to speak at the 2015 funeral of the victims of the mass shooting at the Emanuel African Methodist Episcopal Church in Charleston, South Carolina, he was at first reluctant. As he later told his friend Bruce Springsteen on their *Renegades: Born in the USA* podcast, going to speak to families after mass shootings when Congress had repeatedly refused to act on gun control, especially after the 2012 shooting at Sandy Hook Elementary School in Newtown, Connecticut, was painful. "I had thought that after

Newtown when twenty six-year-olds had been gunned down in this fashion by a deranged young man . . . I thought all right, well, Congress is gonna do something about this. . . . The closest I ever came to just losing hope about this country was probably after efforts for modest gun safety laws were defeated," Obama confessed.

When it happened again in Charleston, Obama initially said he would go south but didn't want to speak, given that nothing he had said previously had brought about any real change. But then he agreed to provide the eulogy for his friend the Reverend Clementa Pinckney, a state senator who had been killed in the shooting.

Aware of the inadequacy of any words he might utter, Obama decided to speak about grace. At the time, he told Springsteen, he and his friend the writer Marilynne Robinson had been corresponding on this subject, and particularly "the notion of grace as a recognition that we are fundamentally flawed and weak and confused. So, we don't deserve grace, but we get it sometimes."

At the funeral, Obama told the congregation how he'd "been reflecting on this idea of grace." To even think about grace at a time when many would contemplate vengeance, he said, would require an open mind but also an open heart. He mentioned his correspondence with Robinson and her notion of grace as "that reservoir of goodness beyond, and of another kind, that we are able to do for each other in the ordinary cause of things." He went on: "If we can find that grace, anything is possible. If we can tap that grace, everything can change. Amazing grace."

Then the first African American president of the United States paused for a long moment, and began to sing, as the clergy around him and the crowd before him rose in unison to join in, to weep and sing and hope. Even now, watching on YouTube, goosebumps prickle my limbs. He ended by saying, "May we find ourselves worthy of that precious and extraordinary gift as long as our lives endure."

✳

THE MAN WHO PENNED the words to "Amazing Grace," in 1772, was former slave trader John Newton, who later repented of his active oppression of other people, and agitated to have the slave trade ended. Today, one of his biographers estimates the song is sung about ten million times a year. Despite its origins, it became a revered song of the African American community, which is why it is so apt that the last stanza was not written by Newton but was first written down and published in 1852 by Harriet Beecher Stowe in *Uncle Tom's Cabin*, an anti-slavery novel. Cheryl Boots, a senior lecturer in Humanities at Boston University, argues that Stowe uses hymns in her novel to elicit sympathy for the abolitionist cause, to "affirm the slaves' humanity (in contrast to their status as chattel property), establish the slaves' equality, and legitimate the slaves' emancipation." The dream of freedom is that of the light of heaven, the way humans infused with grace would shine, "bright shining like the sun."

✳

"AMAZING GRACE" WOULD BECOME an anthem of the civil rights movement, as a song of hope, solidarity, gratitude and yearning. Arlo Guthrie sang it at Woodstock. In the 1960s, says Steve Turner, author of *Amazing Grace: The Story of America's Most Beloved Song*, when people were abandoning the church in droves, it grew in popularity. "It seemed strange to me," he told *Christianity Today*, "that in the midst of the counterculture, you had people standing up singing this song by a Calvinist minister from England." But, he said, "Black church people invest the song with a lot of personal meaning, and they'll talk about how grace has worked in their lives. In addition, the struggles that Black people have come through related very much to the words of the song, that they have felt wretched, [but] they've felt that they've been rescued, both individually and as a people. And quite a lot of them are aware that it had a connection to slavery." It was not just that Newton was involved in the slave trade, Turner says, but also that he had once effectively been a slave, on Plantain Island in Sierra Leone. "He'd been enslaved and he had enslaved people."

❄

WHEN PEOPLE ARE GRASPING for words, like Obama, "Amazing Grace" is, with uncanny regularity, a song they turn to. When a First Nations Australian woman, Ani, was thrown into seclusion by a handful of hospital nurses after telling one of them, "Here's your fucking medication. Now get fucked, I'm not having it," she sang "Amazing Grace," over and over, for more than three hours, until they let her out. In a study of the impact of seclusion on Aboriginal people published in the *International Journal of Mental Health*, Rachel Sambrano and Leonie Cox argue that this singing was a form of resistance that "reclaimed her humanity as against the humanity of secluding her . . . Those within earshot could not merely forget her or experience her as passive as she respectfully disrespected their actions."

Singer Joan Baez led the crowd in a robust rendition at the 1985 Live Aid concert in Philadelphia, held to raise funds for relief of the Ethiopian famine. Broadway actress and singer LaChanze, who was eight months pregnant when her security-trader husband was killed on 9/11 at the World Trade Center, sang it at the dedication of the National September 11 Memorial and Museum. A choir of children and local residents sang it at the Hope for Grenfell Gala in 2018, after fires in the high-rise twenty-four-story Grenfell Tower in North Kensington, London, resulted in the deaths of seventy-two people.

The starting point of the hymn is that we are all wretched.

The end is that we are standing in light.

❄

THE PURSUIT OF AWE, wonder and light is one of the driving principles of my life. After having written about awe for my last book, I allowed myself to devote significant time to hunting it down, to venturing outside and clearing thickets of distractions so I might be more open to it. And so I found myself with a television crew in Tasmania, shooting a program entitled *Awestruck* and looking up into the sky at midnight and marveling. We were on a beach about half an hour out of Hobart called Goat's Beach, having just devoured fried scallops at the local RSL. At our feet, the curling ocean was blue with bioluminescence, and above us the star-strewn sky was smudged pink by an aurora. We tried—and succeeded—to capture it with time-lapse photography, as our eyes do not see color well at night. Standing there for an hour on the windswept sand, my feet grew numb, my toes stiff. It was freezing, but exhilarating. My first aurora!

How can any of us deserve to see such a sight, almost unbearable in its beauty? What did we do to earn it? Nothing, but it is there. Being allowed to dwell in the natural world, and witness its infinite daily miracles, is one of the greatest examples of grace. Not to honor it is unthinkable. Imitate the trees, as May Sarton said.

In *Orwell's Roses*, Rebecca Solnit asks: "What is the goal of social change or political engagement? Can studying what good already exists or has existed be part of the work?" My answer to this, as it must be clear by now, is *yes*. We must study the good that exists, and foment it, hopefully without being cast as ignorant or impossibly idealistic. Solnit goes on to distinguish between "the dour (and widespread) position that we are forever starting from scratch because everything is contaminated or corrupt and the position that the good exists as a kind of seed that needs to be tended more energetically or propagated more widely." Grace is this seed. You may call it something else, which is fine. You may disagree with my definition. But it is very hard to deny what it looks like when you see it, or the power it can wring out of any moment. Debbie McGrath saw it as "a tiny speck of something" after meeting her brother's murderer; Jane Bolitho called it a "glimmer of humanity" seen in restorative justice conferences; Sister Helen Prejean even saw it in a rapist, in "a little part of this soul that could be built."

I am generally allergic to pat recipes for happiness, but I think experiencing and showing grace can open us up to a kind of beauty that we underestimate for its potency and freeing potential. Consider these examples. A 2020 study found that people with a "hostile" attributional style—in other words, people who "assign malicious intent to others' actions"—tend to be less satisfied with their relationships. Research published in the *Journal of Happiness Studies* found they are also less likely to be content more generally. The researchers gathered 707 people from Japan, the United States and Poland, aged between seventeen and sixty, and asked them to read through the following scenarios:

1. You've been at a new job for three weeks. One day, you see one of your new coworkers on the street. You start to walk up to this person and start to say hello, but she/he passes by you without saying hello.

2. You have an appointment with an important person. When you arrive at your appointment, the secretary informs you that the person is not in; they took the day off.

3. You walk past a bunch of teenagers at a mall and you hear them start to laugh.

4. You are supposed to meet a new friend for lunch at a restaurant but she/he never shows up.

5. You call a friend and leave a message on their answering machine, asking them to call you back. One week passes and they have not called you back.

The study participants then reported how much they assigned blame to the person in the story and how angry they were. They also had to fill out a survey on their own levels of happiness. Those who gave people the benefit of the doubt were generally the happiest. So there is an upside to shifting our outlook to a more generous one. That makes sense intuitively, even if there is somewhat of a chicken-and-egg scenario about this—are happier people just more likely to cut others slack? I know that's true of me: when I'm sick, I am a less tolerant human. But surely we can practice this kind of thinking, be conscious of our narrowness.

❄

THERE IS A SMALL mountain of studies showing that when we witness acts of profound virtue or moral beauty, we are uplifted, warmed (sometimes physically), and more likely to behave in the same way (as explained earlier, it's called moral elevation). Other studies show the physical and mental benefits of compassion, kindness, giving people the benefit of the doubt, being selfless. Science can't easily measure grace, largely because ineffability and mystery are core to grace, but many are beginning to try.

As the Franciscan priest and writer Richard Rohr points out in one of his meditations, scientists tell us that when they peer into microscopes and into telescopes, they find "that energy is actually in the space between atomic particles and between the planets and the stars—in the relationships more than [in] the particles." This is what they see, too, when they look at the sun and how its nuclei merge and burn. Likewise, grace occurs in the space between people, and grace brings light.

We chronically underestimate the impact of our kindness, or grace, on others—an attitude that begins when we are children. One recent study, published in 2023, conducted an experiment on two hundred kids and adults, asking them to perform an act of kindness—in this case, giving a pen to a stranger in a museum—then rate afterward how they thought the gift was received. The participants substantially underestimated the impact of their gesture, across all ages, and the researchers found this tendency occurred in children as young as four. But after their random kind act, the participants felt far happier, in a "significantly more positive mood."

As George Eliot wrote in *Middlemarch*, "the growing good of the world is partly dependent on unhistoric acts." The unhistoric act of catching a bus to a blood donation center every second Tuesday afternoon. Of calming a patient with post-surgical psychosis, nightmares and pain. Of placing the hands of a person suffering alone from COVID onto a rubber glove filled with warm water. Of sitting beside the bed of a dying parent, eyes reddening and ears straining to hear their breath, hoping they know you are there and know they are loved. Of driving through empty streets late at night, exhausted, to pick up a teenager to keep them safe. Of promising to operate on a desperate mother one more time, to give her more life. Of teaching someone to sink into nature, by, say, hiking, diving or swimming, to close their eyes and open their senses and breathe the planet in.

The world depends on us treating strangers not just like random lumps of flesh, but creatures of depth, with hearts and frailties. On us giving a stranger the benefit of the doubt, of refraining from flipping the bird, or a stinging rebuke or a glare, because you never know the weight of the pack on that stranger's shoulders, or how much time they have left on earth. On us standing with the oppressed and abused, the vulnerable and ignored, and listening in silence and sympathy. On us allowing for the chest-expanding possibilities of forgiveness. And on us recognizing that none of us deserves to live in a world of such unbearable, fragile beauty, and that miracles can be wrought when we allow people, and ourselves, to be human. To walk alongside each other, despite everything. To sing, even.

To feel the sun on our faces, and know we are alive.

Acknowledgments

This book sent me down hundreds of rabbit holes, and I would like to thank those I either dragged down with me, or stumbled across once inside them. First, the many experts and researchers whose brains I tapped like maples for sap: Professor Jeremy Bailenson, Professor Rob Harcourt, Dr. Brad Norman, Professor Marilyn Francus, Professor Meredith Rossner, Richard Dening, Associate Professor Jane Bolitho, Associate Professor Catherine Suter, Professor Isabelle Mansuy, Thea Deakin-Greenwood, Renee Handsaker, Nareeda Lewers and Tracy Westerman, among others.

There are dozens who gave their time to me so generously in interviews that often spanned months, especially Aunty Hazel Walgar, Aunty Lorraine Peeters, Amani Haydar, Debbie McGrath, Chris Carrier, Aisha Novakovich, Semei Araújo Cunha, Vanessa Formenton and Nila Tanzil. Others, like Jemma Falkenmire from Australian Red Cross Lifeblood and all her super donors, as well as Bree Fuller from NSW Corrective Services, provided critical assistance.

As did those who skillfully helped me navigate Japan and investigate the plight of comfort women: Kumi Taguchi, Shoma Kubo, Ayano Kasajima and Fumiko Yamashita. And all others who provided support in myriad ways: Meagan Gerrard, Shaan Peeters, Alex Wood, Megan Barrow, Jeremy Fernandez, Tim Ayliffe,

Justin Stevens, Hayley Gleeson, Suzana Freitas dos Santos, Samuel Leighton-Dore, Caitlin Brassington, Michelle Johnston, Dr. Cherry Koh, Sally Beath, the wonderful Stephanie Boltje and Ghada Ali, Annie White and my much loved *Drum* team.

I am indebted to those friends who cast their eyes over draft chapters, particularly Tim McGregor, as well as Teela Reid, Declan Roche, Darren Saunders, Leigh Sales, Geoff Broughton, Naomi Priest and Paul Gamblin. My work is richer for their reflections. (Any blunders of course remain my own.)

I consider myself incredibly lucky to have such a supportive team at HarperCollins, including Alice Wood, Lily Capewell, Karen-Maree Griffiths, and Jim Demetriou. The clever Hazel Lam's cover designs continue to shine. My inimitable, long-suffering editor, Scott Forbes, has saved me from many a blooper with his eagle eyes and sharp instincts. The magical Catherine Milne is adored by her authors, and with good reason: her belief is like concrete, her patience infinite, her championing unparalleled. She sees the potential for gold in hay, every time.

And I am always grateful for my agent, Binky Urban, whose ebullience, affection, acumen and candor are rightly the stuff of legend.

I need to thank some friends too. Every one of my books, especially when interrupted by a tough surgery and a lengthy recovery, is made possible because my extraordinary friends remain by my side. I want to especially thank this magnificent crew:

Fellow water-explorers Dave, Cathie, Sophie, Pete, Emma, David and Bec, for salty joy.

Fellow travelers Jen, Naomi and Kylie, for staunch solidarity.

My girls Mia, Leigh and Caroline, for sage advice—and making me cry with laughter.

Annabel, a kindred spirit with an eye for the absurd and the tender in equal measure.

Woody, whose original thoughts and stoic encouragement never fail.

Maureen, a rare bird and a steadfast friend.

Martha, whose crackling mind and massive heart are unswerving.

Briony, who is both wise and true, delightfully full of both sense and nonsense.

Cath, for always accompanying me on mad adventures, whether in Japan, Broadbeach or the NSW South Coast, and for superb custard and true friendship.

Lucie, whose loyalty is unwavering, whose love is fierce, and whose readiness to fight/dance is impressive.

Caitlin, whose heart is so pure you could see through it if you held it up to the light.

Jacquie, my constant sea companion and fellow awe-loving mermaid.

Josie, whose superlative cooking—especially her lasagne— brought me back from the brink.

Jock, who is always there, and always laughing, through everything.

My kind, funny family: Bruce, Mike, Kerryn, Laura, Cate, Harry, Luke, Steve, Anne Maree, Elijah, Oscar, Sebastian, and my mother, Judy, whom I miss every day. And, of course, to Poppy and Sam, my North Stars. It's probably a bit odd, being the kids of a writer. But everything I do is for you.

Notes

Any quotes *not* referenced here are from public statements or from interviews or correspondence with the author.

Epigraphs

vii   *When we've been there ten thousand years*: These anonymous lines were added to the hymn "Amazing Grace" and first recorded in Harriet Beecher Stowe's novel *Uncle Tom's Cabin*. See p. 272.

Author's note

ix   *This book was written*: See Grace Karskens, "Manly Cove, Kal'ymay," *The Dictionary of Sydney*, State Library of New South Wales website, https://dictionaryofsydney.org/entry/manly_cove_kaiymay.

Introduction: When the Shadows Fall Behind You

2   *I had been stunned*: Dacher Keltner, "What's the most common source of awe?" *Greater Good Magazine*, 24 January 2023.

2   *Would it be nature*: Dacher Keltner, *Awe: The New Science of Everyday Wonder and How It Can Transform Your Life*, Penguin, New York, 2023, pp. 75–74.

3   *We report having*: For example, a study in *American Sociological Review* looked at the number of close friends that individuals have. In 1985, the average number was 2.9; by 2004 it was 2.1. The percentage of people who responded that they had no close friends at all tripled over the same period. See Miller McPherson, Lynn Smith-Lovin, and Matthew E. Brashears, "Social isolation in America: Changes in core discussion networks over two decades," *American Sociological Review*, vol. 71, no. 3 (2006), doi:10.1177/000312240607100301.

3   *One study*: Jean M. Twenge et al., "It's beyond my control: A cross-temporal meta-analysis of increasing externality in locus of control, 1960–2002," *Personality and Social Psychology Review*, vol. 8, no. 3 (2004), doi:10.1207/s15327957pspr0803_5.

3   *Over the same period*: Jean M. Twenge et al., "Ego inflating over time: A cross-temporal meta-analysis of the Narcissistic Personality Inventory," *Journal of Personality*, vol. 76, no. 4 (2008), doi:10.1111/j.1467-6494.2008.00507.x.

3   *Asked to find reasons*: See Jamil Zaki, "What, me care? Young are less empathetic," *Scientific American*, 1 January 2011.

4   *We are also, incidentally*: The number of adults who read literature for pleasure sank below 50 percent for the first time ever in the past ten years, with the decrease occurring most sharply among college-age adults. In a study published in early 2023, a team led by psychologist Raymond A. Mar of York University in Toronto demonstrated that the number of stories preschoolers read predicts their ability to understand the emotions of others. See Raymond A. Mar et al., "Exploring the link between reading fiction and empathy: Ruling out individual differences and examining outcomes," available at www .yorku.ca/mar/Mar%20et%20al%202009_reading%20fiction%20and%20 empathy.pdf. Mar has also shown that adults who read less fiction report themselves to be less empathetic.

4   *Lonely people are more likely*: On cheating, see Zaki, "What, me care?"; regarding being less generous, see Steven W. Duck, Kris Pond, and Geoff Leatham, "Loneliness and the evaluation of relational events," *Journal of Social and Personal Relationships*, vol. 11, no. 2 (1994), doi:10.1177/0265407594112006.

4   *loneliness can make us sick*: E. Lee et al., "High prevalence and adverse health effects of loneliness in community-dwelling adults across the lifespan: Role of wisdom as a protective factor," *International Psychogeriatrics*, vol. 31, no. 10, pp. 1447–1462 (2018), doi:10.1017/S1041610218002120.

4   *Researchers compared loneliness*: Dilip V. Jeste et al., "Study of loneliness and wisdom in 482 middle-aged and oldest-old adults: A comparison between people in Cilento, Italy, and San Diego, USA," *Aging & Mental Health*, vol. 25, no. 11, pp. 2149–2159 (2020), doi:10.1080/13607863.2020.1821170.

4   *The designer of the study, Dr. Dilip Jeste*: Holly Lawrence, "Can wisdom protect against loneliness as we age?," *Retirement*, Forbes website, 11 February 2019.

5   *A 2021 study*: Tanya T. Nguyen et al., "Association of loneliness and wisdom with gut microbial diversity and composition: An exploratory study," *Frontiers in Psychiatry*, vol. 12 (2021), doi:10.3389/fpsyt.2021.648475.

5   *Some find empathy*: C.D. Cameron et al., "Empathy is hard work: People choose to avoid empathy because of its cognitive costs," *Journal of Experimental Psychology: General*, vol. 148, no. 6, pp. 962–976 (2019), doi:10.1037/xge0000595.

5   *"an unexplainable goodness"*: Richard Rohr, in *Immortal Diamond: The Search for Our True Self*, Jossey-Bass, 2012, p. 20.

6   *Poet Mary Oliver wrote*: See Mary Oliver, "Sand Dabs, Five," from *Winter Hours: Prose, Prose Poems, and Poems*, Houghton Mifflin Harcourt, 1999, p. 80.

6   *"I do not understand the mystery of grace"*: Anne Lamott, in *Grace (Eventually): Thoughts on Faith*, Riverhead Books, New York, 2008.

6   *"Regardless of the context"*: Peter Wehner, "The uncommon power of grace," *New York Times*, 23 December 2018.

6–7 *When Lutheran pastor Nadia Bolz-Weber*: Bolz-Weber (@Sarcasticluther) on Twitter, https://twitter.com/Sarcasticluther.

7   *According to Helen Garner*: Helen Garner, "Helen Garner on happiness: 'It's taken me 80 years to figure out it's not a tranquil, sunlit realm,'" *The Guardian*, 5 February 2023.

7 *"All things of grace and beauty"*: Cormac McCarthy, *The Road*, Picador, London, 2006, p. 46.

7–8 *Bolz-Weber sees grace evident*: Nadia Bolz-Weber, *Pastrix: The Cranky, Beautiful Faith of a Sinner and Saint*, Jericho Books, New York, 2013, p. 51.

8 *Anne Morrow Lindbergh called it*: Anne Morrow Lindbergh, in *Gift from the Sea*, Pantheon Books, New York, 1955, p. 17.

8 *"When we're called to leave"*: Helen Prejean, "Dead man walking: Sister Helen Prejean on grace, justice, and death row," *The Table* podcast, Biola Center for Christian Thought website, 1 October 2018.

8 *Friedrich Schiller described*: "Friedrich Schiller," Stanford Encyclopedia of Philosophy website, https://plato.stanford.edu/entries/schiller/#toc.

8 *"Love is holy"*: Marilynne Robinson, *Gilead*, Virago Press, London, 2005, p. 238.

8 *She defines grace*: Marilynne Robinson, "Grace and beauty," *Ploughshares*, vol. 44, no. 1 (2018), pp. 157–167, doi:10.1353/plo.2018.003.

12 *"It's really the thing we're fighting for"*: Krista Tippett, "Imani Perry: More beautiful," *On Being with Krista Tippett*, On Being website, 26 September 2019.

13 *"In the bosom of every human"*: Krista Tippett, "John Lewis: Love in action," *On Being with Krista Tippett*, On Being website, 23 July 2020.

14 *"All the natural movements of the soul"*: Simone Weil, from *Gravity and Grace*, Routledge & Kegan Paul, London, 1952.

14 *Robert Macfarlane tells us*: Robert Macfarlane on Twitter, https://twitter.com/RobGMacfarlane/status/1247041449578946561?lang=en, and https://twitter.com/RobGMacfarlane/status/970192187395858432.

PART I: Our Souls, Our Selves
"Really into waterfalls": On a state of daily grace

17 *"All her life she would believe"*: Ann-Marie Priest, *My Tongue Is My Own: A Life of Gwen Harwood*, La Trobe University Press, 2022. Used by permission of Black Inc., Melbourne.

18–19 *"our great prophet of totalitarianism"*: Rebecca Solnit, *Orwell's Roses*, Granta Books, London, 2021, p. 87.

19 *Solnit told The Nation*: John Nichols, "Rebecca Solnit is not giving up hope," *The Nation*, 14 January 2022.

19–20 *Actor and writer Brett Goldstein*: "Ted Lasso actor Brett Goldstein," *Fresh Air*, NPR website, 27 March 2023.

Chapter 1: 21.3 Grams

22 *Nine percent had had "near-death experiences"*: One patient "had a verifiable period of conscious awareness during which time cerebral function was not expected." See Sam Parnia et al, "AWARE–AWAreness during REsuscitation–A prospective study," *Resuscitation*, vol. 85, no. 12 (2014), pp. 1799–1805, doi:10.1016/j.resuscitation.2014.09.004.

22–23 *"Hypothesis concerning soul substance"*: "Soul has weight, physician thinks," *New York Times*, 11 March 1907.

23   *When the study was reported*: Ibid.

23–24   *While attempting to photograph*: Stephanie Pappas, "How much does the soul weigh?," *News*, LiveScience website, 25 July 2022.

24–25   *"Tomorrow when the farm boys find this"*: Laura Gilpin, "Two-headed Calf," from *The Hocus-Pocus of the Universe*, copyright © 1977 by Laura Crafton Gilpin. Used by permission of Doubleday, an imprint of the Knopf Doubleday Publishing Group, a division of Penguin Random House LLC. All rights reserved.

25   *"In the centuries before Hippocrates"*: R.S. Ulrich and L. Gilpin, "Healing arts," in *Putting Patients First: Designing and Practicing Patient-Centered Care*, Jossey Bass, 2003, pp. 117–146.

25–26   *"Evolutionary theory proposes that"*: Ibid., p. 122.

28   *"He touches her so lightly"*: Laura Gilpin, "The Weight of a Soul" from *The Weight of a Soul*, a limited-edition collection of poetry published with funding from the Laura Gilpin Kindness Fund as the Planetree Memorial Edition, 2008, pp. 19–21. Extract published with the permission of the Estate of Laura Gilpin.

28–29   *In the same volume Gilpin writes*: Gilpin, "The Bath," from *The Weight of a Soul*. Extract published with the permission of the Estate of Laura Gilpin.

29   *her death notice in the* New York Times: Paid Notice: Deaths; Gilpin, Laura Crafton, *New York Times*, 6 May 2007.

30–32   *"I have helped babies into the world"*: Caitlin Brassington, "'Just a nurse': Queensland woman writes open letter to woman at corner store," ABC News website, 11 October 2016. Used by permission of the author.

32–33   *The most wrenching part*: Though it did lead to some lovely innovations—like the Canadian woman who created a "hug glove," hanging a plastic tarp with four sleeves on it off a clothesline, so she could hug her mother. See AFP, "Woman's ingenious social distancing hack to hug mother," Yahoo News website, 18 May 2020.

33   *"My biggest trauma"*: Courtney Brogle, "Heartbreaking photo shows 'hand' COVID nurse created for lonely patients," *Newsweek* website, 9 April 2021.

33   *the virus was a "little flu"*: Jake Horton, "Covid Brazil: Why could Bolsonaro face charges?," BBC News website, 27 October 2021.

33   *pushing hospitals to the brink*: Luke Taylor, "Covid-19: Brazil's hospitals close to collapse as cases reach record high," *BMJ*, vol. 372, no. 800 (2021).

33   *22.3 million positive cases*: United Nations CEPAL, *Preliminary Overview of the Economies of Latin America and the Caribbean 2020*, United Nations, 2021.

33–34   *By March 2021*: Célia Landmann Szwarcwald et al., "COVID-19 mortality in Brazil, 2020–21: Consequences of the pandemic inadequate management," *Archives of Public Health*, vol. 80, article 255 (2022).

34   *"crimes against humanity"*: Matt Williams, "Bolsonaro faces 'crimes against humanity' charge over COVID-19 mishandling," The Conversation website, 21 October 2021.

35   *Author Helen Garner wrote*: Helen Garner, "Helen Garner on happiness: 'It's

taken me 80 years to figure out it's not a tranquil, sunlit realm,'" *The Guardian*, 5 February 2023.

Chapter 2: Anonymous Samaritans

38   *our job "is to love others"*: Thomas Merton, "The power and meaning of love," *Disputed Questions*, Farrar Straus & Giroux, New York, 1960.

40   *A recent prevalence survey estimated*: Yasmin Mowat et al., "Prevalence of blood donation eligibility in Australia: A population survey," *Transfusion*, 18 July 2023, pp. 1–9, doi:10.1111/trf.17474.

41–42   *Australia's most legendary donor*: "Meet the lifetime donor with the 'golden arm' who saved millions of lives," CBC Radio website, 17 May 2018.

43   *After all, studies have found*: Liudmila Titova and Kennon M. Sheldon, "Happiness comes from trying to make others feel good, rather than oneself," *Journal of Positive Psychology*, vol. 17, no. 3 (2022), pp. 341–355, doi:10.1080 /17439760.2021.1897867.

44   *"To them it didn't matter if I was rich or poor"*: Gill Hicks, "Gill Hicks," The Forgiveness Project website, www.theforgivenessproject.com/stories-library /gill-hicks/.

45   *In* Middlemarch, *George Eliot described*: George Eliot, *Middlemarch*, CRW Publishing, London (first published 1871), 2007, p. 831.

PART II: Our Circles

Our beating hearts

51   *"You always try to capture people you love"*: "Artist Christian Boltanski tours "Les Archives du Coeur"', *Arts and Culture Incoming*, Dazed Digital website, 16 August 2010.

Chapter 3: Grace Inherited

56   *Harvard professor Imani Perry says*: Imani Perry, *Breathe: A Letter to My Son*, Beacon Press, Boston, 2019, p. 5.

56–57   *"adequate maternal nutrition could counter"*: Dora L. Costa et al., "Intergenerational transmission of paternal trauma among US Civil War ex-POWs," *PNAS*, vol. 115, no. 44 (2018), pp. 11215–11220, doi:10.1073/pnas .1803630115.

57   *In 2016, she published a groundbreaking study*: Katharina Gapp et al., "Potential of environmental enrichment to prevent transgenerational effects of paternal trauma," *Neuropsychopharmacology*, vol. 46 (2016), pp. 2749–2758, doi: 10.1038 /npp.2016.87.

57–58   *"Long after the traumatic experiences themselves"*: University of Zurich, "Not only trauma but also the reversal of trauma is inherited," *Science News*, ScienceDaily website, 23 June 2016.

58   *"Environmental enrichment at the right time"*: Andrew Curry, "Parents' emotional trauma may change their children's biology. Studies in mice show how," *Science*, 18 July 2019. For related analysis on how positive and negative experiences can

impact inflammation, see also Naomi Priest et al., "The effect of adverse and positive experiences on inflammatory markers in Australian and UK children," *Brain, Behavior, & Immunity–Health*, vol. 26, no. 100550 (2022), doi:10.1016/j.bbih.2022.100550.

58   *a study with mice showing*: Jennifer E. Cropley et al., "The penetrance of an epigenetic trait in mice is progressively yet reversibly increased by selection and environment," *Proceedings of the Royal Society B: Biological Sciences*, vol. 279, no. 1737 (2012), pp. 2347–2353, doi:10.1098/rspb.2011.2646.

59   *Meaney's work was controversial*: Ian C.G. Weaver et al., "Epigenetic programming of maternal behavior," *Nature Neuroscience*, vol. 7 (2004), pp. 847–854.

60   *A host of behavioral scientists*: See, for example, Lizzie Buchen, "Neuroscience: In their nurture," *Nature*, vol. 467 (2010), pp. 146–148, doi:10.1038/467146a, and Martha Henriques, "Can the legacy of trauma be passed down the generations?," *BBC Future*, BBC website, 26 March 2019.

60   *"Many Women there are"*: Alicia Andrzejewski, "Monstrous and mindful births: Policing the pregnant imagination," Synapsis website, 4 February 2018.

63   *This was first discovered*: Viviane Caller, "Baby's cells can manipulate mom's body for decades," *Smithsonian Magazine*, 2 September 2015; Katherine Rowland, "We are multitudes," Aeon website, 11 January 2018.

63   *Fetal cells have been found*: William F.N. Chan et al., "Male microchimerism in the human female brain," *PLoS One*, vol. 7, no. 9 (2012), doi:10.1371/journal.pone.0045592.

63   *greater risk of autoimmune disorders*: Hilary S. Gammill et al., "Cellular fetal microchimerism in preeclampsia," *Hypertension*, vol. 62, no. 6 (2013), pp. 1062–1067, doi:10.1161/HYPERTENSIONAHA.113.01486.

63   *protection from rheumatoid arthritis*: Amy M. Boddy et al., "Fetal microchimerism and maternal health: A review and evolutionary analysis of cooperation and conflict beyond the womb," *Bioessays*, vol. 37, no. 10 (2015), pp. 1106–1118. doi:10.1002/bies.201500059.

63–64   *"the bidirectional transfer of genetically foreign cells"*: J. Kinder et al., "Immunological implications of pregnancy-induced microchimerism," *Nature Reviews Immunology*, vol. 17 (2017), pp. 483–494, doi:10.1038/nri.2017.38.

64   *Astonishing*: For a good summary of the research, see Rowland, "We are multitudes."

64   *"Women may have microchimeric cells"*: Robert Martone, "Scientists discover children's cells living in mothers' brains; the connection between mother and child is deeper than thought," *Scientific American*, 4 December 2012.

66–67   *"never to be released"*: *Regina v Knight* [2001], NSWSC 1011 (8 November 2001), Supreme Court of NSW website, www8.austlii.edu.au/cgi-bin/viewdoc/au/cases/nsw/NSWSC/2001/1011.html.

67   *After Victoria Schembri served time*: Candace Sutton, "Queen bee: Cannibal killer Katherine Knight's life in prison where she's known as 'The Nanna,'" news.com.au, 22 July 2017.

67–68   *"She is a gentle soul"*: Ibid. See also James Phelps, *Green Is the New Black*:

Inside Australia's Hardest Women's Jails, Random House Australia, Sydney, 2018, in which Schembri explains how Knight also took on the role of social coordinator: "'She organizes a big catch-up every Friday. She organizes all the food and makes sure that everyone in the wing is a part of it. She includes every single person, even those she doesn't really like. She does it to bring everyone together. It stops a lot of problems from happening.'"

68   *"She is really nurturing"*: "Victoria Schembri on life in prison with infamous killer Katherine Knight," *Daily Telegraph*, 28 February 2020.

69   *"Where the moral failure is"*: Helen Prejean, "Dead man walking: Sister Helen Prejean on grace, justice and death row," *The Table* podcast, Biola Center for Christian Thought website, 1 October 2018.

69–70   *"I said to Robert Lee Willie"*: "Angel on death row," *Frontline*, PBS website, n.d.

70   *A University of Michigan review*: Samuel R. Gross et al., "Rate of false conviction of criminal defendants who are sentenced to death," *Proceedings of National Academy of Sciences*, vol. 111, no. 20 (2014), pp. 7230–7235, doi:10.1073 /pnas.1306417111.

71   *"The story of James Coddington"*: Nicholas Kristof on Twitter, https://twitter .com/NickKristof/status/1554974253988003840.

71–72   *"a story . . . of remarkable transformation"*: Justin Jones, "Why I believe James Coddington is deserving of clemency," *The Oklahoman*, 22 August 2022.

72   *"recognizes our human capacity for change"*: Helen Prejean on Twitter, https://twitter.com/helenprejean/status/1554968233022631936.

72   *in 2023 this slowed to one every sixty days*: Sean Murphy, "Oklahoma appeals court agrees to slow pace of executions," AP News, 25 January 2023. See also "Oklahoma court schedules 25 executions between August 2022 and December 2024," *News*, Death Penalty Information Center website, 6 July 2022.

73   *"I did not get my Spaghetti-O's"*: See Nick Collins, "Last meals: Weird requests on death row," *The Telegraph*, 7 December 2010.

73   *An analysis of death row statements*: Zachary Crockett, "What death row inmates say in their last words," *Priceonomics*, 16 March 2016.

73   *"Oh fuck, oh fuck"*: Michael Erard, "What people actually say before they die," *The Atlantic*, 16 January 2019.

74   *"With their last breath"*: Hajo Schumacher, "Der Milf-Komplex (The MILF Complex)," *Der Spiegel*, 20 September 2018.

74   *In other research*: Roy Lacoursiere, "Dying calls for mother: Factual or fanciful?," *Journal of Aging, Humanities and the Arts*, vol. 4, no. 4. (2010), pp. 415–420, doi: 10.1080/19325614.2010.533397.

74   *One Ukrainian surgeon reported*: Olha Omelyanchuk, "Surgeon from the ATO zone: Before death, all soldiers call for their mothers," *Euromaidan Press*, 4 August 2014.

74   *"You . . . disgraced your own families"*: Sanya Mansoor, "What to know about Tyre Nichols' life as police release videos of his death," *TIME*, 27 January 2023.

76   *"the moon, watching"*: Laura Gilpin, "Night Song," from *The Hocus-Pocus of the*

Universe, copyright © 1977 by Laura Crafton Gilpin. Used by permission of Doubleday, an imprint of the Knopf Doubleday Publishing Group, a division of Penguin Random House LLC. All rights reserved.

Chapter 4: Icarus Flew

77   *"I believe Icarus was not failing as he fell"*: Jack Gilbert, "Failing and Flying," from *Refusing Heaven*, Copyright © 2005 by Jack Gilbert. Used by permission of Alfred A. Knopf, an imprint of the Knopf Doubleday Publishing Group, a division of Penguin Random House LLC. All rights reserved.

81   *"He had a great sense of humor"*: National, "Journalist Mellish farewelled in Sydney," *Sydney Morning Herald*, 21 March 2007.

83–84 *"Everyone forgets that Icarus also flew"*: Gilbert, "Failing and Flying."

86–87 *"This time last year"*: Primo Levi, *If This Is a Man* (aka *Survival in Auschwitz*), Little Brown Book Group, 2014 (first published 1947), ch. 15.

87   *"Actually there is tragedy everywhere you look"*: Jane Cadzow, " 'You can lose so much, and yet be happy': Cynthia Banham's revelation," *Good Weekend*, 17 March 2018.

Chapter 6: On Being Decent Men

99   *"There has been an earthquake warning"*: R.S. Rosenberg, S.L. Baughman, and J.N. Bailenson, (2013) "Virtual superheroes: Using superpowers in virtual reality to encourage prosocial behavior," *PLoS ONE*, vol. 8 no. 1 (2013), doi:10.1371/journal.pone.0055003.

100   *The researchers concluded*: Ibid.

100   *"It's very clear that if you design games"*: Stanford University, "Virtual superpowers encourage real-world empathy," *Science News*, ScienceDaily website, January 31, 2013.

100   *A growing body of research shows*: See J. Haidt, "The moral emotions," in: R.J. Davidson, K.R. Scherer, and H.H. Goldsmith (eds), *The Handbook of Affective Sciences*, Oxford University Press, 2003, pp. 852–870; and Julie van de Vyer and Dominic Abrams, "Is moral elevation an approach-oriented emotion?," *Journal of Positive Psychology*, vol. 12, no. 2 (2017), pp. 178–185.

100–01 *Scientists call this phenomenon "moral elevation"*: Rico Pohling and Rhett Diessner, "Moral elevation and moral beauty: A review of the empirical literature," *Review of General Psychology*, vol. 20, no. 4 (2016), doi:10.1037/gpr0000089.

101   *Those who reported being elevated*: Jonathan Haidt, "Wired to be inspired," *Greater Good Magazine*, 1 March 2005. See also W.T. Piper, L.R. Saslow, and S.R. Saturn, "Autonomic and prefrontal events during moral elevation," *Biological Psychology*, vol. 108 (May 2015), pp. 51–55, doi:10.1016/j.biopsycho.2015 .03.004.

101   *In a study of moral elevation in the workplace*: Michelangelo Vianello, Elisa Maria Galliani, and Jonathan Haidt, "Elevation at work: The effects of leaders' moral excellence," *Journal of Positive Psychology*, vol. 5, no. 5 (2010), pp. 390–411.

101   *In a study published in 2015*: Piper et al., "Autonomic and prefrontal events."

101–02 *"I think we have a tendency to absorb"*: Jill Suttie, "How our bodies react to seeing goodness," *Greater Good Magazine*, 12 May 2015.

105 *"I cannot trust Obama"*: "Flashback: McCain tells supporter Obama is 'a decent family man.'" CNN, YouTube, 20 February 2015.

105–06 *Obama defended a veteran*: "Obama defends heckler at Clinton rally," *Wall Street Journal*, YouTube, 4 November 2016.

PART III: Our Strangers

Random encounters

109 *One poll found*: YPulse, "3 stats to understand what main character energy means to Gen Z and Millennials," YPulse website, 17 May 2022.

109 *"the star at the center"*: John Koenig, "Sonder: The realization that everyone has a story," *Dictionary of Obscure Sorrows*, YouTube, 27 October 2014.

109–10 *"sonder"*: John Koenig, *The Dictionary of Obscure Sorrows*, Simon & Schuster, 2021.

Chapter 7: Other People's Lives

113 *"There are tree branches calling"*: All three poems included by permission of the authors.

116 *But on I went*: Quotes from Brad Aaron Modlin's "What You Missed That Day You Were Absent from Fourth Grade," from *Everyone at This Party Has Two Names*," Southeast Missouri State University Press, 2016, SemoPress.com, BradAaronModlin.com. Used by permission of the author.

Chapter 8: The Comfort of Strangers

119 *Then an old woman came up to me*: For those wondering what happened next, I managed, with the help of a passerby, to get to a hospital and was examined by doctors. It was a virus, they said, as we communicated in broken French. The doctor drew a picture of a pig and said, "Vous devez manger du porc!" ("You must eat more pork!"). Clearly he thought I might have been anemic, but having just become a vegetarian after visiting a pig farm in York, I was not keen on his prescription.

120 *"A small act for her"*: Alisa Bonner (@AlisaBonner11) on Twitter, August 13, 2020.

120 *"such a quiet act of kindness"*: Nick Cave and Sean O'Hagan, *Faith, Hope and Carnage*, Canongate Books Ltd, Edinburgh, 2022, p. 45.

Chapter 9: The Discomfort of Estrangers

126 *With bullying, research has shown*: Kira M. Newman, "Which feels better, forgiveness or revenge?," *Greater Good Magazine*, 18 April 2016. For the particular study, see Hayley Watson, Ronald Rapee, and Natasha Todorov, "Imagery rescripting of revenge, avoidance, and forgiveness for past bullying experiences in young adults," *Cognitive Behavior Therapy*, vol. 45, no. 1 (2016), pp. 73–89, doi:10.1080/16506073.2015.1108360.

130   *"It convinced me she was human after all"*: Julia Baird, "My experience of the harassment that's been missing from the #metoo debate," *Sydney Morning Herald*, 12 January 2018.

130   *"the moments when you get demoralized"*: Maureen Dowd, "The Grande Dame of Documentary is leaving her home at HBO," *New York Times*, 16 December 2017.

131–32 *A Singaporean study found*: Nabilah Awang, "1 in 2 women quit jobs after facing sexual harassment in the workplace, 1 in 4 changed career paths: Aware study," Todayonline website, 8 December 2021.

132   *the United States*: Erika Beras, "Poll: Nearly half of the women who experienced sexual harassment leave their jobs or switch careers," *Economic Anxiety Index*, MarketPlace website, 9 March 2018.

132   *Australia*: Deloitte Access Economics, *The Economic Costs of Sexual Harassment in the Workplace*, final report, Deloitte website, March 2019.

132   *the United Kingdom*: John Carvel, "Harassment victims are forced to quit," *The Guardian*, 30 August 2001.

132   *a "stern, chain-smoking presence"*: Giuseppina Fabiano, "The woman who explained the stars," *Nature*, 24 February 2020.

Chapter 10: *Restlaufzeit*: In the Time We Have Left, We Must Dance

135   *"Do you still wake"*: Sarah Fay, "Jack Gilbert, The Art of Poetry No. 91," *The Paris Review*, no. 175 (fall/winter 2005).

135–36 *In Lisa Taddeo's novel* Animal: Lisa Taddeo, *Animal: A novel*, Avid Reader Press, 2021, pp. 224–228.

137   *Palliative medicine physician Sunita Puri explained*: Sunita Puri, "As a doctor, I know being ready to die is an illusion," *New York Times*, 29 March 2023.

138–39 *Poet Mary Oliver wrote the poem*: Mary Oliver, "The Fourth Sign of the Zodiac," *Blue Horses*, Corsair, London, 2014, pp. 61–64.

139   *"A life, if lived well, is long enough"*: Elliot Dallen, "At 31, I have just weeks to live. Here's what I want to pass on," *The Guardian*, 7 September 2020.

139–40 *"I wish I'd had the courage to live a life true to myself"*: Bronnie Ware, *The Top Five Regrets of the Dying: A Life Transformed by the Dearly Departing*, Hay House, Sydney, 2011, https://bronnieware.com/blog/regrets-of-the-dying; used by permission of Bronnie Ware.

141   *"We shouldn't worry about the things we can't control"*: Georgina Scull, "Having a near-death experience taught me how to live better," *The Guardian*, 10 April 2022.

141–42 *"It's as if the repository of this wisdom"*: Krista Tippett, "Rachel Naomi Remen: How we live with loss," *On Being with Krista Tippett*, On Being website, 11 August 2005.

142   *A 2007 study*: J.C. Coyne et al., "Emotional well-being does not predict survival in head and neck cancer patients: A radiation therapy oncology group study," *Cancer*, vol. 110, no. 11 (2007), pp. 2568–2575, doi:10.1002/cncr.23080 .PMID: 17955501.

142   *Three years later, another study*: J.C. Coyne and H. Tennen, "Positive psychology

in cancer care: Bad science, exaggerated claims, and unproven medicine," *Annals of Behavioral Medicine*, vol. 39, no. 1 (February 2010), pp. 16–26, doi:10.1007/s12160–009–9154–z.

143   *"It has become accepted in popular culture"*: Jillian R. Satin, Wolfgang Lindenk and Melanie J. Phillips, "Depression as a predictor of disease progression and mortality in cancer patients," *Cancer*, vol. 15, no. 22 (November 2009), doi:10.1002/cncr.24561.

143   *They found that depression*: Penelope E. Schofield et al., "Hope, optimism and survival in a randomised trial of chemotherapy for metastatic colorectal cancer," *Support Care in Cancer*, vol. 24, no. 1 (2016), pp. 401–408, doi:10.1007/s00520–015–2792–8.

144   *We seem to have little understanding*: See Amanda Dodson, "5 lessons for the newly chronically ill," *Psychology Today*, 15 September 2022.

144   *Tamika Woods, a clinical nutritionist*: Tamika Woods, "6 life lessons I learned from chronic illness," Nourished Natural Health website, 15 January 2019.

144–45 *Freelance writer Christina Ward*: Christina M. Ward, "The life lessons of chronic illness–pain will teach you," *Essay*, Medium website, 24 May 2020. Used by permission of the author.

147   The Lancet *claims*: See https://twitter.com/TheLancet/status /1398621349824839682. Others say one in five–see, for example, D.S. Goldberg and S.J. McGee, "Pain as a global public health priority," *BMC Public Health*, vol. 11, no. 770 (2006), doi:10.1186/1471-2458-11-770, which notes: "Estimates suggest that 20% of adults suffer from pain globally and 10% are newly diagnosed with chronic pain each year."

147   *The Australian Institute of Health and Welfare reports*: Australian Institute of Health and Welfare, *Chronic Pain in Australia*, 7 May 2020.

149   *"Here lies One whose Name was writ in Water"*: Keats's friends Joseph Severn and Charles Armitage Brown erected his tombstone, which, under a relief of a lyre with broken strings, includes the epitaph: "This Grave / contains all that was Mortal, / of a / YOUNG ENGLISH POET, / Who, / on his Death Bed, / in the Bitterness of his Heart, / at the Malicious Power of his Enemies, / Desired / these Words to be engraven on his Tomb Stone / Here lies One / Whose Name was writ in Water / Feb 24th 1821."

149   *One thing that upset Keats*: Joanna Richardson, *Fanny Brawne: A Biography*, Jarrold and Sons, Norwich, 1952. pp. 31–32.

149–50 *"There are many regrets"*: All quotes from Kerry Egan, *On Living: Life's Greatest Lessons and Last Thoughts from the Dying*, Penguin, Random House UK, 2018, pp. 56–59.

PART IV: Our Sins

Forgive us our sins

155–56 *Heliophysicist Craig DeForest estimates*: Nathaniel Scharping, "What would the sun sound like if we could hear it on Earth?," *The Sciences*, Discover website, 5 February 2020.

156   *astronomers presented research showing*: Jeanna Bryner, "In space, scientists can hear the sun scream," NBC News, 30 May 2007.

Chapter 11: Napoleon's Penis: What We Choose to Remember

159   *He bought it because "fun was being poked at it"*: According to Tony Perrottet, author of *Napoleon's Privates: 2,500 Years of History Unzipped* (It Books, 2008), quoted in "The twisted journey of Napoleon's privates," *The Bryant Park Project*, NPR website, 2 July 2008.

159   *a "maltreated strip of buckskin shoelace"*: Christopher Shay, "Napoleon's penis," *TIME*, 10 May 2011.

159   *After Lattimer died in 2007*: Tony Perrottet, quoted in "The twisted journey of Napoleon's privates."

163   *He later told one he had "let God down"*: David Denby, "The making of Norman Mailer," *New Yorker*, 19 December 2022.

163   *"one of the most original and powerful writers"*: Richard Brody, "The novel that Norman Mailer didn't write," *New Yorker*, 16 October 2013.

164   *three women or girls a day*: Rose Hackman, "Femicides in the US; the silent epidemic few dare to name," *The Guardian*, 26 September 2021.

165   *Coinciding with the COVID pandemic*: United Nations Office on Drugs and Crime, "Killings of women and girls by their intimate partner or other family members: Global estimates 2020," *Data Matters 3*, no. 11 (2021).

165   *Despite some drops in the homicide rates*: Ibid., p. 1.

165   *"I could feel the whole house shake"*: Yamma Brown, "My father was James Brown. I watched him beat my mother. And then I found myself with someone like Dad," *Vulture*, 16 September 2014.

165   *"Regardless of what went on"*: Rick Rubin on James Brown, in "Rolling Stone's 100 greatest artists," *Rolling Stone*, 3 December 2010.

166   *"There was a constant state of fear"*: Althea Legaspi, "Don McLean's daughter alleges mental, emotional abuse by 'American Pie' singer," *Rolling Stone*, 23 June 2021.

166–67   *"My husband has a violent temper"*: Staff and agencies, "Don McLean says he is 'not a villain' following his domestic violence arrest," *The Guardian*, 22 January 2016.

167   *"I can truly say"*: "Don McLean: 'My ex-wife is the worst person I ever knew,'" *The Street Journal*, 26 October 2020.

167   *"subject to every type of physical and mental abuse"*: Nikki Finke, "The tiny spark that survived: The rock 'n' roll life of star's child bride," *LA Times*, 30 June 1989.

168   *In 1990, a lawsuit brought by fifty-nine women*: In 1987, Berry was charged with assaulting a woman at the Gramercy Park Hotel in Manhattan, resulting in "lacerations of the mouth, requiring five stitches, two loose teeth, [and] contusions of the face." He was fined only $250 after he pleaded guilty to harassment, a lesser charge.

169   *"It's not about being physically mature"*: The Newsroom, "Mandy Smith calls for age of consent to rise," *The Scotsman*, 17 April 2010.

169 *"She took my breath away"*: Dan Cairns, "Bill Wyman: The Rolling Stone airbrushed out of history," *The Times*, 24 July 2022.

169 *she dedicated her autobiography*: Lesley-Ann Jones, "'I was there when Bill Wyman dated Mandy Smith. My guilt haunts me me,'" *The Times*, 10 April 2019.

169 *"Stones Withstand Divorce"*: See, for example, Anorak, "The Rolling Stones were proud to withstand 'under-age sex,'" Flashbak website, 19 November 2013.

170 *boasted about bedding a fourteen-year-old girl*: Anthony Kiedis, *Scar Tissue*, Hyperion, New York, 2004, p. 159.

170 *"a beastly people with a beastly religion"*: Shashi Tharoor, "The Ugly Briton," *Time*, 29 November 2010.

170–71 *He ridiculed Mahatma Gandhi*: "Churchill's reputation in the 1930s," Churchill Archives Centre.

171 *He called Chinese people "chinks"*: Dan Jones, "Becoming a Victorian," *The Spectator*, 20 March 2010.

171 *Scholars have argued his views on race*: Priyamvada Gopal, "Why can't Britain handle the truth about Winston Churchill?," *The Guardian*, 17 March 2021.

171 *"On the subject of India, Winston is not quite sane"*: Ibid.

171 *There was no acknowledgment*: "Churchill on Gandhi's death," *The Churchill Project*, Hillsdale College website, 14 February 2016.

171 *Gandhi's legacy has been challenged*: Lauren Frayer, "Gandhi is deeply revered, but his attitudes on race and sex are under scrutiny," *World*, NPR website, 2 October 2019.

172 *"Gandhi believed in the Aryan brotherhood"*: Soutik Biswas, "Was Mahatma Gandhi a racist?," *India*, BBC News website, 17 September 2015.

172 *"He thought in his twenties"*: Lauren Frayer, "Gandhi is 'an object of intense debate': A biographer reflects on the Indian leader," *World*, NPR website, 29 September 2019.

172 *Others have questioned Gandhi's practice*: If he wasn't aroused by their presence, he could be reassured he'd achieved *brahmacharya*, a Hindu concept of celibate self-control. Such a person, Gandhi wrote, would be incapable of lying or harming anyone.

172 *"I object to"*: Dalit Diva, "Why it is time to dump Gandhi," Medium website, 14 June 2017.

173 *"anonymous UK telephone bidder"*: BBC, "Hitler's wife Eva Braun's WW2 knickers sell for £3,700," BBC News website, 19 September 2019.

Chapter 12: When You Can't Forgive

176 *Salma Hayek wrote*: Salma Hayek, "Harvey Weinstein is my monster too," *New York Times*, 12 December 2017.

177 *"a process of reducing negative thoughts"*: K. Kaleta and J. Mróz, "Gender differences in forgiveness and its affective correlates," *Journal of Religion and Health*, vol. 61, no. 4 (2022), pp. 2819–2837, doi:10.1007/s10943-021-01369-5.

177 *"the value of forgiveness lies"*: Joanna North, "Wrongdoing and forgiveness," *Philosophy*, vol. 62, no. 242 (1987), pp. 499–508, doi:10.1017/S003181910003905X.

178 *"our responsibility to keep relationships alive"*: Lucia Osborne-Crowley, "Nothing good can come of this," *Meanjin*, autumn 2022. She quotes Soraya Chemaly's book, *Rage Becomes Her*, in which Chemaly argues that because women have historically been socialized to avoid anger, and fear it, they must embrace it: "Anger has a bad rap, but it is actually one of the most hopeful and forward thinking of all our emotions. It begets transformation, manifesting our passion and keeping us invested in the world."

178–79 *"Women in the Church were pressured"*: Sady Doyle, "A kind of forgiveness," *New York Review of Books*, 31 December 2018.

179 *"keep it sweet"*: Megyn Kelly, "Polygamist cult founder's daughter, Rachel Jeffs, gives her first TV interview," *TODAY*, YouTube.

179 *The current leader of the church*: Roxy Simons, "What has the Mormon Church said about *Keep Sweet: Pray and Obey?*," *Newsweek*, 8 June 2022.

179–80 *The 2022 film* Women Talking: Jean Friedman-Rudovsky, "The ghost rapes of Bolivia," *Vice*, 23 December 2013.

181 *"some of Dad's overseas relations"*: Amani Haydar, *The Mother Wound*, Pan Macmillan, Sydney, 2021, p. 269.

181 *"Some of Dad's nieces and nephews"*: Ibid., p. 270.

181 *"One person commented"*: Ibid., p. 257.

182 *"ongoing matrilineal knowledge"*: Ibid., p. 333.

182 *"I read somewhere that if trauma can be inherited"*: Ibid., p. 327.

182–83 *"They are captivated by these declarations"*: Ibid., p. 300.

183 *A study of 572 college students*: M. Meghan Davidson, Nicole M. Lozano, Brian P. Cole, and Sarah Gervais, "Relations between intimate partner violence and forgiveness among college women," *Journal of Interpersonal Violence*, vol. 30, no. 18 (2015), pp. 3217–3243, doi:10.1177/0886260514555008.

183 *This reluctance to forgive*: A longitudinal study of couples found that partners who were forgiving of both psychological and physical intimate partner violence were more likely to continue experiencing that aggression from their partner; see J.K. McNulty, "The dark side of forgiveness: The tendency to forgive predicts continued psychological and physical aggression in marriage," *Personality and Social Psychology Bulletin*, vol. 37, no. 6 (2011), pp. 770–783, doi:10.1177/0146167211407077 (cited in Davidson et al., "Relations between intimate partner violence and forgiveness").

183 *A 2020 study*: A. Zrihan Weitzman and E. Buchbinder, "Intimate violence forgiveness dynamics in the context of men's positions as victims and perpetrators: A dyadic perspective," *Journal of Family Issues*, vol. 42, no. 7 (2020), pp. 1–24.

183–84 *He found that the tendency to express forgiveness*: McNulty, "The dark side of forgiveness."

184–85   *Women who have been abused*: Haydar, *The Mother Wound*, p. 283.

185   *A 2006 study found*: Susan C. Modesitt et al., "Adverse impact of a history of violence for women with breast, cervical, endometrial, or ovarian cancer," *Journal of Obstetrics & Gynecology*, vol. 107, no. 6 (2006), pp. 1330–1336, doi:10.1097/01.AOG.0000217694.18062.91.

185   *Another study from 2014 found*: Sandra K. Cesario et al., "Linking cancer and intimate partner violence: The importance of screening women in the oncology setting," *Clinical Journal of Oncology Nursing*, vol. 18, no. 1 (2014), pp. 65–73, doi:10.1188/14.CJON.65-73.

185   *A meta-analysis from 2018 confirmed*: J.M. Reingle Gonzalez, K.K. Jetelina, S. Olague, and J.G. Wondrack, "Violence against women increases cancer diagnoses: Results from a meta-analytic review," *Preventive Medicine*, vol. 114 (2018), pp. 168–179, doi:10.1016/j.ypmed.2018.07.008.

185   *A cross-sectional study*: Deborah Loxton et al., "History of domestic violence and physical health in midlife," 2006, *Violence Against Women*, vol. 12, no. 8, pp. 715–731. Men of course suffer from domestic abuse too (though in much smaller numbers); even so, a 2022 Indian study found women suffer from more long-term health problems as a consequence of domestic abuse than men do, even when suffering the same injuries; see B.R. Maruya, "An overview on domestic violence," *Asian Journal of Multidimensional Research*, vol. 10, no. 12, pp. 398–403, doi:10.5958/2278-4853.2021.01139.3.

185–86   *One definition is*: Brittany Loggins, "When is it OK not to forgive someone," *Relationships*, Verywell Mind website, 13 October 2021.

186   *She also hears about it from survivors*: Ijeoma Oluo, "When forgiveness isn't a virtue," *The Establishment*, Huffington Post website, 30 December 2015.

186   *"Instead of focusing on healing and comfort"*: Ibid.

186   *"Even if the intention is coming from a good place"*: Anastasia Pollock, "Why I don't use the word 'forgiveness' in trauma therapy," *Good Therapy*, 20 January 2016.

186   *"a way of wielding boltcutters"*: Nadia Bolz-Weber, "Forgive assholes, have a little faith," YouTube, 31 May 2018.

187–88   *"their own self-preservation"*: Megan Feldman Bettencourt, "How forgiveness has been weaponized against women," *Harper's Bazaar*, 28 September 2016.

Chapter 13: The Stolen Generations: What Does Forgiveness Mean?

191   *Hazel is a member of the Stolen Generations*: Almost three-quarters of the children over twelve who were removed between 1912 and 1928 were girls; they were taken ostensibly to control their sexual behavior, but many clearly became prey. See Peter Read, "The myth of the Stolen Generations—a rebuttal," *Opinion*, ABC News website, 15 February 2008.

191   *The impulse for this cruel and devastating policy*: Ebony Cleland, "Stolen Generations member tired of Aboriginal people being told to 'get over it,'" ABC News website, 1 October 2017.

192   *But her language, Bayungu, is now close to extinction*: Here is a written example:
Ngarri yinhaya Bayungu. Nharnurila bunithu gunjayindiya. Nyinayi bajanma
bilyguru majun. Bunggurdi murla nhurndijarri ngarri guthuwalbuga
thungguranhura nywardi.
This translates as:
This country is Bayungu. We all go to Cardabia Station. We eat plenty of fish,
turtle and this is really important. Also we eat kangaroo and kangaroo tail that
we cook in the ground.
See www.wangkamaya.org.au/pilbara-languages/bayungu.

193   *"Forgiveness is never earned or deserved"*: Scott Morrison, Prime Minister,
"National apology to the Stolen Generations: 14th Anniversary Statement,"
Hansard, 14 February 2022.

194   *"Get in the bin"*: Rachael Knowles and Sarah Collard, "'Get in the bin': PM
under fire for National Apology remarks," *NITV*, SBS website, 15 February 2022.

194   *"I'm horrified"*: Jack Latimore, "PM prompts fury by looking for forgiveness
14 years after Rudd's apology," *Sydney Morning Herald*, 14 February 2022.

194   *"If people have been severely traumatized"*: Ibid.

194–95 *Pastor Ray Minniecon*: Ray Minniecon, The Forgiveness Project website, www
.theforgivenessproject.com/stories-library/ray-minniecon/.

198   *a "giant intellectual fraud"*: Georgina Mitchell, "Andrew Bolt's claim Stolen
Generations a 'myth' spurs Press Council complaint," *Sydney Morning Herald*,
1 August 2015.

198–99 *"A survivor may think"*: Martha Minow, *Between Vengeance and Forgiveness: Facing
History after Genocide and Mass Violence*, 1998, Beacon Press, Boston, 1998, p. 17.
See also the discussion in Declan Roche, *Accountability in Restorative Justice*,
Oxford University Press, 2003, p. 36.

200   *Pope Francis apologized*: Leyland Cecco, "Pope Francis 'begs forgiveness' over
abuse at church schools in Canada," *The Guardian*, 26 July 2022. When Pope
Francis visited Quebec in 2022, protesters held up a sign saying *RESCIND
THE DOCTRINE*, referring to the papal Doctrine of Discovery from the
1400s, which gave the papal imprimatur to the invasion and occupation of
lands not inhabited by Christians. This fully erased the rights of Indigenous
people to their lands and resources. (The Vatican has reportedly said this
doctrine is currently under discussion. See Aleem Maqbool, "Pope Francis:
Did the pontiff's apology in Canada go far enough?," BBC News website,
20 July 2022.) There have been other apologies, all in varying shades of regret
and accountability. In 2018, the same pope expressed regret for the church's
enabling of sex abuse. "We showed no care for the little ones. We abandoned
them," he admitted. In 2015, he apologized to the Indigenous people of
Bolivia. In 2010, Pope Benedict apologized to Irish Catholics for "systemic"
child abuse—but did not punish any leaders. In the 1980s and 1990s, John
Paul II repeatedly apologized for the church's involvement in the slave trade.
He also apologized to women for being marginalized, and for the church's
failures to do more to prevent the Holocaust.

201 *The refusal of the Japanese government*: In 1993, Chief Cabinet Secretary Yohei Kono, the government spokesman, apologized for the "comfort women" system and acknowledged the Japanese military's involvement in taking women against their will, but did not admit guilt or take responsibility.

Chapter 14: "We Will Wear You Down with Our Love"

203 *Grant's great-aunt*: Stan Grant, "Stan Grant in Cootamundra: Revisiting a place of stolen lives," *The Point*, NITV website, 4 April 2016.

207 *the king had asked*: Jacquelin Magnay, "'But will I be welcome?' King's fears over a potential visit to Australia amid republic push," *The Australian*, 3 May 2023.

209 *a man has since been charged*: Olivia Ireland and Nick Bonyhady, "Man charged for alleged threats against Stan Grant as ombudsman clears ABC," *Sydney Morning Herald*, 25 May 2023.

209 *Radio host Neil Mitchell said*: Adriana Mageros, "'Not the time': Radio host Neil Mitchell says ABC's coverage of King Charles' coronation 'totally misread the mood,'" *Australia News*, Sky News website, 8 May 2023.

209 *It was also called*: Josh Taylor, "Stan Grant faced 'unrelenting racism,' fellow ABC panelists say, as scale of conservative coverage revealed," *The Guardian*, 20 May 2023.

209 *Former conservative politician Cory Bernardi*: Cory Bernardi, "Stan Grant was appointed 'whiner in chief' for ABC's coverage of King's coronation," Sky News, 7 May 2023.

209–10 *"tried to depict me as hate-filled"*: Stan Grant, "For years I've been a media target for racism and paid a heavy price. For now, I want no part of it—I'm stepping away," ABC News website, 19 May 2023.

210 *"a growing mood among academics"*: Janet Albrechtson and Tom Switzer, "We stand with Stan? Give us a break. Stand for quality journalism," *The Australian*, 24 May 2023.

210–11 *Just a month before the coronation*: David Conn, Aamna Mohdin, and Maya Wolfe-Robinson, "King Charles signals first explicit support for research into monarchy's slavery ties," *The Guardian*, 6 April 2023.

211 *It was also shown*: David Conn and Rachel Hall, "Direct ancestors of King Charles owned slave plantation, documents reveal," *The Guardian*, 27 April 2023.

212 *But according to ABC*: "Coronation panel discussion complaints," ABC Statement, 28 May 2023.

212 *"Australians have been taught"*: Craig Foster, Instagram, www.instagram.com/p/CscRImGSlXa/?hl=en.

212 *As did the false claims*: Amanda Meade, "ABC coverage of King Charles III coronation tops Australian ratings despite being attacked by monarchists," *The Guardian*, 9 May 2023.

213 *"To those who have abused me and my family"*: Martin Luther King actually said, "We will wear you down with our capacity to suffer," not love. See the Reverend Dr. Martin Luther King, Jr., *A Gift of Love: Sermons from* Strength to Love *and Other Preachings*, Penguin, New York, 2012, ch. 5.

Notes

Chapter 15: The Callus: On Restorative Justice

218   *"I looked up and I saw him walk past"*: The quotes from Debbie McGrath come from a series of interviews with me on 24 and 25 June 2023, and a speech she has delivered to restorative justice conferences.

221   *The focus is not what can be proved*: Rachael Dexter, Simone Fox Koob, and Tammy Mills, "'I felt lighter': Restorative justice gives sex crime survivors a different way forward," *The Age*, 29 August 2021.

224   *Tracey told ABC News*: Ashleigh Barraclough, "Talking to the driver that killed her daughter," ABC News website, 6 February 2023.

224–25   *"Oh, you're right, mate, no worries"*: Meredith Rossner, "Restorative justice, anger, and the transformative energy of forgiveness," *International Journal of Restorative Justice*, vol. 2, no. 3 (2019), pp. 368–388, doi:10.5553/IJRJ.000005. Here she is drawing on the work of Australia's "godfather" of restorative justice, John Braithwaite; see, for example, J. Braithwaite, "Redeeming the 'F' word in restorative justice," *Oxford Journal of Law and Religion*, vol. 5, no. 1 (2016), pp. 79–93, doi:10.1093/ojlr/rwv049.

225   *One study found*: M. Armour and M. Umbreit, *Violence, Restorative Justice, and Forgiveness: Dyadic Forgiveness and Energy Shifts in Restorative Justice Dialogue*, Jessica Kingsley Publishers, London, 2018.

225   *"Participants and practitioners told me"*: Meredith Rossner, *Just Emotions: Rituals of Restorative Justice*, Oxford University Press, Oxford, 2013; and H. Strang, *Repair or Revenge: Victims and Restorative Justice*, Clarendon Press, Oxford, 2002.

225   *"subtle energy of forgiveness"*: Rossner, "Restorative justice."

225   *"While apologies can restore"*: Some remarkable and thought-provoking work is being done in this area by Thea Deakin-Greenwood, who founded Transforming Justice Australia, a survivor-led restorative justice program for sexual assault, with Jane Bolitho. She says one of the biggest stumbling blocks can be self-compassion, both on the part of the victim, who has been unable to stem the damage to their lives—feeling like a bad parent for not being able to hold down a job, for example—as well as the person responsible. Thea speaks of a woman who met with a sexually abusive stepfather who was jailed for what he'd done to her. She went to see him every month, peppering him with questions, demanding responses until one moment, without minimizing or excusing anything, he told her he had been badly abused as a child, and "she understood how broken he was, she saw him in a different light, as damaged and a weight was lifted from her." Somehow released from the weight of the trauma, she did not see him again.

225   *so-called circle sentencing*: Steve Yeong and Elizabeth Moore, "Circle sentencing, incarceration and recidivism," *Crime and Justice Bulletin*, no. 226 (April 2020).

228   *"creating a new narrative"*: See also Shadd Maruna, "How ex-convicts reform and rebuild their lives," American Psychological Association, Washington, 2001.

229   *In his excellent TED Talk*: Dan Reisel, "The neuroscience of restorative justice," TED2013, February 2013.

302

Chapter 16: "A Broken Place": People Who Have Forgiven

233 *"all people are capable of being perpetrators or victims"*: Michael Lapsley, The Forgiveness Project, www.theforgivenessproject.com/stories-library/michael -lapsley/.

236–37 *"people of both genders are more forgiving"*: Julie Juola Exline in "Men have a harder time forgiving than women do," *Science News*, ScienceDaily website, 3 March 2008.

239 *"Forgiveness is more for the forgiver"*: Elizabeth Daoud, "Danny Abdallah's tragic revelation about day his kids died: 'I choose to forgive myself,'" *Social Affairs*, 7News website, 27 June 2022.

239 *"I have decided to forgive you"*: Tim Brown, "Christchurch mosque shooter appears moved as victim's mother offers forgiveness," *Crime*, RNZ website, 24 August 2020.

240 *Research shows the benefits of forgiveness*: A.C.D. Cheadle and L.L. Toussaint, "Forgiveness and physical health in healthy populations," in L.L. Toussaint, E.L. Worthington, and D.R. Williams (eds), *Forgiveness and Health: Scientific Evidence and Theories Relating Forgiveness to Better Health*, Springer, Dordrecht, 2015, pp. 91–106, doi:10.1007/978-94-017-9993-5_7; see also M.E. McCullough, L.M. Root, B.A. Tabak, and C. vanOyen Witvliet, "Forgiveness," in S.J. Lopez and C.R. Snyder (eds), *The Oxford Handbook of Positive Psychology*, Oxford University Press, Oxford, 2009; and N.G. Wade, W.T. Hoyt, J.E.M. Kidwell, and E.L. Worthington, "Efficacy of psychotherapeutic interventions to promote forgiveness: A meta-analysis," *Journal of Consulting and Clinical Psychology*, vol. 82, no. 1 (2014), pp. 154–170.

240 *There is also some evidence*: Toussaint et al., *Forgiveness and Health*, pp. 91–106.

240 *In one experiment*: Charlotte vanOyen Witvliet and Thomas Ethan Ludwig, "Granting forgiveness or harboring grudges: Implications for emotion, physiology, and health," *Psychological Science*, vol. 12, no. 2 (2001), pp. 117–123, doi:10.1111/1467-9280.00320.

241 *"A lack of forgiveness"*: Anne Lamott, *Small Victories: Spotting Improbable Moments of Grace*, Riverhead Books, New York, 2014.

241 *The editors of the book*: *Forgiveness and Health*: Toussaint et al., *Forgiveness and Health*, pp. 91–106.

241 *His team found*: L.L. Toussaint, G.S. Shields, G. Dorn, and G.M. Slavich, "Effects of lifetime stress exposure on mental and physical health in young adulthood: How stress degrades and forgiveness protects health," *Journal of Health Psychology*, vol. 21, no. 6 (2016), pp. 1004–1014, doi:10.1177/1359105314544132.

241 *Toussaint told the American Psychological Association*: Kirsten Weir, "Forgiveness can improve mental and physical health," *CE Corner*, American Psychological Association website, vol. 48, no. 1 (2017).

241 *Toussaint also conducted a study*: L.L. Toussaint, G.S. Shields, G. Dorn, and G.M. Slavich, "Forgiveness, stress, and health: A 5-week dynamic parallel process study," *Annals of Behavioral Medicine*, vol. 50, no. 5 (2016), pp. 727–735, doi:10.1007/s12160-016-9796-6.

242 *Professor Frederic Luskin*: Emily Laurence, "Forgiveness: How to forgive yourself and others," *Mind*, Forbes website, 27 January 2023.

242 *Evidence shows that global forgiveness*: Stephen Lichtenfeld, Markus A. Meier, Vanessa L. Buechner, and Maria Fernández Capo, "The influence of decisional and emotional forgiveness on attributions," *Frontiers in Psychology*, vol. 10 (2019), doi:10.3389/fpsyg.2019.01425.

242 *Through this process, says Enright*: Weir, "Forgiveness can improve mental and physical health."

243–44 *"Forgiveness is an act of self-healing"*: Eva Kor, "We can heal with forgiveness," *Jewish Chronicle*, 30 April 2015.

244–45 *In an article on repentance and forgiveness*: Michael Dobkowski, "Forgiveness and repentance in Judaism after the Shoah," *Ultimate Reality and Meaning*, vol. 27, no. 2, pp. 94–107 (2004), doi: 10.3138/uram.27.2.94.

245 *"Once someone has been branded a rapist"*: Thordis Elva and Tom Stranger, "Our story of rape and reconciliation," TEDWomen, October 2016.

245–46 *"Many people feel that forgiveness"*: A.H. Cayley, "South of Forgiveness: A rape. A book. A conversation," Neighborhood website, n.d.

246 *"Why didn't I just get myself a bottle of vodka"*: Elva and Stranger, "Our Story."

247 *Black civil rights leader John Lewis argued*: John Lewis, "Forgiving George Wallace," *New York Times*, 16 September 1998.

247 *"If you forgive you may indeed still not understand"*: Marilynne Robinson, *Home*, Farrar, Straus and Giroux, New York, 2008.

247 *In her essay "Grace and Beauty"*: Marilynne Robinson, "Grace and beauty," *Ploughshares*, vol. 44, no. 1 (2018), pp. 157–167, doi:10.1353/plo.2018.0031.

Part V: Our Senses

Flukeprint

251 *"We're the only things"*: Sarah Fay, "Jack Gilbert, The Art of Poetry No. 91," *Paris Review*, no. 175 (fall/winter 2005).

255 *It is through solitude*: Anne Morrow Lindbergh, *Gift From the Sea*, Pantheon Books, New York, 1955, 1975, pp. 38, 45.

255 *Sarton described loneliness*: May Sarton, *Journal of a Solitude*, W.W. Norton & Co., New York, 1992.

256 *"I think of the trees"*: Ibid.

256 *A FLUKEPRINT*: Samuel Leighton-Dore, "A Flukeprint," https://twitter .com/SamLeightonDore/status/1688775816946298880; used with the permission of the author.

Chapter 17: Fever Dreams

264 *"Whatever peace I know"*: May Sarton, *Journal of a Solitude*, W.W. Norton & Co., New York, 1992.

265 *their world, that needed protecting*: Green turtles live for up to fifty years and weigh up to 70 kilograms, but, after decades of illegal hunting for their shells and eggs, they are now under threat. Turtles were "harvested"—caught and

killed—in Western Australia, mostly around Coral Bay and Exmouth, from the 1870s. In the 1960s, the hunting became a full industry, with an estimated 55,000 to 69,000 green turtles killed between 1960 and 1973, when the harvesting was shut down. Turtle-shell hunting has declined but still continues illegally, fueled by the black market. Today green turtles are still considered endangered.

265   *The 1980s were a time of reckoning*: J. Roman et al., "Whales as marine ecosystem engineers," *Frontiers in Ecology and the Environment*, vol. 12 (2014), pp. 377–385, doi:10.1890/130220. Scientists estimate that the number of great whale numbers has declined between 66 and 90 percent since the slaughter of whales began (the first recorded commercial whaling took place around 100 AD).

266   *a remarkable story of renewal*: The Australian east coast population has recovered as fast (10.8 percent per year) as it is possible for any humpback whale population to recover, given that the mother must swim to and from Antarctica each year to feed and nourish her calf.

266   *removed from the endangered species list*: Rob Harcourt, Honorary Professor of Marine Ecology at Macquarie University, says: "This is testimony to the resilience of nature when humans allow them to lead their lives without interference. Australia's humpbacks are now in a comfortable state and this same picture is seen around the globe for these gentle giants of the sea." Note that Norway, Iceland, and Japan still hunt whales, though Iceland vowed in 2022 to stop commercial whaling by 2024.

266   *Marine scientist Brad Norman found*: There is a certain poetry in the way these creatures have been traced by Norman—modifying an algorithm created by NASA to allow the Hubble Space Telescope scientists to map the night sky. Whale sharks have patterns of splotches, stripes, and spots on them that look like stars and are unique, like fingerprints. Norman has encouraged people diving or swimming with whale sharks to take photographs of them, especially in the area behind their gills, and send it in to his "Sharkbook" to add to the global identification database to help monitor their numbers, movements and activities.

Chapter 18: A Grace Note

270–71   *"I had thought that after Newtown"*: Barack Obama, Bruce Springsteen, *Renegades: Born in the USA*, Higher Ground, Spotify, ep. 3, "Amazing Grace: American Music," March 2021.

271   *"the notion of grace"*: Ibid.

271–72   *At the funeral, Obama told the congregation*: President Barack Obama, "Remarks by the president in eulogy for the Honorable Reverend Clementa Pinckney," *Speeches & Remarks*, The White House: President Barack Obama website, 26 June 2015.

272   *to "affirm the slaves' humanity"*: Cheryl C. Boots, "Harriet Beecher Stowe's abolition soundtrack in Uncle Tom's Cabin," *Forum on Public Policy: A Journal of the Oxford Round Table*, summer 2010.

272   *"bright shining like the sun"*: Beecher Stowe reportedly took the "ten thousand times" from another hymn, "Jerusalem, My Happy Home."

273   *"It seemed strange to me"*: David Neff, "An interview with an 'Amazing Grace' historian," *Christianity Today*, 1 March 2003.

273–74   *In a study of the impact of seclusion*: Rachel Sambrano and Leonie Cox, "'I sang Amazing Grace for about 3 hours that day': Understanding Indigenous Australians' experience of seclusion," *International Journal of Mental Health Nursing*, vol. 22, no. 6 (2013), p. 527, doi:10.1111/inm.12015.

275   *"What is the goal of social change or political engagement?"*: Rebecca Solnit, *Orwell's Roses*, Granta Books, London, 2021, p. 180.

276   *A 2020 study found*: T.N. Bradbury and F.D. Fincham, "Attributions in marriage: Review and critique," *Psychological Bulletin*, vol. 107, no. 1 (1990), pp. 3–33, doi:10.1037/0033-2909.107.1.3.

276   *Research published in the* Journal of Happiness Studies *found*: D. Jasielska et al., "Happiness and hostile attributions in a cross-cultural context: The importance of interdependence," *Journal of Happiness Studies: An Interdisciplinary Forum on Subjective Well-Being*, vol. 22, no. 1, (2021) pp. 163–179, doi:10.1007/s10902-020-00224-w.

277   *But surely we can practice this kind of thinking*: The authors pointed out that "the fact that our findings are consistent with extant theoretical and empirical literature, and that this pattern was found in a cross-cultural sample suggests that these patterns might be generalizable."

278   *As the Franciscan priest and writer Richard Rohr points out*: Richard Rohr, "Considering the Trinity," *Daily Meditations*, Center for Action and Contemplation website, 5 June 2023.

278   *One recent study*: M. Echelbarger and N. Epley, "Undervaluing the positive impact of kindness starts early," *Journal of Experimental Psychology*: General, doi:10.1037/xge0001433; and N. Epley et al., "Undersociality: Miscalibrated social cognition can inhibit social connection," *Trends in Cognitive Sciences*, vol. 26, no. 5 (2022), pp. 406–418, doi:10.1016/j.tics.2022.02.007.

Alex Ellingshausen

Julia Baird is a bestselling author and an award-winning journalist based in Sydney, Australia. She is a columnist for the *Sydney Morning Herald* and cohosts the ABC podcast *Not Stupid* (Australia). She has also been an op-ed contributor for the *New York Times* and the *Philadelphia Inquirer*; the deputy editor of *Newsweek* in New York; and a Joan Shorenstein Fellow at the Harvard Kennedy School, Harvard University. Her first book, *Media Tarts*, was based on her PhD in history about the portrayal of female politicians. *Victoria*, her biography of Queen Victoria, was published to critical acclaim and was one of the *New York Times's* top ten books of 2016. Her third book, *Phosphorescence*, was a multi-award-winning international bestseller. Baird lives near the sea with her two children and an abnormally large dog.